THE PARADOX OF PARADISE

The Paradox of Paradise

*Creative Destruction
and the Rise of Urban
Coastal Tourism in
Contemporary Spanish Culture*

WILLIAM J. NICHOLS

VANDERBILT UNIVERSITY PRESS

Nashville, Tennessee

Library of Congress Cataloging-in-Publication Data

Names: Nichols, William J, 1970- author.
Title: The paradox of paradise : creative destruction and the rise of urban
 coastal tourism in contemporary Spanish culture / William J Nichols.
Description: Nashville, Tennessee : Vanderbilt University Press, [2023] |
 Includes bibliographical references and index.
Identifiers: LCCN 2023035291 (print) | LCCN 2023035292 (ebook) | ISBN
 9780826506221 (hardcover) | ISBN 9780826506214 (paperback) | ISBN
 9780826506238 (epub) | ISBN 9780826506245 (pdf)
Subjects: LCSH: Culture and tourism--Spain--History. | Urban
 tourism--Spain--History.
Classification: LCC G155.S6 N534 2023 (print) | LCC G155.S6 (ebook) | DDC
 914.6/09732--dc23/eng/20231016
LC record available at https://lccn.loc.gov/2023035291
LC ebook record available at https://lccn.loc.gov/2023035292

Cover image: Plate on stand, Focal Start/Shutterstock.com; Postcard, Eastern Beach,
Benidorm. Ediciones Hermanos Galiana

For Silvia and Marina, my inspiration in all endeavors, every day.

CONTENTS

ACKNOWLEDGMENTS

This project started as a vague idea many years ago when I was on the Costa del Sol overlooking the coastline and in awe of the construction cranes that seemed to forge a skyline on top of the existing skyline. This book is the result of many conversations with friends, colleagues, and family whose support has not only informed my approach and my analysis but has served as the lifeline that pulled me through moments of self-doubt and disorientation. I dedicate this book to my wife, Silvia, and our tenacious daughter, Marina. They sacrificed many hours so that I could read, think, and write to bring this all together. My parents are always present in all I do, and my work ethic and resilience is due in no small part to the model they have set for me.

Many others along the way have provided that emotional support that got me through during the dark moments that creep in late at night like gremlins seeking to erode confidence. I thank Kaitlin and Courtney who guided me through some tough moments with sage perspectives.

Ana Corbalán inspired me to write this book after reading the article I provided for her edited book with Ellen Mayock titled *Toward a Multicultural Configuration of Spain: Local Cities, Global Spaces*. Great friends like H. Rosi Song, Susan Larson, Malcolm Compitello, Marc Greenberg, Dennis Looney, Denis Provencher, Leigh Mercer, Elena Delgado, Michelle Murray, Jeffrey Coleman, Ben Fraser, Judy Nantell, Bob Davidson, Íñaki Prádanos, Jordi Marí, Jessica Folkart, Kathy Everly, Jorge Pérez, and Sam Amago provided incredible insights and invaluable *ánimo* to keep me focused and motivated. Silvia Bermúdez advised me with the proposal and provided vital feedback that helped me reframe it.

One of the great benefits of this project was the ability to develop closer ties with amazing scholars at the University of Málaga from a wide range

of disciplines including art history, architecture, tourism, and communication. I look forward to future projects with these amazing people. I especially want to recognize Maite Méndez Baiges, Alberto García, María José
Márquez Ballesteros, Juan Francisco Lozano, María Dolores Joyanes, Antonio Guevara, and Juan Antonio Perles. As much as I would love to keep the
jewel that is Málaga all to myself, I want to acknowledge the great artists and
thinkers who reside there and have been so generous with their time (and
patient with my questions): Diego Santos, Tecla Lumbreras, Alberto Llamas,
Eduardo Jiménez Urdiales, Daniel Natoli, and the late Pablo Aranda. I especially want to recognize Enrique del Río, owner of Librería Áncora. Enrique
was always on the lookout for titles for me, suggested ingenious strategies
to hunt down difficult-to-find texts, and would always be willing to introduce
me to authors and other scholars. I also want to thank architect José Seguí
Pérez as well as everyone at the Obervatorio del Medio Ambiente Urbano
(OMAU), especially Paloma Sanz Hernández. Outside of Málaga, I was fortu-
nate to rely on the support of colleagues like Tomás Mazón at the University
of Alicante, Luz C. Souto at the University of Valencia, and Juan Pablo Wert
Ortega at the University of Castilla-La Mancha. I also deeply appreciate the
openness and generosity of artists like María Moldes, Roberto Alcaraz, and
Rogelio López Cuenca. I certainly hope that one outcome of this project is
that their amazing and impactful work draws more attention by scholars in
the field of Iberian cultural studies.

I would be remiss if I did not recognize the colleagues at Georgia State
University who have contributed to the successful completion of this book
project through their support, moral as well as administrative. Foremost,
Sara Rosen, Dean of the College of Arts and Sciences, provided for a Research
Intensive Semester (RISe) at a crucial moment that diminished my duties as
department chair to allow me the time to focus and the space to think. I also
express my deepest gratitude to Dean Rosen and vice-president for research
and economic development at GSU, Tim Denning; their generosity enabled us
to include color images in this book. Early in the project, Jan Nijman, director
of the Urban Studies Institute at GSU, invited me to participate in a research
roundtable that helped me immensely to frame my research question and
to contemplate the Spanish coasts as "sites of consumption." Similarly, Lou
Ruprecht extended a kind invitation to present at the "Europe and Beyond"
colloquium hosted at Emory University that aided me in framing the initial
steps of the project. At that event I came to know Ema Guano, in the Anthropology Department at GSU, who works on tourism in northern Italy. I have
enjoyed our conversations since and I look forward to exploring projects

about the Mediterranean imaginary in tourism more broadly. When she was associate dean of the College of Arts and Sciences, Carol Winkler offered unwavering support as well as reality checks, when appropriate. Her prompt for me to "carve out the time" to get this book written impelled me to find a way to build writing time into my daily schedule. I would like to acknowledge Kavita Pandit, with whom I enjoyed talking through ideas to develop a writing schedule and for implementing writing accountability. I also want to thank Tim Jansa, David Cotter, Kristy Winkler, Trish Nolde and others who have worked with the Center for Urban Language Teaching and Research. Their dedication to the center and their deep and lasting friendship have meant so much. Last, but certainly not least, when I began my role as interim associate dean in the Honors College, Sarah Cook, then interim dean, allowed me to work from home once a week to focus exclusively on writing. Sarah epitomizes the notion of "generous thinking," and her support not only allowed me the time to finish the project but also inspires me as a leader.

Lastly, I want to thank Zack Gresham at Vanderbilt UP. He provided invaluable feedback throughout the entire process and opened innovative avenues that I would have otherwise left unexplored. I also want to thank Gianna Mosser for her belief in and support of this project. I also appreciate the quick responses and patience of Michael Shulman at Magnum Photos, Guillermo Carazo in the communication department for Greenpeace España, Dan Trujillo at Artists Rights Society, New York, and the great people at the Centro Pérez Siquier in Olula del Río, Almería.

Introduction

Concrete Coasts and Liquid Tourism

"El turismo fue nuestro *Plan Marshall*"

MANUEL FRAGA IRIBARNE, Minister of Information and Tourism, Spain (1962–1969)

This book argues that the story of Spain's development since the 1950s is the story of the Global South within the narrative of modernity. Through the exploitation of natural resources—sand, sun, and sea—Spain sought to entice tourist gaze of the Global North to offer a narrative of exotic escape and authenticity. Yet the destruction of the natural landscape through the urban development of the Mediterranean coasts and the islands not only reconfigures the physical built environment but also commodifies local cultural identity and heritage for foreign consumption by the global tourist. The paradox, then, is the perception that the natural landscape and authentic local cultures can reap miraculous economic benefits only when they are destroyed and reconstituted as an earthly paradise. As sites of consumption, these idyllic spaces attract tourist capital with the promise of spiritual salvation and physical rejuvenation which, in turn, promises economic salvation to the local residents and frames the modernization project on a national level. The story of Spain's urban development along the coasts since the 1950s sets the blueprint for the urban renewal projects throughout the Peninsula that reimagine cities like Madrid, Barcelona, Valencia, Sevilla, Bilbao, and Málaga where the identity of working-class neighborhoods has been redefined through gentrification projects that seek to appeal to the tourist gaze. The story of Spain's coasts that were built and marketed as an earthly paradise for the consumption of foreign visitors is also the story of sites around the globe from Bali to Cancún to Negril to Goa to Macau that exploit and export the same kind of utopic imaginary as sites for consumption. But the story of Spain's tourism cities (and other similar sites around the world) and the country's journey into modernity invite us to ponder the paradox of paradise through a series of questions: Who is the author of that story? Who is the intended audience? Who is part of the story and what is their role? Who is left out of the story and why? And most importantly, what is the possibility for proposing a different story, an alternative narrative to the dominant discourse of economic development through the so-called creative destruction of the natural landscape, large-scale urban renewal projects, and unregulated land speculation through corruption and collusion?

Through my focus on the urbanization of the Spanish coasts for tourism I offer here a critique to the "narrative of development" that originated during the so-called era of *desarrollismo* in the late Franco years and has informed modernization projects in Spain since. Because we are talking about "narratives" and the "story" of the modernization project, the field of cultural studies offers the most appropriate lens through which to examine representations of the built environment in Spain from Marbella and Torremolinos in the Costa de Sol (near Málaga) to Benidorm in the Costa Blanca (between Valencia and Alicante) and Girona in the Costa Brava near Barcelona (as well as the Canary and Balearic Islands). Since the early 1960s, this stretch of coastline has undergone (and continues to undergo) tremendous transformations that have urbanized the Mediterranean littoral in order to attract international tourism capital.

Dean MacCannell writes in his classic book *The Tourist: A New Theory of the Leisure Class* that modernity and the processes of modernization do not present themselves with a clear purpose and an understandable utility for all but that they are perceived as a project composed of fragments that are unorganized, wasteful, violent, superficial, unplanned, uneven, and inauthentic.[1] MacCannell recognizes, however, that while the individual and collective experience in society may convey an unequal, unorganized, and alarming sensation, under this disordered exterior there is a firm intention to establish "modern values" on a global level.[2] The sensation of instability and inauthenticity in modern society is, ironically, what propels the processes of modernization as an attempt to alleviate the feeling of disorder. But it is also this feeling of disorder in the modern world that creates a "unifying consciousness" in which modern society believes what is real and what is authentic resides in another place, in other historic times, in other cultures, in other lifestyles that are thought to be simpler and purer.³ From the perspective of the West, that "pure" place tends to be located in the so-called Global South, in regions like Asia, Latin America, and Africa that are perceived to be untouched by modernity. The central thesis MacCannell posits is that the empirical and ideological expansion of modern society is intimately connected in diverse ways with the development of international tourism and the phenomenon of "sightseeing" as a fundamental element of mass leisure culture in the modern world. What MacCanell has discovered is that the act of traveling should be considered a kind of ritual, typically for the middle classes, that is done as a means to contest differentiations within society. That is, sightseeing is an attempt on an individual and collective level to transcend the discontinuity of the modern experience through another that is unifying and totalizing. The differentiations in the world—be they cultural, economic, geographic, ethnic, historic, etc.—are displaced from their social, natural, and original context to be reconstituted and reintegrated in a narrative that affirms their authenticity in the reconstruction of a social identity and a cultural heritage.⁴

To contribute to the fields of tourism studies and urban studies, I call attention to a variety of forms of cultural production that along with film and literature also includes postcards and tourism propaganda, material productions that have received little or no attention previously. I also examine photographic images and how new media like Instagram both offer new avenues for distribution that democratize access and production at the same time they ironically reinforce traditional visual tropes associated with tourist spaces. While many critics in peninsular urban studies tend to focus on Madrid and Barcelona, I aim to upend the center/periphery dichotomy by looking at the Mediterranean coast in Spain, hence my focus on what transpired in Torremolinos and Benidorm as the model for unregulated speculation, political collusion and corruption, and the commodification of space in which the so-called Spanish Economic Miracle was "built," launching the country's modernization project. By building the coasts, Spain engaged in mostly corrupt practices in order to appeal to the foreign gaze of a "modern" Europe that sought escape from the pressures of the developed world in the Spanish beaches and hotels. In the years leading up to the economic crisis of 2008, a number of corruption investigations like Operación Hidalgo and Operación Ballena Blanca exposed vast global criminal networks of money laundering and drug trafficking in connection to urban development projects and real estate along the Costa del Sol. Operación Malaya, the largest urban corruption scandal in Spanish history, exposed an endemic corruption within the fiscal, juridical, and political institutions that guide modernization and

urbanization projects in Spain. I argue that Operación Malaya can be understood retrospectively as a prelude to the economic crisis of 2008. Today the
vulnerability of precarious (often seasonal labor), the urban protests of the
Indignados, the widespread housing evictions across the country, and the
growing backlash of "turistofobia" may be understood as symptoms of crisis
that evoke the endgame of Spain's modernization project started more than
fifty years ago on the coasts with the *desarrollismo* (development-ism) of the
1960s, when coastal towns like Torremolinos and Benidorm were transformed
into the epicenters of Spain's tourism industry. The many so-called "ghost
hotels" that pepper the Spanish coastlines, tourism-focused building projects that were abandoned in the wake of the 2008 financial meltdown, stand
today I argue as monuments of crisis that embody the paradox of paradise
and reify the impact of the ideology that has guided Spain's modernization
project since the early 1960s.

A salient contribution of this study is to dismantle the facile and static
boundaries that often separate the study of contemporary Spanish culture
into pre-Franco, Franco, and post-Franco. What I demonstrate is that the
design and construction of cities like Torremolinos and Benidorm, once
sleepy fishing villages, into fetishized and commodified spaces meant to
attract the consumptive gaze of the foreign tourist infused Spain with an
inherent contradiction. While many have asserted that Spain enters the
global stage with the 1992 Olympics in Barcelona, I argue that the country
sought to entice a foreign if not global gaze much earlier by selling Spain as
"different" in the 1960s. This marketing strategy allowed the Franco regime
to preserve its conservative ideology at the same time it embraced a more
liberal economic paradigm. Northern Europeans were offered an escape from
the stresses of modern life in the exotic landscapes and primitive culture of
the Mediterranean coasts. Lastly, by examining cultural production beyond
novel and film this book places various forms of cultural representations into
dialogue by focusing on their underlying discourse of development (whether
critique or defense). While many of these "texts" traditionally have been dis-
missed as frivolous or unworthy of academic study because they are so often
associated with popular culture, especially the perceived kitschy superficiality
evocative of coastal tourism, my approach understands them as social artifacts that not only offer a keen insight into a society's collective psychology
in a given era but also assert the validity of the humanities to offer a unique
critical perspective that complements the approaches of the social sciences.

Publications related to the topic of tourism in Spain include Justin Crumbaugh's *Destination Dictatorship: The Spectacle of Spain's Tourist Boom and the*

Reinvention of Difference (2009), Sasha Pack's *Tourism and Dictatorship: Europe's Peaceful Invasion of Franco's Spain* (2006), and *Spain Is (Still) Different: Tourism and Discourse in Spanish Identity* edited by Eugenia Afinoguénova and Jaume Martí-Olivella (2008). Likewise, urban studies in Spain has become a rich area of study as demonstrated by recent books such as Malcolm Compitello's *De Fortunata a la M40: Un siglo de cultura de Madrid* (2003), Ann Davies's *Spanish Spaces: Landscape, Space and Place in Contemporary Spanish Culture* (2012), Benjamin Fraser's *Henri Lefebvre and the Spanish Urban Experience* (2011) and *Toward an Urban Cultural Studies: Henri Lefebvre and the Humanities* (2015), Susan Larson's *Constructing and Resisting Modernity: Madrid 1900–1936* (2011), Stephen Vilaseca's *Barcelonan Okupas: Squatter Power!* (2013), and Silvia Bermúdez and Anthony Geist's *Cartographies of Madrid* (2019). *The Paradox of Paradise: Creative Destruction and the Rise of Urban Coastal Tourism in Contemporary Spanish Culture* breaks new ground by integrating tourism studies with urbanism to examine and critique the narrative of development in Spain. While critics associated with tourism studies discuss the economic and political impact of tourism on Spanish culture and society, there has been no discussion of the role of the city and urban development. Inversely, critics who focus on urban studies have not given attention to the Mediterranean coasts and tend instead to write about Madrid and Barcelona, the two largest cities in Spain often considered the political and cultural centers of the country.

This book builds on the foundation laid by Sasha Pack, Eugenia Afinoguénova and Jaume Martí-Olivella, and Justin Crumbaugh through their seminal works on Spanish tourism studies. These early works on Spanish tourism studies tended to focus on the question of identity in Spain—be it economic, political, or national—and how it adapted, or not, to cross-cultural interactions or resisted, or not, existing cultural stereotypes. In *Tourism and Dictatorship: Europe's Peaceful Invasion of Franco's Spain*, Pack, a European historian, explores what he calls Spain's "tourism policy" that formulated during the Franco regime to extract wealth from Northern European nations through the precipitous acceleration of tourism in the 1960s.[5] Pack notes that Spain marketed its coasts to Northern Europeans as a sand and sun playground not by accident. Europeans, he asserts, had a long history of tourism and in a reconstructed post-war Europe they also possessed "unprecedented disposable income and time."[6] The sun-soaked Mediterranean for its part, he continues, offered a more attractive travel destination for the European leisure class than the frigid beaches of the North Atlantic. Moreover, Spain's proximity, the progressive liberalization of border policies in Europe during the 1950s, and the expansion of cheap charter flights made travel to the warm

Mediteranean beaches irresistible. All of these factors along with the advent of jet travel in the late 1960s exploded tourism in Spain that grew from 993,100 tourists in 1954 to 10,506,675 in 1964, and 31,335,806 in 1973.[7] Such tourism policy not only catalyzed the modernization projects of Spain during the second half of the dictatorship, but also wrought a prolonged struggle between reformists like Fraga who advocated for the rising class of tourism interests and more conservative technocrats affiliated with the Opus Dei who favored more traditional industries. Additionally, Pack notes that as tourism grew in importance for the Spanish economy, it ironically strengthened existing tensions between the center and periphery as funds from the lucrative tourism industry along the coasts were diverted to subsidize an impoverished interior. Pack concludes that Spain's experience with international tourism lends support to the notion that mass leisure and personal mobility have played critical roles in global society that have provoked changes in commercial policy, altered standards of social decorum, and shifted conceptions of Spain's national and European identities.[8] While Pack approaches Spanish tourism from a historical and policy vantage point, Afinoguénova and Martí-Olivella's *Spain Is (Still) Different: Tourism and Discourse in Spanish Identity* examines cultural encounters in tourism through approaches to cultural production, namely literature and film.[9] Whereas Pack is focused on the explosion of tourism and its rapid escalation as the primary economic driver in Spain, Afinoguénova and Martí-Olivella's edited collection brings together a range of essays that focus on the theme of tourism from the nineteenth century through the early twentieth-century through the Franco regime. The title of the book re-frames the famous Spanish tourism slogan from the 1960s, "Spain is different," to examine the discourses about Spanish identity and the role tourism has played in producing and circulating concepts of difference related to Spanish culture. The editors state that the aim of their volume is to reconsider the success of Spain and Spanish-ness and to interrogate the discourses and practices related to tourism that tend to "obscure the social roles, interests, and consensuses inherent in the definition of Spain as a tourist destination."[10] They add that the book is inspired also by a need to counter the official triumphalist discourses of the successes of tourism in Spain by examining the linkages between tourism, the organization of economic and cultural fields, and Spanish identity. At the same time, however, they have sought to avoid the trap of viewing tourism as simply a vehicle for the transmission of identity by understanding both tourism and identity as processes and practices that operate together to produce a sense of self individually and collectively. Lastly, Crumbaugh's *Destination Dictatorship: The Spectacle of Spain's Tourist Boom and the Reinvention of Difference* focuses on the years of desarrollismo during the 1960s in Spain and examines the symbolic practices that underlied the burgeoning tourism industry.[11] Crumbaugh analyzes the ways in which films like Lazaga's *El turismo es un gran invento* offered a "meta-theoretical blueprint" to recast the Franco regime as a champion of progress, prosperity, and modernization that worked in collaboration with Western democracies to improve the lives of Spaniards.[12] He also includes the understudied writings of Manuel Fraga that highlighted the importance of mass media and tourism, and he analyzed the ideological implications and commercial impact of the marketing campaign "Spain is different." Lastly, Crumbaugh's approach to the films of Manolo Escobar examines the commercial appeal of Escobar; at the same time, it traces the ideological dimensions of the fixation that underlie Spanish film in the 1960s on sexual transgressions with tourists, specifically through the figure of the "Sueca."

While I am not aware of any single-authored or edited books centered on Spanish tourism published in the US in at least a decade, there have been recent publications in Spain that have focused on cultural production, specifically visual culture, associated with tourism. Alicia Fuentes Vega with *Bienvenido, Mr. Turismo: Cultura visual del boom en España* examines the visual culture of the boom years of Spanish tourism including brochures, advertisements, cartoons, and, to a lesser extent, postcards.[13] Vega studies the visual selling of Spain through iconography throughout the Peninsula, not just along the coasts. My approach to postcards builds on her study of visual culture by analyzing the ideological implications of the materiality of a cultural product so emblematic of tourism, while also exploring the contradictions and obstacles that one encounters in the study of a product so ubiquitous within tourism, especially along the coasts. Moreover, where Vega offers incisive analysis on visual culture in the 1960s tied to tourism in Spain, I seek to draw connections to the contemporary social, economic, and political situation in Spain through the lens of cultural studies. In *1960s–1970s Costa Brava: Postals, Postales, Cartes Postales, Postcards*, Jordi Puig Castellano presents postcards of the Costa Brava region from the 1960s and 1970s.[14] A travel writer, Puig Castellano seeks to capture and evoke the essence of an era through a documentary approach to postcards. Through the images he presents the contradictions and paradoxes of a time in Spain when society witnessed rapid and tremendous change. Yet, he also offers a careful documentation and classification of the more than fifteen thousand postcards he consulted for this project, thus endowing the book with a kind of archival purpose. With this said, Puig Castellano's book is less academic and more artistic, imbued with a nostalgic tone of a bygone era that attests to the power of the lowly post-card and its strong hold on individual and collective identity and memory.

The ways this book builds on previous publications centered on Spanish tourism are several. First, I am able to expand the discussion temporally beyond the end of the Franco regime and the early years of the democracy to track a trajectory that maps onto current post-2008 crises that challenge Spanish society. Secondly, I expand the discussion of tourism in Spain by integrating it with urban studies and the need to mount infrastructure to support the influx of tourists from Northern Europe. None of the texts that I mention here has addressed the ideological, cultural, economic, or political implications of urbanizing the Mediterranean coasts in Spain as a key component of tourism policies. Lastly, I incorporate into this book an examination of understudied texts, novels and film, but also other forms of cultural production including travel brochures, postcards, and photography. Not only do I expand the study of tourism in cultural fields beyond literature and film, but I also incorporate a consideration of material culture—architecture, interior design, postcards, brochures, souvenirs, and the urban space itself—as texts that may be read as social artifacts. Additionally, I incorporate new media, such as Instagram and Facebook, into my discussion of visual culture and the ideological implications for the story of tourism in Spain and the narrative of modernization.

The Spanish Economic Miracle and the Urbanization of Spain's Mediterranean Coasts

In a 1967 brochure promoting the Costa del Sol, the Ministry of Tourism extols both the modern ambience of the coast that offers the tourist a culture of leisure through "playas magníficas (y) centros turísticos de fuerte atmósfera cosmopolita" (magnificent beaches and tourist sites with a strong cosmopolitan atmosphere) as well as the quaint primitive feel of "pueblecitos de pescadores, de ambiente sencillo y primitivo, espléndidas vegas tropicales y las montañas que la protegen de los fríos del interior" (small fishing villages with a simple, primitive atmosphere surrounded by tropical meadows and mountains that protect it from the cold climate of the Peninsula's interior). Characterized by vibrant colors, exuberant flora, lively people, and a bright Mediterranean sun, the brochure boasts that the Costa del Sol offers visitors access to the monumental splendor of ancient civilizations and the deep emotions of folkloric culture like flamenco and religious celebrations like Semana Santa. At the same time, tourists may take advantage of the "mil oportunidades deportivas" (a thousand opportunities for sports) such as water-skiing, deep-sea fishing, hiking, and golf. The Costa del Sol, moreover, possesses an unparalleled gastronomy typified by gazpacho, many varieties of fresh fish from the Mediterranean, and typical Málaga moscatel sweet wine. More importantly, a "amplia, modernísima y numerosa" (vast, super-modern, numerous) network of hotels extends all along the coast from Málaga to Tarifa with tourist resorts and "urbanizaciones" (housing developments) of the highest quality and comfort as well as an intricate system of rail and motorways along with continuous direct flights and various seaports that facilitate the tourist's arrival by any means of transportation. A similar brochure from the same year for the Costa Blanca, which stretches from Murcia through Alicante to Valencia, is not only structured similarly to extol the history, folklore and gastronomy but also repeats similar phrasing as the brochure for the Costa del Sol. The blinding Mediterranean sun, paradisaical beaches, and colorful landscapes beckon to the tourist while an extensive network of hotels "en continuo crecimiento" (in constant growth) offer breathtaking views of the sea. Highways and railways as well as air and seaports allow tourists the ability to arrive by any form of transportation but also offer mobility to the Balear Islands, other cities in southern Spain, and even Africa which the brochure describes as a "continente en período de desarrollo" (continent in a period of development). Both the brochure for the Costa del Sol and the one for the Costa Blanca engage the gaze of the tourist with professional color photos of the landscapes and seascapes, activities, and food that would characterize their experience along the coast along with maps that entice the cartographic imagination of the tourist.

That these brochures (and many others published over the last fifty years) highlight the urban amenities and transportation networks is far from accidental. The 1963 Ley de Centros y Zonas de Interés Turístico Nacional (Law for Centers and Zones of National Tourist Interest) acknowledges the inherent appeal of Spain's natural resources, specifically its Mediterranean coastline, to attract foreign tourists. However, the same document recognizes that those areas are ill-prepared to accommodate a mass influx of visitors because they lack the services and infrastructure needed, especially with regard to water, sanitation, and, most especially, housing development. Through this law Manuel Fraga, the Minister of Information and Tourism during the dictatorship of Francisco Franco, sought to establish an official public policy to foment and direct development along the coasts to complement private efforts and facilitate the "explotación turística" (exploitation of tourism) while also imposing regulations that hoped to impede possible rampant, uncontrolled overbuilding.[15] Even in the early years of Spain's coastal tourism boom, Fraga and others in the Franco regime recognized that the lack of urban development along the coasts imposed serious impediments to the expected annual growth of "la afluencia turística extranjera" (influx of foreign tourism). The law proposes a "cuidada planificación técnica" (meticulous technical planification) of the coastal areas that would not only accommodate but actually hoped to stimulate a controlled growth of the tourism industry to guarantee immediate profitability for any investments. In *Ordenación Territorial y Urbanística de las Zonas Turísticas*, Javier Sola Teyssiere asserts that Spain enacted this law as an urgent response to the rapid exponential increase in tourist demand in the late 1950s and early 1960s.[16] The law, he states, sought "resquicios oportunos" (opportune chinks) that would allow authorities to "bordear" (skirt), if not ignore completely, the prevailing urbanism legislation of the time established by the 1956 Ley del Suelo that imposed a slower rhythm of planning regulation.[17] Facing the enormous need to address tourism demand, authorities prioritized the "desarrollo cuantitativo del fenómeno turístico frente a una planificación territorial del mismo" (quantitative development of the tourist phenomenon over a territorial planification of it).[18] Nevertheless, adds Sola Teyssiere, within the framework of development planning and the public interventions related to the promotion of tourism, one begins to perceive certain measures related to the zoning ordinances and urban planning of tourist locations that aimed to "evitar la saturación incipiente de ciertas zonas o bien, más frecuentemente, promover la oferta de nuevas localizaciones" (avoid the incipient saturation of certain zones or, more frequently, to promote offerings in new locations).[19] If, he continues, the directives about tourism policy outlined in the *I Plan de Desarrollo Económico y Social (1964–1967)* urged a programmed evolution of tourism through a better exploitation of natural resources to expand tourism offerings (as well as increased tourism marketing campaigns) through the *Ley de Zonas y Centros de Interés Turístico Nacional*, then the *Ley 197/1963 de Centros y Zonas de Interés Turístico Nacional*, he asserts, is a foundational text as "uno de los antecedentes más sobresalientes en materia de ordenación territorial del turismo" in Spain (one of the most outstanding precursors in terms of zoning ordinances related to tourism).[20]

The expressed objective of this law is to erect ordinances that map the urban planning and development of coastal tourism (and in some cases tourism in Spanish cities in the Peninsula's interior) through concepts that are both precise enough to guide the trajectory of said development yet elastic enough to allow entrepreneurial innovation. The law specifies that all tourist centers must present a Plan de Ordenación (Ordinance Plan) that maps the geographical area for development and addresses the needs for water and sanitation, electricity, and transportation as well as anticipated demands for postal service, telegraph and telephone, and other kinds of communication. Additionally, tourist centers must also compose a Plan de Promoción Turística (Tourism Promotion Plan) that delimits the physical area to be developed and estimates the minimum and maximum number of housing needs along with the categories of lodging, enumerates additional facilities needed that are considered "imprescindibles" (essential), anticipates any improvements or modifications to beautify the landscape, and offers additional economic studies that address the costs of development. Moreover, existing industries would need to implement "correcciones precisas" (precise corrections) to adapt their operations in ways that contribute to tourism. In *Tourism and Dictatorship: Europe's Peaceful Invasion of Franco's Spain*, Sasha Pack specifies the industries considered to be "anti-touristic" and whose presence near or within tourist areas could create nuisances large and small.[21] Among those industries, Pack points to cement factories, fertilizer plants, petrochemicals, metallurgy, foundries, mining, fishing, and livestock raising. Up to 1963, conflicts between resort tourism and conventional industries would be handled at the municipal level. However, the Ministry of Information and Tourism, Pack asserts, argued that the effective resolution of such conflicts would require very careful zoning on a national scale. Pack states that such zoning was attractive to Fraga for two reasons: first, it would resolve the perpetual conflict between tourist and "anti-tourist" industries in favor of the former, and second, comprehensive zoning would expand state control over infrastructural quality and over the developers themselves.[22]

Once declared a Zone of National Tourism Interest, any future businesses in the area as well as any assets belonging to the State, regional government, or municipality must focus their activities on tourism or risk expropriation. Those who contribute to the creation of an area with the "National Tourism Interest" designation through investments, construction, services or other activities related to tourism will enjoy benefits that range from reduced taxes, special amortization rates, up to ninety percent discounts on customs duties for the importation of construction machinery, special preference to obtain credit, access to public assets, and receipt of forced transfers of title for property not developed with sufficient efficacy. The law also specifies that the Commissioner of the Economic Development Plan will work in coordination with other State entities ranging from sanitation and water works to port authorities, housing and urban development to architecture, and state heritage offices to tourism agencies. The law concludes by mapping the blueprint for such widespread mobilization of State offices and agencies whose charge, especially through the ministries of housing and urban development, is the acquisition of plots of land under the adequate economic conditions, through forced expropriation if necessary, to build the necessary infrastructure both to meet and stimulate the demand of foreign tourism in Spain, especially along the coasts.

If Spain's 1959 Plan de Estabilización (Stabilization Plan) marks a watershed in which the government shifts from the autarkic Falangist ideology toward economic liberalization directed by authoritarian Catholic technocrats and focused on an already burgeoning tourism industry, then the 1963 Ley de Centros y Zonas de Interés Turístico erects an ideological framework about the space of the coasts, exploitation of natural resources, infrastructure and facilty needs, and the guiding purpose of the built environment on the Mediterranean littoral. While tourism may have saved Spain from economic collapse in the late 1950s and brought the country's so-called "economic miracle" in the 1960s, the urbanization of the coasts not only facilitates the exponential increase of foreign tourism in Spain but, more importantly, establishes an intimate connection between urban renewal and the desire to attract the gaze, and subsequently the capital, of the foreign tourist. Ángel Palomino in *El milagro turístico* pierces the notion of a monolithic Spanish economic miracle that derived from the tourism boom of the 1960s.[23] From his point of view, a series of miracles based on illusionism and magic fostered the conditions for the tourism boom to become possible. Palomino notes that between 1926 (when the Hotel Miramar opened in Málaga) and 1959 (when the iconic Hotel Pez Espada was constructed in Torremolinos), no luxury hotels had been established along the Costa del Sol. The miracle was not, he asserts, the economic revitalization in Spain that resulted from the tourism boom of the 1960s, but what he finds miraculous is that anyone thought to erect "palacios en el desierto" (palaces in the desert) when no rational expectation justified such vast investments of capital along the coasts.[24] Without even a rudimentary market analysis or a clear sense of how to address telecommunication, sanitation, sewage, water and electricity, and other needs, Palomino contends that the miraculous origins of coastal tourism in Spain lie in the desire to build an "industry" where one had not existed before, that offered no objective method to calculate possible earnings, nor presented signs of any return on investment. With the opening of the Hotel Pez Espada, "amanece la nueva era" (the new era dawns) of the Costa del Sol in which Palomino notes a 1400 percent increase in the number of luxury hotels between 1959 and 1969 that is accompanied by a 510 percent increase in visitors.[25] Palomino coincides with Lefebvre and understands the Costa del Sol as a constructed space in a sense that transcends the physical built environment along the Mediterranean Sea. More than the hotels, restaurants, and attractions, Palomino states that the Costa del Sol is the result of "gigantescas inversiones" (gigantic investments) clearly, but more so the confluence of the "mercado mundial del Ocio" (global market of leisure) with the market of real estate speculation to re-create the Costa del Sol as a space of consumption that marketed (and continues to market) the illusion of a "paraíso terrenal" (earthly paradise).[26] In *Ocio, Turismo y Hoteles en la Costa del Sol*, Rafael Esteve Secall refers to the confluence noted by Palomino as "la revolución del ocio" (the revolution of leisure), which connotes a new cultural and ideological models and facilitates a collective shift from "homo faber" to "homo ludens."[27] Secall asserts that technological advances in mass media, the abandonment of agricultural and a rural lifestyle, and the predominance of employment in industrial and service industries with higher wages and more clearly defined workdays have provoked economic and social transformations but also spatial and temporal changes that have sharpened the need for leisure as well as the possibility to enjoy it. If everyday life has become more urban and days are defined by work, then the need for spaces and time defined by leisure has likewise grown in importance. The urban growth along the Mediterranean coasts, Secall continues, is evidence of the social, economic, and technological transformations that have facilitated travel and leisure, but it also imposes a "lógica nueva" (new logic) in urban policies that serve private interests, adhere to the desire to generate capital through flexible accumulation, and convert urban centers into sites of consumption.[28]

The political and economic policies ushered in by technocrats such as Manuel Fraga that focused almost exclusively on tourism to generate revenue not only set into motion large-scale development of the urban, built environments along the Spanish coasts but also conceptualized the Mediterranean beaches as spaces of consumption that entice the gaze of foreign tourists, in particular those from Northern Europe. Remote fishing villages in the 1950s, towns like Torremolinos and Benidorm became the epicenters of the Spanish tourism industry in the 1960s and 70s. In an article from *El País* about the ecological impact of coastal urbanization, Manuel Planelles cites some shocking statistics from a 2016 report developed by the Observatorio de Sostenibilidad.

According to the authors of the report, 27.8 percent of the 7,898 kilometers of coastline in Spain have been urbanized or transformed by humans. In twenty-four years, between 1987 and 2011, the occupancy within 500 meters of the sea has grown 32.9 percent at a velocity of 22.7 kilometers every twelve months. The report states that, at that rate, in 251 years 100 percent of the coast will be completely urbanized. The authors of the report signal that an increase in resident population parallels the expansion of urbanized space along the coasts and highlights that between 1991 and 2011 the number of inhabitants there grew 22.6 percent, passing 15 million and approaching 20 million. 35.2 percent of the 3,829 kilometers along the Atlantic and Mediterranean have been transformed into housing, commercial zones, infrastructure, or strip mining. The areas that are hardest hit are the Costa del Sol and the Costa Blanca where 81 percent and 67 percent of the coastline, respectively, have been urbanized. Planelles concludes the article by quoting the authors of the report—Fernando Prieto, Raúl Estévez, and Carlos Alfonso—who worry that the rapid transformation of the coasts propels Spain toward an ecological and economic collapse. They comment that the overdevelopment of the coasts to accommodate and stimulate tourism in Spain ironically endangers the viability of the tourism industry by degrading the quality of the beaches that attract those foreign visitors.[29] On the Costa del Sol today, there is hardly a break in the coastline development from Málaga to Gibraltar. This developed area is not only the epitome of sprawl but is now so big it is being referred to as Spain's second biggest "city." Benidorm, on the other hand, was a once-sleepy seaside village that is now the model for vertical growth and second only to Manhattan in skyscraper density. Tomás Mazón, a disciple of sociologist Mario Gaviria who was a key architect of Benidorm, describes the city as one of the most spectacular examples of tourism development one can imagine. In "Benidorm: un destino turístico de altura," Mazón plays on the word "altura" to point to Benidorm's vertical altitude as well as its stature as a tourist destination. He references the more than five million international tourists who visit Benidorm annually and combine with Spanish tourists and residential tourists for sixty million overnight stays per year, the second greatest in Europe. Mazón outlines the installations and facilities of the urban environment that accommodate such high tourist demand: 150 hotels and 40,000 vacancies; tens of thousands of apartments; 383 restaurants; more than 1,000 bars and cafés; 60 banquet halls, discos, and gambling halls; 170 disco bars; 63 travel agencies, 1 cable ski; 11 camping resorts with close to 12,000 vacancies; more than 2,000 businesses; 6 consulates; 69 banks; more than 200 real estate agencies; 4,600 hammocks and 1,400 parasols; 1 water park and 6 mini-golf courses. In 1950, he states, the population of Benidorm was 1,720 inhabitants and in 2010 it was counted at 75,000. Mazón notes, however, that in reality the population never descends below 150,000 people in any month of the year and in the peak months the population reaches more than 600,000 people.[30]

Torremolinos and Benidorm, then, epitomize fetishized urban spaces and falsified landscapes that "learned from Las Vegas," to borrow from Venturi, where leisure masks the machinations of capital with a ludic narrative and accentuates the effects of capital on cultural identity during the years of Spain's "desarrollismo" in the 1960s. The commodification of cultural identity (through the images of flamenco dancers, bullfighters, guitars and other "typically" Spanish markers) to attract international capital, specifically that of Western and Northern Europe where countries saw an economic boom after World War II through reconstruction policies such as the Marshall Plan, mirrored the conversion of Torremolinos and Benidorm into sites of consumption.

Creative Destruction and Spaces of Consumption along the Spanish Coasts

Torremolinos and Benidorm, along with many other urbanized centers along the Mediterranean coasts as well as the Canary and Balearic Islands, exemplify what Manuel Vázquez Montalbán calls a "ciudad democrática" (democratic city) that is open only in appearance.[31] For Vázquez Montalbán, such urban spaces stage a "dramatization" of modernity that excludes alternative ideologies, subverts agency through simulacra, and adheres to the logic of the market. Pleasure and leisure, especially through mass media technologies, replace direct political repression to control individual consciousness and thus transform "el gran Hermano" (Big Brother) into "el gran Consumidor" (Big Consumer). By establishing consumption, of ideas as much as products, as an overarching social and cultural value, a market-driven paradigm, he posits, controls consciousness by instilling individuals with the false perception that their purchasing power is proof of their agency and free will if not their political power. In a similar vein, Sharon Zukin examines the social power at play in the shopping experience at sites of consumption from ancient marketplaces to designer boutiques and big-box stores like Walmart to online websites in *Point of Purchase: How Shopping Changed American Culture*.[32] What

Zukin calls the "discourse of democratic rights" parallels Vázquez Montalbán's "democratic city" and asserts that what is marketed and sold is not a
product or even an experience but the lure of "true value" where the consumer, free from work and politics, believes they may exert individual agency
and find emotional validation through their power to purchase.[33] She notes
that the accumulation of "social spaces, cultural labels, and critical guides"
around consumerist behaviors and activities carry deep ideological implications that have wielded tremendous power over our imagination.[34] Vázquez
Montalbán points to Seville and Barcelona as examples of cities that literally
have redesigned their physical spaces through a kind of plastic surgery in
preparation for the Expo and the Olympics, respectively, in 1992.[35] Through the
transformation of their physical spaces, Seville and Barcelona transformed
also their underlying ideology to epitomize the "democratic city" that "está
conquistada y autoregulada por su cerebro de ciudad mercado, de la ciudad
espectáculo, de la ciudad simulacro" (is conquered and self-regulated by its
mind as a market city, as the city of spectacle, as the city of simulacra).[36] In *El
tsunami urbanizador español y mundial*, Ramón Fernández Durán expands the
notion of the "ciudad espectáculo" (city of spectacle) beyond the macro-events
of 1992 described by Vázquez Montalbán.[37] He includes the creation of transportation infrastructure (i.e. highways, high velocity train rails, airports, sea
ports, etc.), the construction of so-called "parques de tecnología" (technology
parks) that house business offices and commercial centers at the outskirts of
metropolitan zones, large-scale civil engineering projects that lead to further
privatization and gentrification of public spaces, urban restructuring justified
in the name of culture (through the Prado, the Guggenheim, MACBA, Mata-
dero, etc.) yet accompanied by the proliferation of transnational companies
(Starbucks, McDonalds, Tony Roma, etc.), the creation of new buildings for
Spanish transnational companies (Ciudad Bancaria del Santander, Endesa,
Repsol, Telefónica, etc.), and other macro-projects and macro-events like
the Copa de América in Valencia, Madrid Ciudad Olímpica, la Expo de Agua
in Zaragoza, Forum de las Culturas in Barcelona, and more.[38] The result of
such "operaciones de cirugía urbana" (urban surgery operations), Fernández Durán states, is the reconfiguration of cities and urban spaces as sites
of consumption where luxury appears accessible to all and public space has
been privatized, commercialized, and is controlled through surveillance.[39]

   In Spain, the notion that economic growth results from urban construction projects intimately tied to land speculation, international tourism,
and consumer culture did not originate in 1992 nor even after the death of
Franco but was born on the coasts.[40] For Henri Lefebvre, the Mediterranean

coast epitomizes the kind of commodified and fetishized space akin to a theme park where the "consumption of space" transforms into a "space of consumption." *Todo bajo el sol*, a graphic novel by Ana Penyas, explores the transformation of the Spanish coasts since the 1950s into a "space of consumption" and how that shift impacts the lives of families and individuals across generations. Penyas opens the text with a dedication that reads, "A quienes tuvieron que abandoner su lugar y a quienes que se quedaron como extraños en su propia tierra" (To those who had to abandon their place and to those who remained as if foreigners in their own land).[41] The first page presents four panels with black and white drawings that evoke a bygone era and depict the actions of a fisherman who is pulling his boat onto shore. In one panel, all the viewer sees are feet anchored in the sand and in the others various angles of the man's torso as he pulls and pushes the boat onto the sand. Taken together, the panels convey the labor and motion that underlie the actions and define the space of the beach during that time. On the next page, another four-panel series offers color images in a poignant juxtaposition with the black and white drawings. These latter images capture the sense of space today as it is defined by tourist activity. Again, disjointed images of feet in the sand, a torso pushing a parasol into the beach, hands opening it, and another hand grasping a beach bag suggest actions associated with tourism and leisure that have come to define the space as it is now. On the next page, a wide shot shows the viewer a group of fishermen working together to get the boat up onto the sand while the page facing it depicts an overweight solitary tourist under the parasol who is pulling a tourist guidebook from his beach bag. These first pages set the context of the deep transformations of the "space" of the coasts and its effects on the individuals of a singular family across generations, who lose their "place" as tourism becomes the dominant economic activity along the Spanish coasts.

In *The Production of Space*, Lefebvre states that the attraction of sun, sea, and sand may lure tourists initially but then it becomes a qualitative demand for "materiality and naturalness" to be rediscovered and consumed through their "real or apparent immediacy."[42] Thus, he concludes, space is split into two kinds of regions, both of which uphold neo-capitalist and neo-imperialist ideologies: regions exploited for the purpose of production of consumer goods and regions exploited for the purpose of the *consumption of space*. As a result, he continues, tourism and leisure become major areas of investment and profitability by integrating with the construction sector, property speculation, and general urbanization but also intertwining with the capitalism of agriculture and food production. The construction of the Mediterranean coasts, then, is at once physical and ideological, infused with an inherent dialectic between liberation and repression in which middle-class tourists seek escape from the mundane realities of everyday life in the industrialized societies of Northern Europe, especially those where wealth flourished from the impact of the Marshall Plan, by fleeing to the commodified spaces of the Spanish coasts designed for their consumption.[43] In *España a Go-Go*, the notable Spanish urban sociologist, Mario Gaviria (who was also a student and friend of Lefebvre) calls the dialectic between the production of space and the consumption of said space a "estrategia neocolonialista" (neocolonialist strategy) that manifests in the material construction of hotels and apartments as well as the speculation and land development that is implied.[44] Gaviria notes the irony of Spanish tourist spaces whose natural geophysical and climactic characteristics offer ideal natural conditions, especially for those from the colder environs of Northern Europe. However, for such natural spaces to be "utilized," they must first be dominated, habilitated, and urbanized in ways that attract tourists from the advanced industrialized European societies yet that also degrade natural spaces and make them scarcer. Tourism, Gaviria asserts, destroys the natural landscape in two ways: through the physical transformation of the natural environment but also through promotional materials for tour companies that "sell" Spain (as we see in the brochures earlier in this chapter) as a paradise. Moreover, he concludes, tourism not only destroys the natural landscape but also aggravates class differences between wealthy regions where investments have built infrastructure to accommodate and attract foreign tourists while residents in poorer areas lack schools, sewage systems, electricity, etc.[45] The benefits of these inauthentic landscapes designed to attract the foreign capital of tourists often do not, then, impact the everyday lives of the residents who live there.[46] Gaviria was a pioneer in tourism studies and a key figure in the design of Benidorm since the dawn of charter tourism in Spain in the early 1970s. Unlike the Costa del Sol that expanded without a clear or intentional plan to guide urban development, Gaviria viewed Benidorm as a kind of social experiment in which the planning of urban space to attract tourism intersected with marketing to create the notion of the city as a "materialization of welfare." The happiness associated with the economic welfare (often used interchangeably with the term well-being by normative economists) resulting from the so-called Spanish Economic Miracle manifested, Gaviria argued, in Spain's physical urban landscape, especially through costal tourism. For Gaviria, Benidorm epitomizes the idea of welfare because of its density and verticality as well as its efficient use of space and its ecological sustainability. If tourism is the key to economic success, he reasoned, then it was important to embrace it and design tourist centers to be efficient as well as inviting. Rather than sprawling over hundreds of square miles, Benidorm extends vertically (covering only seven kilometers of coastline) so the ecological footprint is minimized by avoiding large "urbanizaciones" (housing developments) that degrade the land and consume tremendous amounts of water. Benidorm, from Gaviria's perspective, is the ideal model for what a Mediterranean city should be: a theme park that understands its utopian purpose and is designed to attract and accommodate intensive tourism with all of its contradictions and nuances.

Lefebvre wrote *Toward an Architecture of Enjoyment* after visiting Mario Gaviria in Spain and contemplating the built environment of Benidorm. Leisure activities, he states, occur in "empty spaces" like beaches or snow-covered mountains.[47] In such spaces, the everyday is separated from the "non-everyday," and work distinguished from leisure. Thus, space must be reconfigured and turned into a space of enjoyment resulting, he concludes, in the "domination of preexisting spaces" and the "destruction of the abruptly dominated space."[48] Lefebvre concludes that leisure spaces ultimately seek to create a sense of utopia and share certain characteristics. First, they occupy transitional zones between labor and non-labor. Secondly, use is sharply contrasted with exchange, yet this contrast is dissimulated through myths of personal discovery and spiritual fulfillment (often communicated through promotional materials and brochures). Lastly, leisure spaces are contradictory where what spiritual salvation has been promised ends up being ephemeral and illusory. Lefebvre's reference to the "empty spaces" where leisure activities happen evokes the title of Dean MacCannell's book *Empty Meeting Grounds*.[49] MacCannell approaches the question of tourist space from a semiological perspective in which such spaces and the sights that accompany them may be understood as signs encoded with meaning that define the tourist experience and the contours of the tourist's emotional responses. For MacCannell, tourist experiences then become routinized and reinforce the semiological and ideological significance of the tourist space.[50] The "emptiness" of urban spaces designed for tourist consumption to which Lefebvre and MacCannell refer connects to what Manuel Delgado calls "la ciudad mentirosa" (the lying city) where rationalist urbanism is supplanted with the search for immediate economic benefits by converting empty public space into revenue-generating sites of consumption.[51] Through such a transformation, Delgado asserts, these public spaces are "aseado y bien peinado" (cleaned up and well-groomed) in ways that legitimize the discourse of urban development and gentrification by making these areas "apetecibles para especulación, el turismo y las demandas institucionales en materia de legitimidad" (appetizing for speculation, tourism, and institutional demands in matters of legitimacy).[52] The "illusion of transparency" as Lefebvre calls it in *The Production of Space*, masks the contradictions of capitalism with a sleek, luminous, innocent urban space that appears as a mirage (or a paradise as Palomino refers to the Spanish coasts) offering the individual a promise of escape from everyday life and the possibility of creating a new self through spectacle and consumption.[53] In the interest of capital and flexible accumulation, then, public space is reconfigured to appear devoid of conflict, exorcised of markers of class inequalities, and "emptied" of meaning such that leisure and pleasure define individual and collective experiences of these spaces. In *Place and Placelessness*, Edward Relph describes the "homogenizing influence" of tourism that destroys local and regional landscapes (which ironically often first attracted tourism) and replaces them with conventional tourist architecture that fabricates "synthetic landscapes and pseudo-places."[54] He calls such locations "touristscapes" that are characterized by "other-directed architecture" that deliberately aim toward outsiders, spectators, passers-by, and especially consumers. The effect of such architecture, Edwards continues, is the creation of other-directed places that suggest nothing of the people who live and work there but declare themselves unequivocally to be "Vacationland" or "Consumerland," characterized by "exotic decoration, gaudy colors, grotesque adornments, and the indiscriminate borrowing of styles and names from the most popular places of the world."[55]

David Harvey calls such individual and collective experiences of built environments an "urbanization of consciousness," in which the organization of the developed urban space conditions individuals and society according to the demands of the market.[56] The processes of consumption and accumulation not only construct urban spaces, but Harvey declares that they inform the individual's everyday experiences in those spaces. According to Harvey, the individual reads the symbolic order of the urban environment and internalizes it in such a way that spaces—whether they be forbidden, feared, ignored, or redundant space or shared, comfortable, or challenging spaces— define who we are, how we understand ourselves, and how we interact with others.[57] Capitalism, Harvey affirms, creates the conditions that facilitate the fetishization of the city by impelling the processes of "creative destruction" where working class communities are erased from the urban landscape and along with them the imprint of their history and memory in favor of property development, gentrification that appeals to the gaze of the consumer (especially that of the tourist).[58] The fusion of consumerist narcissism and the desire for self-realization foster, according to Harvey, an urbanization of consciousness that intoxicates the individual with fetishisms that perpetuate the contradictions of capitalism and reproduce structures of dominance. Harvey echoes the assertions of Vázquez Montalbán, Zukin, and others that the rhetoric of individual liberty and the subject's agency as it manifests through their capacity to purchase and consume not only masks the mechanisms of power but also subverts the possibility for political mobilization to resist the processes of capitalism.

The Mediterreanean coasts in Spain epitomize Harvey's notion of "creative destruction" where the virgin beaches have been urbanized into sites of consumption that have been "deterritorialized," literally and figuratively. For China C. Cabrerizo, tourism is the catalyst that drives the physical transformation of cities and the reconfiguration of undeveloped territories both as an economic stimulus and as a vehicle for political and social control. In *La ciudad negocio: Turismo y movilización social en pugna*, Cabrerizo recognizes tourism as an economic "salvavidas" (lifesaver) that offers an entry point into the global economic system for developing nations through the "habilitación" (habilitation) of spaces, urban and rural, into places that attract visitors and consumption with an inviting "cara amable" (a friendly face) that masks any negative impact.[59] The author points to a 2005 report from the World Tourism Organization (WTO) that advocates tourism as a change agent for impoverished countries, especially those in the Global South, to create a market that will attract consumers and serve as a motor for economic development. Spain's own "economic miracle" confirms the WTO's exultation of tourism as a vehicle for economic mobility within a global market. Spain's marginal economic and political status within Europe during the 1950s and 1960s (and Andalucía's marginalization within Spain) typifies the kind of developing country the WTO addresses and its economic transformation, moreover, models the social impact the WTO envisions.[60] Where the industrialization of the nineteenth and early twentieth centuries brought the creation of factories and industrial warehouses at the outskirts of cities along with nearby working-class neighborhoods and the reconfiguration of urban centers to accommodate the bourgeoisie, Cabrerizo sees the same kind of urban transformation and expansion through which cities and territories reconfigure themselves as sites of consumption to attract tourism. Through economic and cultural exploitation, tourism devours rural landscapes and coastal ecosystems and appropriates local culture and symbolic capital to convert them into products and commodities for consumption that attract desire by appealing to the tourist's gaze. As Cabrerizo asserts, anything and everything may be assimilated into the discourse and ideology of tourism and any space may be transformed into its protagonist: "Son los hoteles, las urbanizaciones con o sin campo de golf, los centros comerciales y de ocio, los parques temáticos, los museos, los puertos deportivos, los casinos y las zonas de fiesta, los aeropuertos y las grandes vías de movilidad. Pero también son los paraísos perdidos, las selvas tropicales, las playas vírgenes, la ciudad de los rascacielos, las millas de oro, de plata y de bronce, los paseos de arte, la meca del futbol, la ciudad de las tres culturas, la isla bonita, la costa azul, la blanca y la brava" (It is the hotels, the urban developments with or without a golf course, the shopping malls and entertainment centers, the museums, the marinas, the casinos and night clubs, the airports and the highways. But it is also the lost paradises, the tropical jungles, the virgin beaches, the cities of skyscrapers, the golden miles, and silver, and bronze, the art strolls, the football meccas, the city of three cultures, the beautiful island, the blue coast, and the white one, and the wild one).[61]

As Cabrerizo implies here, the urbanization of the Mediterranean coasts may be understood as a discourse that rewrites and renames the beachfront spaces, infusing and inscribing them with the logic, as well as the contradictions, of consumer capitalism. Although the discourse of urban development in the name of tourism may have begun in Spain along the coasts in the early 1960s, it has persisted over the last half-century as the guiding ideology for Spain's modernization project in which urban renewal, gentrification, and tourism have been intimately intertwined. Moreover, I argue, the current atmosphere of crisis in Spain—economic, ecological, cultural, and political—may be understood as the endgame of the impetus to build the coasts as sites of consumption. In *Capitalismo y turismo en España del "milagro económico" a la "gran crisis,"* Iván Murray Mas asserts that the focus on "capital turístico" (tourism capital) on the Mediterranean coasts as well as the Canary and Balearic Islands set Spain on a trajectory that has not only radically changed Spanish society but set the model for "procesos de deslocalización productiva" (processes for productive dislocation) through the colonization of new tourist peripheries in the Global South.[62] The "fiesta del ladrillo" (festival of bricks) in the 1960s and 1970s became the "fiebre del cemento" (cement fever) in the 1990s and 2000s, he states, as real estate speculation expanded like a virus where financial liberalization, monopolistic rents, and political deregulation created the conditions for a real estate bubble of "dimensiones mastodónicas" (Mastodonic dimensions).[63] The prioritization of what he calls the "negocio del ocio" (business of leisure) has reformulated Spain through the reconfiguration of urban spaces in such a way that tourism is implicated in all sectors of Spanish society and, as a consequence, is likewise implicated in the various manifestations of crisis in Spain today.

Construction, Consumption, and Crisis in Spain

From precarious labor to ecological impacts to social movements like the Indignados to political corruption scandals, the imprint of tourism, and especially urbanization related to tourism, can be found on all aspects of crisis that confront Spanish society today. Without a doubt, tourism is considered the driving force that is responsible for the Economic Miracle in the 1960s and continues to be the cornerstone of the Spanish economy, generating 11 percent of the country's GDP (about 178 billion euros in 2018) and almost 3 million jobs. However, the seasonal nature of the tourism industry and proliferation of service-oriented employment in restaurants, hotels, night clubs, etc. epitomize the shift away from traditional economies such as agriculture, mining, and manufacturing toward a post-Fordist, post-industrial system of production dependent on information and communication networks. Despite the economic boost of tourism, the nature of employment within a seasonal service industry depends on labor that is by nature precarious and exacerbates the deep vulnerabilities of an already insecure job market in Spain. Unconstrained and unregulated urban growth, especially on the Mediterranean coasts, has exacerbated land erosion and overextended infrastructure capacity to handle the ever-increasing quantities of solid waste that accompany the ever-increasing numbers of tourists. The increased traffic of ferries, tankers, and cruise ships have contributed to higher levels of water pollution, while the increase in ground and air traffic have likewise contributed to air contamination. Moreover, overfishing to meet the gastronomic consumption needs of tourism threaten maritime flora and fauna with practices that are unsustainable. The rise of what the UN World Tourism Organization (UNWTO) has called "overtourism" and the emergence of "turistofobia" in Spanish coastal cities (as well as interior locales) exposes the deep fear of loss and captures the inherent contradictions of Spain's dependence on tourism over the last sixty years.[64] The reconfiguration of urban spaces into commodified sites of consumption designed to attract a foreign gaze has instilled residents in Spain with a perceived loss of cultural identity within the fabric of local communities and neighborhoods. The construction of hotels initiates a reconceptualization of space defined by pleasure and leisure, yet more recently the proliferation of Airbnb appeals to tourists seeking an "authentic" experience at the same time local residents perceive the rise of "pisos turísticos" (tourist apartments) as a threat to the cultural fabric of residential neighborhoods.[65] Similarly, opaque political processes and pervasive practices of bribery and collusion undermine faith in democratic tenets and reinforce the perception that elitist interests guide urban development, that citizens are intentionally disenfranchised from their own city, and that corruption is endemic to the political system, especially as it relates to land speculation.

The aftermath of the economic crisis of 2008 exposed such vulnerabilities when foreign tourism plummeted, propelling Spain into a deep, long-lasting recession that spiked unemployment and led to austerity measures that resulted in millions of evictions. If the 2008 economic recession exposed the vulnerabilities of Spain's economic model centered on tourism, then more recently the COVID-19 pandemic has laid bare its utter fragility as health concerns and financial constraints have brought foreign mobility to a standstill, dropping close to 75 percent. The credit frenzy that resulted from the vicious circle of ever-increasing tax revenues derived from ever-expanding land speculation exposed the banking industry to extreme risk and ultimately propelled Spain into the worst economic crisis of the last fifty years. Often referred to as the Great Spanish Depression, the impact of the economic meltdown in Spain was far-reaching and long-lasting. Spain's GDP fell 6.3 percent, unemployment rose from 8.3 percent in late 2007 to 20.1 percent in 2010 (43.5 percent among youth 16–25 years of age), domestic demand fell 7.6 percent (contrasted with 1.6 percent in the eurozone), investment in housing dropped 41 percent, and household debt skyrocketed 130 percent, and the Spanish economy went from a 1.9 percent surplus to an 11.1 percent deficit.[66] In "Causes and Consequences of the Spanish Economic Crisis: Why the Recovery Is Taken [sic] So Long?," Carballo-Cruz states in no uncertain terms that the construction and property development sectors played an essential role in the "detonation" of the economic crisis and the disproportionate growth of housing prices led to a housing bubble of "enormous proportions."[67]

Consequently, urban development and land speculation came to a standstill and funding evaporated for many projects throughout the Iberian Peninsula, especially hotels and other constructions related to tourism, and to this day stand incomplete—serving as monuments to the crisis. In response to the austerity measures implemented by the Spanish government that led to mass evictions and, subsequently, many thousands of suicides, Spanish citizens took back their "right to the city," as Harvey would say, by transforming public urban space into sites of resistance. Considered a precursor to the "Occupy" movements seen around the world and inspired in some ways by the uprisings referred to as the "Arab Spring," the Indignados (Incensed) movement (also referred to as 15-M because it began on May 15, 2011), is especially poignant as a political response because the social mobilization they fomented held a direct connection to the occupation of public spaces that had been steadily developed according to private interests over the previous fifty years. As Puneet Dhaliwal notes, the desire to reconceptualize the political and economic systems of Spain manifest through an attempt to reappropriate, reconfigure, and reimagine an alternative public space that offers a much different and more inclusive narrative than the discourse of development that has dominated the modernization of Spain since the 1950s.[68] A manifesto published in August 2014 by the Asamblea de Raval, a working-class neighborhood in Barcelona that has undergone a profound demographic transition, denounces the real estate speculation and so-called urban renewal that has transformed residential neighborhoods in towns all throughout Spain into gentrified tourist theme parks. The manifesto pierces the transparency of official discourse that extols the economic benefits of tourism by noting the nefarious effects of the "desequilibrio insostenible" (unsustainable inequality) underlying the urban development that has expelled residents from and reconstructed space, from the Barceloneta to the Ciutat Vella to the Raval in order to accommodate and expand tourism. Tourism is not the salvation of Spanish society, the manifesto concludes, but an abyss toward which a "proyecto de ciudad" (city project) propels itself and whose logical extension is the "destrucción de nuestra convivencia y de nuestra vida cotidiana" (destruction of our coexistence and of our everyday life).[69]

If the city is a palimpsest whose urban spaces are rewritten and inscribed with the discourse of tourism, then its narrative engages the dialectic between the local and the global by selling its spaces as sites for consumption. As residents are displaced physically and are marginalized figuratively from the narrative of modernity, the question becomes, as Dean MacCannell suggests in *Empty Meeting Grounds* and the Indignados movement in Spain continues to ask, "Who is 'out of place?'"[70] MacCannell asserts that as culture, and all it implies, is subsumed into the logic of tourism, it leads to the formation of new cultural subjects through the powerful manipulation of "symbols, human consciousness, and political processes for the purpose of creating democracies within the narrowest of interests."[71] The symbolic order of the city that frames Harvey's urbanization of consciousness can be understood to expand beyond the language of a city's spaces to encompass a wider range of cultural production that reproduce the dominant narrative through their representation of the city. For example, tourist brochures, like the ones mentioned at the beginning of this chapter, market the spaces of tourism and prepare the potential visitor for what they will find through a narrative that outlines the ideological contours of the destinations along the coast. If representations of a city's urban spaces in diverse forms of cultural production (brochures, postcards, souvenirs, etc) can reinforce the "fetishisms" to which Harvey refers and can reproduce specific urban experiences of capitalism that uphold structures of power in the city, then what is the space in which alternative narratives to the discourse of cement, speculation, and development may be articulated and advanced?

The Paradox of Paradise

Each chapter in this book examines ways in which various forms of cultural production reinforce or resist an ideological construction of the Spanish coasts as a paradisiacal space of consumption that mirrors the construction of the built environment. The sequence of chapters follows a loose timeline that begins with cultural production from the 1960s and early 1970s and concludes with the financial crisis of 2008. The purpose of this organization is to offer a critique of Spain's coastal development through the lens of cultural studies to expose the latent (and oftentimes not so latent) paradoxes that permeated the policies that built the coasts as a tourist paradise. By focusing on diverse forms of cultural expression over the last sixty years, I not only seek to draw connections about the representation of the Spanish coasts between them, but also hope to demonstrate how critiques and fears about over-development early on have ultimately come to pass. Each chapter offers an approach to "paradise" and explores the paradoxes it presents through different forms of culture such as film, literature, postcards, photography, and even historical figures who become cultural icons that reify the social values of an era.

Titled "Designing Desire: Hotels and the Architecture of Paradise as the Foundation of Spanish Modernity," Chapter 1 examines the representation of the hotel in early novels and films to expose how filmic and literary productions simultaneously reified and contested the modern feel of the space most connected with leisure, travel, and the tourist experience. I start with an analysis of two understudied novels from the early years of coastal tourism in Spain that offer unique and poignant, if not prophetic, insights into the current economic, political, social, and cultural landscape of Spanish society:

Spanish Show (1965) by Julio Manegat and *Torremolinos Gran Hotel* (1971) by Ángel Palomino. I then examine the hotel in two films by Pedro Lazaga, *El turismo es un gran invento* (1968) and *El abominable hombre de la Costa del Sol* (1970), not merely as a backdrop or mise en scéne but as a complex ideological space in which physical, mental, and social elements engage each other and interact to "cement" the paradisiacal imaginary of the coasts. I examine the hotel as the iconic monumental embodiment of the urban transformations along the Mediterranean coast in Spain. From the origins of the tourism industry along the coasts, interior and architectural design have played a central role in framing the aesthetic values of the built environment by extolling both the modern feel and consumerist nature of the spaces connected with the tourist experience such as hotels, restaurants, and the beach itself. The hotel's physical space, understood as a cultural construction, entices the subject's gaze with an underlying imaginary in a destination that promises self-realization and self-fulfillment. Dreams are realized through unbridled consumption and the desire to flee the mundane and the emotional void of modern life to embrace the alluring luxury of the hotel as an earthly paradise.

In Chapter 2, "Scenes from Paradise: Postcards, the Tourist's Gaze, and the Generation of Dreams," I analyze how the narrative of the tourist experience was promoted visually through the most ubiquitous cultural product associated with tourism. By examining images of urban spaces along the Spanish coasts in tourist postcards from Spain, we move from the 1960s and 1970s into the 1980s and 1990s. Postcards have sought to attract and engage the foreigner's gaze with the promise of a Spain that was folkloric, rustic, and exotic yet also luxurious, modern, and sexualized. Tourist postcards offer a burgeoning field that expands the study of photography by examining images designed to be intentionally circulated within a capitalist framework. Postcards may be studied both for the latent ideology of the visual representation as well as examples of material culture that directly connects with consumerist tenets of tourism that complement the ideological impact of the image itself. No other aspect of visual culture does more to engage and commodify the tourist's gaze than the images found on postcards. Postcards (as well as brochures and other tourist souvenirs) offer the first instance of promises to fulfill one's desires for fulfillment and salvation by projecting the Spanish coasts as a utopian escape from the pressures of modern society. While many images on postcards depict the luxury of high-rise hotels or the idyllic locales of exotic beaches, many include images of women, often in bikinis or in folkloric flamenco dresses. The prevalence of the (sexualized) female body in tourist postcards from Spain implies the desire to appeal to a heteronormative male gaze that commodifies the female body and "reconstructs" it through its assimilation into consumer capitalism. Thus, while the Spanish coasts have undergone a physical transformation where high-rise hotels have replaced sleepy fishing villages, images of the female body in postcards have constructed the coasts as gendered, sexualized sites of consumption. Moreover, the viewer becomes an active participant in constructing the meaning of the postcard as material culture purchased in a transactional experience. Ironically the viewer seems to acquire agency in creating significance precisely through their consumptive gaze and the act of circulating the image globally.

With Chapter 3, "Empty Tourist Spaces: Paradise, Satire, and the Photography of Martin Parr and Carlos Pérez Siquier," I study the work of photographers like Martin Parr from England and Carlos Pérez Siquier (often referred to as the Spanish Martin Parr) who appropriate the visual language and engage with the visual stereotypes (most prevalent in postcards and tourism propaganda) that frame the representation of urban coastal spaces and the tourist experience there. These photographers not only offer a critical engagement with postcards and tourism propaganda, but they move us along the timeline into the late 1990s and into the 2000s, especially with visual artists who follow in their footsteps. Although Pérez Siquier worked actively in the 1950s and 1960s, his color photography of tourist spaces did not acquire fame or critical recognition until the 2000s. Through satire and self-awareness, these photographers question the discourse of luxury, leisure, and prosperity so intimately tied with the success of tourism industry and the "miracles" it has achieved for the Spanish economy. This chapter's title evokes Dean MacCannell's *Empty Meeting Grounds* and examines how photographers like Parr and Pérez Siquier demystify the tourist gaze to lay bare the underlying values of consumption associated with global tourism, especially at coastal resorts. I examine Parr's *Benidorm: About the World* (1999) and Pérez Siquier's *La Playa:1972–1996* (2019). Especially in Pérez Siquier's case, this collection of previously unpublished photos chronicles the urban transformations of the coastal areas in Almería that began in the early 1970s after the inauguration of its airport and the start of the first tourist charter flights. I also study the legacy of Parr and Pérez Siquier in more recent photography of contemporary visual artists such as María Moldes (especially in her Instagram collaborations with the model Miss Beige) and Roberto Alcaraz. Like Parr and Pérez Siquier, Moldes's photographs similarly question the accepted narrative of Spanish tourism and the ideological constructions that undergird its discourse. Photographer Roberto Alcaraz shares oneiric images of buildings in Benidorm that are devoid of people (and thus humanity) and highlight the city as an ornamental if otherworldly backdrop that has been fabricated for tourism and lacks its own identity where there is an atmosphere that is both anonymous and deceptively amiable.

Finally, in Chapter 4, titled "From Tourist Paradise to "Paraíso Fiscal": Construction, Corruption, and the Legacy of Jesús Gil," I examine the ideological, and even existential, emptiness to which visual artists allude in Chapter 3, an emptiness that acquires an economic, political, and moral dimension by examining urban corruption in Chapter 4. This chapter analyzes the prevalence of crime and corruption along the Mediterranean coasts as the core principles that have literally built modern Spain but also invited volatility and instability that brought about the economic crisis of 2008. Urban corruption has been a common practice in which politicians, mafiosos, lawyers, police, and construction companies curry favor with each other through bribes, tax fraud, money laundering, and more to facilitate permits and award bids for hotels and recreational sites related to the tourism industry creating a "paraíso fiscal" (fiscal paradise). Yet, the built environment of the Spanish coasts designed for tourism has also facilitated a space for the expansion of a lucrative but violent drug industry of narco gangs from all over the world. Beneath the façade of a tourist paradise, a world of mafias, bribes, greed, corruption, and crime not only undergird Spain's modernization project but have steered it into the vortex of economic and political crises that have dominated Spanish society in the last two decades. I focus on the infamous figure of the charismatic property tycoon, soccer mogul, and former mayor of Marbella Jesús Gil y Gil (often referred to as "Trump before Trump"), who can be considered a cultural icon who personifies the vast urban corruption scandals such as Caso Malaya, a prelude to the 2008 financial collapse. Hardly an anomaly, such scandals have flourished within the political and economic ecosystem of urban coastal tourism in Spain. I conclude this chapter with a discussion of so-called ghost hotels and construction projects abandoned in the wake of the 2008 economic crisis. Their hollowness reifies the ideological emptiness of urban coastal tourism, and they stand today, I argue, as monuments of the crisis that attest to the endgame of Spain's modernization project since the 1960s.

CHAPTER 1

Designing Desire

Hotels and the Architecture of Paradise
as the Foundation of Spanish Modernity

As one strolls along the beach, he can count eleven hotels under construction. Their steel and concrete frameworks, six and more stories high, stand as dramatic symbols of the change taking place here. This seacoast, which harbors 3,000 years of human history, has become a year-round vacation spa of swimming pools, bikinis (no topless suits here), water-skiing, golf, tennis and hordes of suntanned British, German, French, Scandinavian and American tourists.

"SPAIN'S COSTA DEL SOL SAYS 'SÍ' TO TOURISM," *New York Times,* 1964

At the Global Tourism Forum in January 2015, the then prime minister of Spain, Mariano Rajoy, underscored the economic and political importance of tourism, and inadvertently corroborated the blurred line between private industry and public service, when he described it as a "sector estratégico para el estado" (strategic sector for the state). This view is confirmed by Turespaña's *Turismo 2020: Plan de turismo español horizonte 2020* in which the organization outlines its "política turística" (tourism policies) with some baseline data: Spain is the number one destination in the world for vacational tourism with 58.1 million international tourists in 2006. The tourism industry generates just under 30 billion euros (about 11 percent of Spain's GDP) and employs more than 2.5 million people (12.4 percent of Spain's population).[1] In his letter the Minister of Industry, Tourism, and Commerce, Joan Clos I Matheu, frames the objectives of the strategic plan that was signed on November 8, 2007, with unanimous approval by the tourism representatives from each of the seventeen regional governments. *Turismo 2020,* he states, maps strategies for the tourism industry over the subsequent decade that combine public and private initiatives to achieve the "máximo bienestar social" (maximum social well-being) within "un entorno económico globalizado, de gran incertidumbre y profundamente cambiante" (a globalized economic context of great uncertainty and ever-changing).[2] The reference to an uncertain global economy could not have been more prophetic. Within the timeframe the document establishes as its horizon, 2008 to 2020, the Spanish economy would be devastated in the aftermath of the worldwide financial crisis. Spanish citizens would reclaim urban spaces during the 11-M Indignados protests against the politics of austerity, hundreds of thousands of people would be forcibly evicted from their homes in successive waves of "desahuicios" (evictions), and tourism would languish first during the Great Recession and then even more so under travel restrictions and fears of contagion during the global COVID-19 pandemic. Nevertheless, despite an awareness of potential economic uncertainty, the *Turismo 2020* plan anticipated an economic growth of 2.4 percent, greater than that projected for any other European country (especially those from which the greatest number of tourists arrive to Spain: United Kingdom, France, Germany). In its "diagnóstico" (diagnostic) of Spain's tourism industry, the report examines the strengths and weaknesses in four areas: competitiveness, destinations, supply and products, and human resources. The success of tourism in Spain, the report asserts, is due entirely to the centralization of efforts since the 1960s to attract mass tourism by offering the product of sand and beach with a high level of standardization all along the Spanish Mediterranean coast. The high quality of tourism resources along with ample infrastructure and installations have made Spanish beaches, the authors assert, the top tourist destination for the European middle class by systematically replicating the model throughout the Mediterranean coast and on the Canary and Balearic islands. Despite the environmental deterioration wrought by excessive and uncontrolled urban growth, the report recognizes that the ample offerings, capacity, and variety of hotel offerings, especially those of four- and five-star quality, have been, and continue to be, the driving force for the economic success of the tourism model in Spain.[3]

In its Plan Nacional e Integral de Turismo (2012–2015), the Ministerio de Industria, Energía, y Turismo similarly recognized the catalyst driving the economic motor of tourism is the hotel, and the quality of the tourist experience, and by extension the so called "marca España" (Spanish brand) is measured by the quality of the services, infrastructure, gastronomy, beaches, and cultural offerings that surround the nucleus of the tourist experience:

the hotel. The PNIT distills this concept to one phrase: un hotel de 4 estrellas debe estar en un entorno de 4 estrellas (a four-star hotel should find itself in four-star surroundings).[4] The mayor of Málaga, Francisco de la Torre, reiterated this notion in May 2015 when he pleaded for "agilidad administrativa (. . .) con la máxima velocidad y seguridad jurídica" (administrative agility with the maximum juridical velocity and security) to open the path for the construction of a five-star luxury hotel in the Port of Málaga. Not only would such a hotel benefit the city with employment opportunities and increased tourist offerings, he asserted, but the edifice itself (35 stories, 130 meters, with 350 rooms) would create a visual impact with a skyscraper that would serve as a "nuevo icono de la Bahía" (new icon of the Bay).[5] Moreover, Paulino Plata, the president of Málaga's Port Authority, asserted that a 5-star luxury hotel of the highest aesthetic and architectural quality would benefit the city immeasurably by expanding its capacity to generate employment and vastly improve the tourist offerings there. Plata compared the hotel planned for Málaga's port with the W Barcelona Hotel, also known as the Hotel Vela due to its sail-like shape, designed by Ricardo Bofill and built in 2009 on the so-called Barceloneta near the beaches.[6]

Beyond its practical function to offer lodging, the hotel's status as "icon" establishes it as a symbolic beacon whose modern design draws the gaze of the tourist with the enticing promise of escape through luxury and leisure. If we accept the hotel as an "icon," then it is no surprise that it has figured prominently in various forms of cultural production from postcards to novels, film, music, and more as the epicenter around which the tourism industry revolves. More than a mere backdrop for various tourism activities, the hotel often acts as a protagonist that moves people, economies, and even ideology by simultaneously crystallizing and instilling the values of consumer capitalism. In this chapter, I examine the hotel as the iconic monumental embodiment of urban transformations along the Mediterranean coast in Spain that epitomize what Henri Lefebvre calls an "architecture of enjoyment" and Mario Gaviria "the materialization of welfare." As a catalyst for economic and urban development, the hotel exemplifies a "non-place" that creates a space of consumption that destabilizes the subject's gaze and assimilates it into the logic of capital through pleasure.

In *Non-places: An Introduction to Supermodernity*, the French anthropologist Marc Augé asserts that non-places proliferate and typify human experience in the age of what he calls "supermodernity."[7] For Augé, supermodernity is characterized by wild extremes of "temporary abodes" from luxurious hotel chains and vacation resorts to inhuman refugee camps and makeshift shantytowns.⁸ Dense networks of transport hubs, by-ways, and transit points deprive supermodernity from a sense of place or past and endow individuals with a sense of ephemeral temporality and anonymity. However, what does anchor identity, Augé states, are the gestures of unmediated commerce and dense communication networks where individuals assert their sense of self through travel, leisure, and consumption. For Augé, hotels and resorts, airports, commercial centers, attractions, theme parks, etc. not only offer spectacles devoid of a past but posit the traveler as a spectator and their own spectacle. Augé points to the traveler brochure that frames the tourist experience with advance images to be anticipated and even reproduced. The traveler's space, Augé declares, is "the archetype of *non-place.*"⁹ The hotel, I argue, can be viewed as both a metaphoric, metonymic, and synecdochic example of the modernization project in Spain that began in the 1960s and extends through the current political and economic crisis. The physical space of the hotel, understood as a cultural construction, entices the subject's gaze with spectacle and offers an underlying imaginary in a destination that promises self-realization and self-fulfillment. Dreams are realized through unbridled capitalist consumption and the desire to flee the mundane emotional void of modern life—to embrace the alluring luxury of the hotel as an earthly paradise.¹⁰

The physical structure of the hotel itself serves as a monumental space that reifies both the demands of and desires for capital that have impelled the urbanization of the Spanish coasts since the 1960s. From the origins of the coastal tourism industry, interior and architectural design have played a central role in framing the aesthetic values of the built environment by extoling both the modern feel and ludic nature of the spaces connected with the tourist experience such as hotels, restaurants, and the beach itself. I will explore the interplay between public and private spaces and the ideological implications of what Diego Santos has called "el estilo del relax," a neo-deco kind of design that characterizes the interior spaces as well as exterior forms of buildings in Torremolinos like the Hotel Pez Espada, Hotel Cervantes, and Hotel Miami among many others.¹¹ Today these hotels serve as monuments that recall the Golden Age of tourism before the boom of charters and monolithic cheap constructions. Moreover, social media sites like torremolinoschic.com offer a collective virtual *lieux de mémoire* that represents, reconstructs, and reiterates the narrative of the tourist boom and Spain's transition to democracy through images of the places, especially hotels, most closely associated with this period of tourism in Spain. Similarly, the recent 2016 opening of the five-star luxury hotel Gran Hotel Miramar in Málaga was billed as the "rebirth of a classic" that not only re-asserts the "monumental splendor" of the hotel, but also represents an overt desire to return to tourism that evokes "the jet set" rather than the masses of sunburned, middle-class tourists. Yet, abandoned hotels such as the Hotel Crusier Tres Carabelas Gran Lujo and the Hotel Algarrobico present icons of a different sort as monuments, which do not seek solace in a perceived utopian past but offer a testament to Spain's crisis, economic as well as ecological, and may be viewed as emblems of the endgame of the modernization project of the last sixty years.

Construction, Consumption and Culture in José Manegat's *Spanish Show* and Ángel Palomino's *Torremolinos Gran Hotel*

The visual, symbolic, and economic importance of the hotel, firmly established and widespread in postcards, infiltrates other forms of cultural production as well in sometimes contradictory ways that both critique yet celebrate the hotel and its effects on Spain's economy and culture. Two novels from the early years of coastal tourism in Spain offer a unique and poignant, if not prophetic, insight into the current economic, political, social, and cultural landscape of Spanish society. Both *Spanish Show* (1965) by Julio Manegat and *Torremolinos Gran Hotel* (1971) by Ángel Palomino were critically acclaimed in their time, the former a finalist for the 1965 Premio Planeta and the latter awarded the 1971 Premio Nacional de Literatura. Yet neither author forms part of the canon of contemporary Spanish literature and both novels have received scant scholarly attention almost to the point of oblivion. Perhaps these novels have been understudied and overlooked because they are perceived to be of less literary quality than other Spanish novels from the 1960s and 1970s that exhibited more experimental avant-garde techniques. Perhaps the conservative politics of the authors seemed out of step with the cultural moment as Spanish society became more open economically as well as artistically, if not yet politically, and the so-called "pactos de olvido" (pacts of forgetting) after Franco's death contributed to a lack of recognition. Or perhaps these novels are thought to lack the seriousness of high-minded literature because the focus on tourism with all its kitschy frivolity seems to lack an exploration of universal themes about the human experience. My interest in these authors and these two specific novels derives not from an interest to recover forgotten literary figures or to reassess the canonical value of their writing. Rather, these texts not only offer a window into the social anxiety about tourism as the catalyst and primary vehicle for Spain's modernization in the 1960s and 1970s, but they also acquire a prescient quality within the current context of Spanish society. By revisiting these novels, the critiques raised by Manegat and Palomino about the commodification of cultural identity, unregulated and unbridled urbanization of the coasts, and the prevalence of corporate corruption make it possible to delineate a clear trajectory to the current atmosphere of social, economic, political, and cultural crisis in Spain. Ironically, the work of these authors may offer a more important commentary about twenty-first-century Spain than about the time when they were writing. And if this is true, then *Spanish Show* and *Torremolinos Gran Hotel* would in fact have much to say about the human condition, especially within the logic of late capitalism.

Julio Manegat structured his novel *Spanish Show* as a series of vignettes that trace characters who are tangential to each other, often observe each other, and whose paths often intersect and even collide with one another. Set in a coastal tourist town along the Costa Brava near Barcelona, Manegat's novel centers on the experiences of Louise Burton, a middle-aged Belgian woman at the fictional Hotel Bahía who is on vacation in Spain for the first time. While the narrator guides the reader through a traditional third-person omniscient voice, the temporal structure of the novel engages the reader with Iserian gaps through jumps in time that oscillate between a before and after a climactic event in the plot.[12] Scenes alternate between the police recovery of an automobile, their investigation of a fatal crash, and other scenes before the accident where characters enjoy the ludic atmosphere of the hotel and the surrounding area.[13] The reader infers that Louise is the victim of the crash and the anticipation of the climactic scene overshadows and tempers her enthusiastic childlike encounters with Spanish culture with a sense of impending doom. Moreover, a heteroglossic multitude of voices from construction workers who emigrated to the coast for employment, to local residents who have lived the physical and economic transformations of the area, to performers and members of the service industry whose responsibility is the entertainment of visiting international tourists captures the widespread impact of tourism, or lack thereof, across social class and geographical location. These voices articulate Manegat's critique of tourism and its perceived subversion of the authenticity of Spanish culture that is converted into spectacle to attract and entertain the tourist's gaze. For Manegat, the so-called "invasión turística" (tourist invasion) poses a double threat that both provokes social disintegration by undermining that which is perceived as truly Spanish and debilitates the perceived Catholic morality of Spanish society by promoting promiscuous and decadent behavior. While Manegat's desire to preserve the social and religious essence of Spain, synonymous terms for the author, derives from an ultra-conservative if not fascist ideology, the sense of loss expressed in his novel resonates with current day "turismo-fobia" that fears damage to the social fabric of local communities, especially in urban settings with the expansion of "pisos turísticos" (tourist rentals) through Airbnb and other platforms.

That the title of Manegat's novel is in English signals the supposed contamination of Spanish culture through the linguistic adoption of a phrase that markets flamenco shows to tourists as authentic experiences. On one hand, the use of English points to the infiltration of foreign influence through a language that is thought to be universally recognized and understood, especially by a more educated European leisure class. English may also signal the need for signage that speaks to the large influx of working-class British tourists that flock to the Spanish coasts as mass charter tourism expands in the 1960 and 1970s. On another hand, the phrase "Spanish Show" to refer to a flamenco dance performance reveals the tendency to sell Spain's exotic otherness through stereotypes of Andalusian identity that are assimilated into a capitalist framework to design desire as part of a marketing campaign. The notion then of a "marca España" is not a new phenomenon but one that has been present since the early days of Spanish tourism to brand the nation in ways that ironically anticipate concerns over authenticity and the postmodern condition examined by theorists such as Baudrillard, Debord, Lyotard, Jameson, Harvey, and others. Hal Foster in *Recodings: Art, Spectacle, and Cultural Politics* asserts that we become trapped in the logic of spectacle because it both induces the loss of the real but also offers fetishized images that alleviate our sense of loss and alienation. Social processes, he continues, become opaque and ideological domination is assured through one-dimensional images that epitomize "the very nadir of capitalist reification."[14] In *Spanish Show*, Spain itself becomes a spectacle for visual consumption. Manegat laments the potential alienating ideological effects of the economic and urban transformations in the 1960s when traditional cultural markers become souvenirs for purchase, authentic forms of folkloric culture are stripped from their context for tourist consumption of stereotypical Spanish-ness, historic forms of labor disappear and workers adapt to meet the needs construction and service industries, and local residents are displaced from the physical environment along the coasts so that foreign visitors may relax in the sand and sun.

Like Ángel Palomino in *Torremolinos Gran Hotel*, Manegat situates the plot of his *Spanish Show* in a fictional hotel along an ambiguous area of the Costa Brava. In a note from the author that precedes the novel, he recognizes that certain elements may be familiar to some readers but their symbolic value rests not in their connection to specific locations but that the events, places, and experiences of the novel "se encuentran en gran número de poblaciónes de la costa mediterránea" (may be found in the vast majority of towns along the Mediterranean coast). What began as an "hilillo de oro" (trickle of gold) became an unstoppable flow of tourists and with them "dinero y más dinero, osadía tras osadía" (money and more money, audacity upon audacity).[15] Early in the novel, the narrator recounts the origins of don Feliciano García, owner of several hotels in the area, whose "miraculous" trajectory into prosperity mirrors that of Spain itself. When he arrived at the Costa Brava in 1949, don Feliciano encountered only a handful of foreign tourists and he could not imagine that Europeans or Americans would be interested in a Spain that was still suffering misery, tragedy, and hunger in the aftermath of the Spanish Civil War. Yet, the narrator explains, as long as no bombs were exploding in the streets there would be those who, for better or for worse, would want to forget the painful past and forge a path to prosperity.[16] The hotel, explains don Feliciano, is at the epicenter of this economic transformation on both a personal and societal level, "El que construya un hotel se hincha" (He who constructs a hotel will get rich).[17] Don Feliciano himself recognized early on the opportunities the hotel industry presented when he started as a lowly bellhop. His ascent to waiter, bartender, receptionist, and manager ultimately leads to his own ownership of three hotels: the España Cañí, the Hotel Bahía, and the Hotel Rex. Don Feliciano's personal story of success and his climb up the social ladder from bellhop to hotel mogul parallels the economic shift in Spain from the "Años de Hambre" (Years of Hunger) after the Spanish Civil War, especially brutal in Cataluña where the novel is situated, to the economic boom of the "Milagro español" (Spanish Miracle) in the 1960s. Moreover, his radius of political influence expands as his footprint on the physical landscape of this town in the Costa Brava grows; his story serves as a metaphorical and metonymical microcosm of the land speculation, construction, and urban expansion all along the Mediterranean coastline in Spain.[18]

The hotel, then, serves as the epicenter and catalyst for the economic, geographic, and ideological transformations of the country. The fabric of the physical environment that radiates outwardly from the hotel is rewritten as a kind of palimpsest that inscribes the town with the ludic narrative of tourism. Don Feliciano complements his hotels with ownership of a night club and restaurants with future plans to partner with other hotel owners to construct a "complejo urbanístico" (urban complex) whose amenities would include a large swimming pool, a concert venue, apartments, bars and restaurants, discos and night clubs, and more. Later, the narrator reaffirms the visible impact of tourism on the town's geography where cafés and restaurants, hotels and apartments, dance halls and souvenir shops emerge. Since sun and sand are the most valued commodities in Spain's tourist industry, the real estate closest to the sea, affirms the narrator, is the most valued property whose worth increases as the influx of tourists grows. While the cafés, restaurants, hotels, and night clubs may generate revenue through tourism, land speculation and the importance of owning coastal territory conferred power as well as wealth as the narrator affirms, "poseer tierras costeras, se convirtió en titulos de riqueza y poderío" (possessing coastal land converted into titles of riches and privilege).[19] The narrator notes that with the accumulation of properties and his increasing affluence, don Feliciano's substantial imprint on the town leads to tremendous financial and political influence. Yet, despite his business acumen and entrepreneurial instincts, the narrator criticizes don Feliciano's greed and that of others like him who have urbanized the coasts to "llenar su bolsillo" (line their pockets) without conscience.[20] Although don Feliciano reflects on his own humble beginnings as a bellhop, he does so uncritically and as a means to justify his own individual merit as well as to demonstrate his patriotic contributions to the economic good of the country as one of the "fuentes esenciales del fondo español de divisas" (key source of foreign capital investment in Spain).[21]

Don Feliciano's self-serving superficial view of his individual past acts as a vehicle through which Manegat indicts the dominant classes of Spain's new technocratic society of the 1960s, those he feels have undertaken a project to modernize the county by burying its own past of misery and hunger. Later in the novel, Louise joins a group of Spaniards who invite her to a night club named "El infierno" (The inferno) where they drink gin, dance, smoke and give in to the Dionysian atmosphere. As Santi, one of the Spaniards, contemplates the scene he recites a verse from Antono Machado's "El mañana efímero." Machado's poem criticizes a stagnant Spanish society that he considers morally bankrupt and intellectually mediocre in the wake of the so-called "desastre" (disaster) of 1898. He notes a divided Spain and attacks the sectors that impede the country's development by adhering blindly to religious beliefs and traditions over reason, science, and education that would bring modernity to Spanish society. Within the context of Spain in the 1960s, Manegat's reference to Machado's famous poem redirects the critique to question the blind faith in tourism and the pursuit of pleasure and prosperity without regard to the costs, both individual and collective. In another scene, as a judge and a forensic doctor prepare for Louise Burton's autopsy, they discuss the perceived costs of tourism as they observe the town through the window of the courthouse. The doctor marvels at the economic impact of tourism that has saved the country from bankruptcy yet his comment, "Poderoso caballero es don Dinero" appears to miss the biting satire of Quevedo's poem that denounces the corrupting power of money and its effect on the moral and political decay of seventeenth-century Spain. The judge's reply signals the material costs of the tourist boom by pointing to agricultural absenteeism where thousands of farmers have abandoned the countryside to become bellhops, waiters, or construction workers.[22] Tourism, he continues, is the "tentación del oro fácil" (temptation of easy money) and what he laments about the "fiebre económica del turismo" (economic fever of tourism) is the ideological impact of Spain's rapid economic transformation.[23] Spain itself, he asserts, has become a commodity to sell and to consume, "Nos hemos convertido en un espectáculo, en un show, como se dice ahora" (we have transformed ourselves into a spectacle, a show, as they say nowadays). Despite the economic gains, what the judge fears is that "estemos creando una España que no existe, que hemos inventado entre todos y que nuestro público, el turismo, los extranjeros, aplauden" (we are creating a Spain that doesn't exist, that we have invented amongst all of us and that our public, tourism, and foreigners, applaud).[24] The comments of the judge offer a curious juxtaposition between the physical, built environment of hotels, cafés, restaurants, and night clubs and the conceptual, ideological construction of Spanish identity that is fabricated and sold to northern Europeans. The great irony of Spain's modernization project, he asserts to the doctor, is "para europeizar a España, como usted dice, vendemos a los extranjeros la españolada" (to Europe-ize Spain, as you say, we market stereotypical Spanish-ness to foreigners).[25] Moreover, he invokes the concepts of "engaño" (illusion) and "espejismo" (mirage), notions closely associated with Golden Age authors like Quevedo who rely on satire to pierce the delusion of Spanish exceptionalism, to expose the self-deception that the rewards of tourism benefit all sectors of society when vast zones of desperate poverty still exist, even in their own region and in their own town. The judge captures the unequal impact of modernization in Spain when he concludes, "No todo el país es la costa" (The whole country is not the coast).[26]

The urban, economic, and labor transformations that Spanish society undergoes in the 1960s through tourism provoke a deep cultural and ideological contradiction in which Spain re-invents itself as an illusion that one character in Manegat's novel compares to a magic trick where "abráis con asombro los ojos y os lo creáis" (you open your eyes and you believe it).[27]

Stereotypical markers of Andalusian folkloric identity—flamenco, bull-fighting, guitars—become the scaffolding upon which the spectacle of the "españolada" mentioned earlier sells Spain to foreigners, particularly Americans and northern Europeans, as exotic escape from their modern world. The narrator describes the first tourists who arrived to Spain as if they were explorers who passed from their civilized society into the primitive culture of "los toros y de las mueres bravías, de las panderetas y del hambre, de la miseria y de las guitarras" (bulls and fierce women, of tambourines and hunger, of misery and guitars).[28] A confluence of branding, marketing, culture, and identity produces what John and Jean Comaroff call in *Ethnicity, Inc.* an "ethno-commodity" that defies, they assert, conventional assumptions about price and value or supply and demand. The process of cultural commodification not only resists the rationality of classic economic theory that would have us believe raw materials are depleted when widely circulated. Quite the opposite in the case of an ethno-commodity, mass circulation underscores the apparent ideological validity of ethnicity and ironically reaffirms the value of difference through the objects that embody cultural identity at the same time they perpetuate cultural alienation. Ironically, the aura of an ethno-commodity is magnified through its reproduction, both material and ideological, such that "greater supply entails greater demand."[29]

By appropriating images stereotypical of Andalusian identity, coastal tourism fabricates sites of consumption that project images of Spanish culture they believe foreigners expect to see as part of the interior décor of hotels and bars but also to purchase as souvenirs.[30] The narrator remarks on the irony of the importance Andalusia has acquired in tourism marketing strategies when for so long it had been a "lejana, ignorada region" (distant, ignored region) that wallowed in poverty and rarely felt the impact of modernity.[31] In his first hotel "España Cañí," don Feliciano sells an experience of Spanish otherness by offering a tourist package that combines sun, sand, and fresh air with typical fried fish and tickets to a bullfight. The strategy of selling the so-called "marca España" entices the tourist gaze by offering images of Spanish-ness that exploit the exotic stereotypes that foreigners already had of Spain, specifically romanticized notions of flamenco, bullfighting, and other markers associated with Andalusian regional identity. Beyond the name of the hotel that invokes ideas of "Gypsy Spain," don Feliciano adorns the interior of the hotel bar-restaurant with framed bullfight posters, the stuffed head of a steer, and criss-crossed banderillas and christens it "La plaza" (The Bullfight Ring). Similarly, Miguel Olives, a veteran of the Spanish Civil War, finds a solution to his impoverished situation in Madrid by moving with his wife María to the

coast where he works in a luxurious bar as a waiter. With hopes of convinc-
ing his wife they should invest in their own business, he reads to her from
a government propaganda pamphlet that touts tourism as a "gran empresa
nacional" (great national enterprise) that increases employment opportunities, helps alleviate the national deficit, and plays a vital role in balancing
the country's budget. Yet, what convinces his wife that they need to invest
their capital and "establecerse" (go into business) more than the official
discourse of the State that promotes tourism as a venture that benefits the
common collective good is the prospect that they as individuals could pocket
"un puñado de esos dólares" (a fistful of those dollars).[32] After purchasing the
locale from the owner of the bar where Miguel worked as a waiter, he rewrites
its identity by renaming it El Torito Bravo: Taberna del Toreador (The Fierce
Bull: The Bullfighter's Tavern) and designing a very carefully curated mise
en scène that sells the Andalusian stereotypes associated with bullfighting
culture even though he had never been in Andalusia.[33] Just like don Feliciano's bar, posters advertising bullfights, banderillas, and a stuffed bull's head
decorate the interior of El Torito Bravo along with bottles of manzanilla,
castañuelas, and tambourines. Even the bar itself resembles a "burladero,"
the barrier that offers a site of refuge for bullfighters and protects them from
attack.[34] At the same time the cultural signifiers that decorate the Torito Bravo
project exotic stereotypes of Spanish identity, signage in English promotes
non-Spanish gastronomical offerings so that both language and food offer a
sense of familiarity. Similarly, when another bar changes its name from La
Taberna del Pueblo to Taberna del Turista-Snack Bar, the linguistic shift not
only supplants Spanish identity but also signals a reprioritization that values
the foreign tourist over the local resident. Additionally, the focus on "snacks"
also suggests a different gastronomical priority that appeals to the tastes and
needs of a beachgoing tourist in search of quick bites. The impact of tourism
on the gastronomical profile along the coasts and this focus on "fast food"
is reflected in the replacement of marble tables and solid wooden seats with
the ubiquitous red plastic tables and chairs that suggest a decline in quality
and mirror the boom of mass tourism that prioritizes quantity over quality.

   This kind of cultural plastification associated with mass tourism is most
readily visible in souvenirs, the embodiment of tourist consumption that
epitomize Baudrillard's "loss of the real" yet also ironically serve as "icons of
meaning" that distill the tourist's cultural experience. Baudrillard describes
an urban "morphogenesis" in which cities lose a sense of functional centers
(commerce, work, knowledge, leisure) and adhere to a "model of disintegration" with hypermarkets that are disconnected from the social fabric of urban

spaces, stripped of history and authenticity.[35] In *Spanish Show*, the narrator describes the progressive transformation of the coastal town that began with the first hotels and then, in the surrounding areas, commercial streets with tourist shops that offered an eclectic array of "objetos típicos" from swords and daggers to Talavera ceramic, Toledo damascene jewelry, and statues of Don Quijote to postcards, perfume, and water guns. When Louise discovers the "calle comercial" (commercial street) just behind the Hotel Bahía she describes it as a "tierra prometida" (promised land) in which lights, lights, colors, music, and voices along with the bustle of tourists strolling assault her senses with a carnivalesque atmosphere and a succession of window displays entice her gaze with infinite objects that tempt her desire.[36] Although Louise realizes that these objects present her with a vision of Spain that confirms what she had expected to find and that similar souvenirs may be found all along the coast, her state of "euforia, de alegría, de exaltación" (euphoria, joy, exaltation) compels her to ascribe authenticity to the objects as a true reflection of the Spanish spirit and the reality of the town that constructs and sells them. Louise literally inscribes the images and ideas of Spanish identity in a letter to her sister where she describes Spain as primitive and exotic, whose people may not be well-educated but are warm and hospitable.[37] Her confirmation that "mucho de lo que nosotros habíamos oído de este país es cierto" (much of what we had heard about this country is true) establishes a dialectic in which production and consumption of ideology compound each other infinitely in a kind of mise en abyme.[38] Contrary to Benjamin's critique of the mechanical reproduction of art that strips away authenticity, John and Jean Camaroff assert that the aura of ethno-commodities does not simply evaporate when it enters the market place but ironically it may be "rediscovered, reanimated, regained."[39] In the case of coastal tourism in Spain, however, local cultural identity is displaced, literally and figuratively, in order to entice the tourist's gaze through the reconstruction of rural seaside villages into spaces of consumption populated by hotels and night clubs, the redesign of interior spaces, and the redefinition of urban areas into commercial zones. The appropriation of stereotypical Andalusian cultural identity to market Spain's difference both fabricates and answers a desire for exotic otherness by projecting it literally as a commodified "show" that renders any attempt to rediscover, reanimate, or regain the authenticity of such ethno-commodities futile.

In his novel *Torremolinos Gran Hotel* (1971), Ángel Palomino captures the "atmósfera mágica" (magical atmosphere) in the Costa del Sol in the 1970s through a fictional hotel "de super lujo," (super-luxury) one of only seven hotels in Spain, that serves as a "palacio en el que cada huésped se le provee, al entrar, de una lámpara de Aladino eficaz y prodigiosa siempre" (palace in which every guest is provided an efficient and prodigious lamp of Aladdin upon arrival).[40] Not simply the backdrop for the characters, the hotel itself is a "coloso" (colossus) that doesn't sleep. With six hundred rooms, a restaurant that can serve up to eight hundred, a bar, a discoteque, and a staff of more than three hundred employees, the hotel itself is not a response to market demand for tourism but is in and of itself the "mercado de ocio" (leisure market). The colossal dimensions of the Torremolinos Gran Hotel is a physical indication of the expansion and the impact of the tourist market in Spain when compared to the "mundo brillante y animado" (brilliant and animated world) of the Pez Espada where the "bomba Torremolinos" (Torremolinos bomb) exploded when someone erected on a deserted beach "la estructura insólita y atrevida de un edificio enorme, entonces en la soledad: ocho pisos" (a most unusual and daring structure of an enormous isolated building: 8 floors).[41]

Awarded the Premio Nacional de Literatura in 1971, *Torremolinos Gran Hotel* relates the events over a ten-day period in a traditional third-person omniscient narrative voice combined with a spatial fragmentation that shifts the perspective from one set of characters and their circumstances to another. Such shifts in narrative focus not only exert hermeneutic demands on the reader and also invite the anticipation of how these various micro-stories may intertwine, but they also endow the imposing physical dimensions of the hotel described here with a sense of complexity by detailing the lived experiences of so many varied characters. In *Torremolinos Gran Hotel,* Palomino offers (as we saw that Manegat does in *Spanish Show*) a kind of Bahktinian heteroglossia that conveys the lived social space through the relations and discourses (along with their underlying ideologies) of the many characters that inhabit the physical space of the hotel and its surroundings. The ludic atmosphere of coastal tourism acquires depth and dimension in Palomino's novel through spatial shifts and diverse, often competing, perspectives of characters to explore the tension between what is visible and what is hidden in the larger discourse of development in Spain throughout the 1960s and 1970s. On one hand, Palomino reveals the machinery of the hotel, the invisible labor and the interconnected systems (both human and technological) in service to the composition of a spectacle designed for consumption through what Lefebvre in *The Production of Space* calls an "illusion of transparency."[42] Palomino describes the "milagro turístico" (tourist miracle) as one built on illusions in two different senses: the dreams of those who built the virgin beaches of the Costa del Sol into the epicenter of the tourism industry as well as the ludic spectacle that offers visitors a fabricated reality that is "amable y falsa" (friendly yet false).[43]

In *Torremolinos Gran Hotel*, Palomino pierces this illusion to reveal what is hidden behind what is openly in view both in terms of the machinery of the hotel itself, especially human labor as vital cogs in the production of the spectacle consumed by tourists, as well as the questionable financial machinations of the hotel's board hidden from the scrutiny of the Ministro de Hacienda (Ministry of Internal Revenue) and whose motto "a forrarse, caballeros" (let's make a killing, gentlemen!) distills the motivation of its members.[44] Clearly, the fictional hotel in Palomino's novel serves as a microcosm that embodies and epitomizes the discourse of development that has impelled coastal tourism from the beginning. Yet, from the opening pages of *Torremolinos Gran Hotel* Palomino asserts a tone through the narrative voice that is not only critical of the unethical and illegal practices of the hotel's board but also questions the sustainability of an economic model that expands, territorially as well as financially, without direction or conscience. As don Carlos Moraleda, owner of the three-star Hotel Estrella del Pacífico, contemplates the lights and sounds emanating from Torremolinos his physical distance suggests an economic marginalization from the ludic lifestyle of the coastal imaginary. Yet, while the Dionysian atmosphere of Torremolinos celebrates an eternal present, don Carlos's position outside the geographic, economic, and ideological space of the tourist city allows him to contextualize the urban expansion of the coast historically and question its future trajectory. The narrative voice describes that every time don Carlos sees a new hotel erected along the coast he thinks the world is run by lunatics "que no saben a dónde van" (who don't know where they are heading) but believes firmly that what awaits is a "desastre financiero" (financial disaster).[45] In the wake of the 2008 financial crash and the 2020 global coronavirus pandemic, the observations of don Carlos at the beginning of *Torremolinos Gran Hotel* acquire an eerily prophetic resonance.

While tourist ambience along the coast may seem superficial, frivolous, and one-dimensional, what Palomino's novel reveals is a carefully designed spectacle comprised of three interdependent embedded worlds that experience, interact with, and contribute to this space of consumption at very different altitudes. At the most superficial level are the tourists themselves whose interest is the consumption of a space fabricated for their leisure where "el día nunca empieza, nunca termina" (the day never begins because it never ends), long faces are forbidden, individual desires are filled through courtesy and attention, and the only obligation is to "divertirse hasta el agotamiento" (enjoy until exhaustion).[46] The narrator describes the hedonistic world of the Costa del Sol as a festive mosaic of bodies (safely understood as female bodies through the metonymic reference to "caderas" (hips) and "ombligos" (navels)), beautiful blonde boys and imposing Nordic women adorned in brightly colored blouses, hotels and apartments, and automobiles of many different colors and many different origins.[47] These elements melt together under the Mediterranean sun to create "un mundo brillante, desenfadado, un estallido de colores de alegría, de vida (a shiny carefree world, a colorful explosion of joy, of life).[48] The sun plays an especially important role in the design of the spectacle where the beach and the pool ironically acquire a divine (if pagan) dimension as the "altar del ocio" (altar of leisure) where a panorama of "carnes al aire" (exposed flesh) sacrifice themselves by suffering first and second degree sunburns in ascetic adoration of ultraviolet rays.[49] Yet, even after the sun has set, the hedonistic lifestyle continues throughout the Torremolinos night life in the "ambiente licencioso" (licentious atmosphere) of discotheques like El Colorado.[50] If discotheques offers a space to continue the hedonistic tendencies of the pools and beaches, then a new profession arises that both embodies and catalyzes the high-energy, sexualized, free-spirited atmosphere of those spaces: the go-go girl. The frenetic contortions and rocking, paradoxically disordered yet rhythmic, of Mónica and Marga, dressed in red and black leather mini-skirts, both mirror and propel the cha-otic atmosphere of the discotheque. Like a flame on a torch or the water in a fountain, the go-go girls literally become a spectacle that seizes the gaze of onlookers and hypnotizes them. The only way to free oneself of the spell, asserts the narrator, is "ponerse a bailar" (to start dancing).[51] The go-go girls, then, offer a kind of mise en abyme in which they not only reflect and repro-duce the hedonistic energy of the crowd in the discotheque but also come to represent the latent ideology of the Costa del Sol.

Within this hyperreal environment, Palomino notes a deterioration in the traditional markers that we rely upon to endow identity and culture with meaning or, at the least, context. Time, for example, ceases to hold any true signifying power and Saturday night, the narrator asserts, is like any other night because "en la Costa del Sol todos los días son día de fiesta, todas las noches, noches de sábado" (on the Costa del Sol every day is a day to party, every night is Saturday night), evoking Jameson's description of a world that is understood through pure material signifiers "as a series of pure and unre-lated presents in time."[52] Palomino acknowledges the assimilation of cul-tural markers into the logic of late capitalism where everyday life has ceded structure to individualistic desires to satisfy the whims of the Freudian id, "En la Costa del Sol no hay hipocresía ni gregarismo; ni siquiera hay todavía costumbres. Todo se hace porque se quiere, porque se siente (. . .)" (In the Costa del Sol there is no hypocrisy nor community; there are not even customs anymore. Everybody does whatever they want whenever they want because they feel like it . . .).[53] From the flamenco show to Spanish Sangría Party welcome receptions at the Torremolinos Gran Hotel, cultural elements of the so-called "España cañí" become empty signifiers that are subsumed into the logic of the marketplace and packaged for consumption as supposedly authentic markers of Spanish identity.[54] A seemingly innocuous and minor detail as the tourist postcard may seem silly, but as the narrator emphasizes "en el negocio turístico no hay bobadas" (in the tourist industry there are no trite details).[55] On one hand, the narrator points out that the tourist postcard serves a distinctly commercial function by generating daily revenues of 800 pesetas with margins, the narrator emphasizes, of 500 percent that total an annual revenue at the Torremolinos Gran Hotel of over 300,000 pesetas. On the other hand, postcards serve a vital ideological function that generate the "space of the dream" as Lefebvre calls it by enticing the gaze of the viewer with images that reproduce and reinforce the Torremolinos imaginary.[56] As a guest in the Torremolinos Gran Hotel browses the postcards in the lobby, scenes of bullfighters and flamenco dancers, panoramic views of Málaga, traditional fishermen, and the Mijas burro-taxi entice her gaze and assimilate cultural markers to sell Spain as an exotic escape that offers an illusion of agency through spectacle designed for consumption. Similarly, when two characters view a film set in the Costa del Sol in which Spanish men act as bumbling "paletos" (bumpkins) around sexually liberated Nordic women, the narrator recognizes the role that Spanish cinema has played in fabricating the "mito de la sueca" (the myth of the Swedish woman) to promote coastal tourism and the hedonistic ideology associated with it.[57] The narrator suggests ironically that what is noticeably absent in the Costa del Sol is a statue of a slender, bikini-clad Northern European woman that would serve as a monument to the stereotypical "Sueca Desconocida" (Unknown Swedish Woman) who had contributed so much to the promotion of tourism along the Costa del Sol.[58]

The generation of the hyperreal, Disneyfied environment of the Costa del Sol is far from natural but rather a carefully designed artifice, and Palomino's novel details the machinery as well as the human labor required to maintain the ludic spectacle and the "atmósfera mágica" of the hotel he depicts. Personified as a colossus that never sleeps, the narrator reveals that at all hours thousands of kilowatts, rivers of water, streams of oil, and hundreds of "criaturas" (creatures) bustle about inside the walls of the hotel. All the while "la gran máquina contable" (the great accounting machine) records data from each department and anticipates the revenue generated from every area and every activity of every day. That the narrator invokes a kind of industrial imagery is no accident, and throughout the novel Palomino offers the reader a look into the inner workings of the machinery needed to fabricate the spectacle enjoyed by the hotel guests. For example, the narrator describes an unbearably chaotic, avant-garde symphony of whistles, snaps, roars, and squeals that powers freon gas through a labyrinth of pipes with hundreds of horse power and thousands of pounds of force to create a cool environment that contribute to the "bienestar y bienestar al ocio" (well-being and well-being to leisure).[59] The dialectic in which the unseen industrial systems and human labor directly construct the space designed for tourist consumption evokes the tension between everyday life and the tourist's "unreflexive bliss" that underlies Minca and Oakes's idea of the "traveler's paradox."[60] While visitors enjoy themselves in the refreshing interior and exterior spaces of the hotel, a cadre of service technicians including electricians, plumbers, carpenters, and other laborers stand at the ready to repair any aspect of the system that may break down. The head of service technicians, meanwhile, monitors the lights, gauges, and displays on a wall of instruments that measure and control water pressure, electrical currents, and more. The hotel, in this aspect, becomes a panopticon in which the purpose of surveillance is not to exert punitive control as Foucault described but to guarantee the ideological order of the illusion through detailed observation of the physical environment.[61]

Other scenes similarly emphasize the reality, both in terms of labor and the machinery, behind the appearances that undergirds the hedonistic spectacle of leisure enjoyed by the tourists. By enumerating the vast operations and quantifying the material resources required to propel the many intertwined systems, Palomino not only conveys to the reader the colossal dimensions of the hotel operations but also clarifies and emphasizes the hotel, and coastal tourism in Spain by extension, as a literal space of consumption. During the down time in the late afternoon when hotel guests transition from a day of sun and sand to an evening of dinner and dancing in the Torremolinos night life, "la vida sigue" (life goes on) affirms the narrator.[62] While the lobby, pool area, and lounge areas are deserted, the narrator quantifies the unseen activities by enumerating the ongoing operations from the number of showers running to the number of housekeeping staff that "restituyen el orden" (restore order) while a cadre of chefs prepare rows of chicken and sirloin steak, blocks of butter, and mountains of lettuce for "consumo inmediato" (immediate consumption) in anticipation of guests literally seeking fast food as they venture out into the Torremolinos night life.[63] In another scene, when a guest complains that his bill seems high, the assistant director of the Torremolinos Gran Hotel pierces the illusion of transparency to offer the guest (and the reader) a look behind the scenes at the unseen machinery, the invisible services, and the hidden labor needed to construct the spectacle that constitutes the tourist experience. The assistant director guides the guest on a tour that begins in the engine room and continues through the laundry, kitchen, meat locker, and concludes in the bakery. The narrator describes a "mundo difícil de imaginar" (world difficult to imagine) where the two swinging doors that separate the ordered chaos of voices, movement, whistles, and alarms from the cool, quiet ambience of the dining room seem a "túnel cósmico" (cosmic tunnel) that passes to a whole other dimension where guests are blissfully ignorant of the simulacra that surrounds them.[64]

While the labor and machinery described maintain the inward illusion for hotel guests, of equal importance is the manipulation of mass media to project an outward impression through a carefully curated control of a public narrative. The same aseptic image that hides reality and bans negative emotions within the hotel to propel the ludic atmosphere for the comfort and pleasure of guests is projected outwardly through mass communication and the press to maintain the appearance and uphold the reputation of the hotel. When a British tourist suffers a heart attack on the premises, the hotel director's primary concern is to move the guest out of the hotel to avoid any possible report of a death in one of the rooms. Then, when an Italian actor enters another guest room illegally and attempts to pass off fake checks, the hotel director convinces the press to frame the story in praise of the authorities and to suppress the name of the hotel. Or, when an assistant in the kitchen accidentally cuts off the tip of his left thumb, he is escorted home to avoid any possibility that the happy world of the Torremolinos Gran Hotel might crack and demystify the appearance for the guests. On the contrary, to promote the image of luxury where international cinema icons, renowned performers, and beautiful Nordic women lounge poolside, the Torremolinos Gran Hotel depends on the media to fortify the mystique of the spectacle with headlines that relate gossip and frivolous news about possible romances among the jet set. Not only is the press a means through which to control the external image of the hotel, but early in the novel the hotel board of directors understands journalism as a medium that can be manipulated to uphold class hegemony by legitimizing and normalizing the discourse of development through uncritically reporting the board's plans for expansion through hotels, resorts, and golf courses all along the Costa del Sol. What Palomino underscores is the notion that David Harvey explores in "The Right to the City," where the normalization of neoliberal discourse via media outlets (the press but also cinema and postcards as was discussed earlier) reaffirms the intimate ties between urbanization and capitalism, but also asserts the hegemony of the dominant classes by exerting social control to shape urban processes and to reproduce the logic of capital on an ideological level. The discourse of revitalization, especially in the name of tourism, through finance capital colonizes space for the affluent through collusion between state and corporate interests (as we saw at the beginning of this chapter) and raises the question about who truly has the right to the city.[65]

While Manegat's novel criticizes the moral dangers the libertine atmosphere associated with tourism pose to the Catholic and cultural integrity of Spain, Palomino perceives a deeper threat in the culture of corporate greed and corruption that directs the tourism industry. In *Torremolinos Gran Hotel*, the hotel becomes the epicenter of a space of consumption designed for the pleasure of tourists but beyond the fabricated illusion that stokes and sates the Dionysian desires of the hotel guests the so-called miracle of Spain's economic model resides in the generation of revenue through what David Harvey calls "monopoly rent."[66] Palomino demystifies what De Soto refers to as the "mysteries" of capitalism by exposing the imperceptible corporate machinations of the Sociedad Anónima (Public Limited Company) whose shareholders are often literally unseen and unknown.[67] Early in the novel, the narrator explains that Díaz Perez S A , founded by its president Don Arturo Díaz, generates profit through the post-Fordist practices of flexible accumulation, an economic model that Harvey asserts epitomizes the condition of postmodernity and the transition away from traditional manufacturing. The company's mission, the narrator attests, is "tomarle el pelo legalmente al Ministro de Hacienda" (to pull the wool over the eyes of the Internal Revenue Service legally) by transforming the purchase of land through real estate speculation into the trade of shares in the company itself. It is much easier, the narrator explains, to mask the sale of shares than it is land under the scrutinizing eye of "el Gran Hermano Fiscal" (Fiscal Big Brother).[68] The Costa del Sol, the narrator continues, is a free trade zone where anything goes and business agreements are protected through tacit agreements, under the table exchanges, and back-room deals. The shareholder company exemplifies Alfred Chandler's idea of the "visible hand" that contradicts Smith's "invisible hand," by not only reifying the transparent flows of capital in the free market but serving as the catalyst to stoke the demands of and desire for capital by controlling its direction.[69]

Through a relatively simple formula, the fictional shareholder company in Palomino's novel exemplifies an economic model that repeats itself all along the Costa del Sol: borrow money short term, invest in property near the beach, construct a hotel, reappraise the value of the land, sell shares, quintuple (or more) the original investment with additional revenue through the services at the hotel, interest, and rent. However, Palomino also highlights that a key component that underlies this economic model are the illegal practices such as bribery and contraband that facilitate the acquisition of land and lower the cost of construction through cheap materials like stolen cement from Italy.[70] One prominent sub-plot in the novel revolves around the diversion of funds from the hotel in an elaborate tax evasion scheme that Arturo Díaz himself calls "Operación Fuga de Capitales." His intention is not to pocket that money because, he reasons, to do so would not fulfill the primary mission of capital which he explains, "El dinero debe estar sudando intereses, criando dinero. En una maleta ni suda ni cría" (Money should be sweating interest and growing more money. In a briefcase it doesn't sweat and it doesn't grow).[71] At the conclusion of *Torremolinos Gran Hotel*, the narrator draws a parallel between the sea and capital, not just through the double understanding of liquidity but also their similar dynamic surges, their ebbs and flows, their stormy squalls and dead calms as well as the intimate connection between the rise of costal tourism and its economic impact in Spain. The narrator, however, echoes the concern of don Carlos, owner of the three-star "Estrella del Pacífico," from the opening pages of the novel about the directionless singularity of the economic model forged on the Costa del Sol. Along with oil in the Middle East, bananas in Central America, and uranium in Katanga, Spanish tourism attracts the global gaze of "grupos avispados" (cunning groups) of foreign investors. Financiers from North America, Switzerland, Belgium, France, and Germany arrive to the Spanish coasts not for the sea, sun, and sand but to swim in "esa gran masa líquida del dinero que no sabe quedarse en casa, no sabe qué hacer" (that vast liquid mass of capital that doesn't know how to stay at home, that doesn't know what it is doing).[72]

The Hotel as Thirdspace in Pedro Lazaga's *El turismo es un gran invento* and *El abominable hombre de la Costa del Sol*

Similar to the novels examined already in this chapter, Spanish film of the 1960s and 1970s offers a contradictory consideration of tourism that both celebrates Spain's newfound modernity and the comforts offered, yet also critiques the perceived loss of traditional Spanish cultural values (most often associated with Catholic morals). As the title of Sally Faulkner's *A Cinema of Contradiction: Spanish Film in the 1960s* suggests the inclusion an representation of "foreign" liberal ideas about sex, pleasure, leisure, and accumulation in the so-called "comedias desarrollistas" of the 1960s presents a paradox in which the elements offered as objects of criticism are also celebrated as values to embrace.[73] Spanish films from the 1960s and 1970s that situate their plots along the coasts mine comedic gold from the cultural clashes between Spain's traditional conservative Catholic values, especially during the dictatorship, and the libertine, ludic, freewheeling, amoral, consumerist atmosphere of coastal tourism. At the same time many of the films from this era convey a conservative message that upholds the moral superiority of Spanish culture and institutions, many scholars have studied the films that offer images of tourism as strategic marketing campaigns that serve as vehicles to promote tourism through place branding. In *Destination Dictatorship*, Justin Crumbaugh refers to the discursive strategies in films that depict Spanish coastal tourism as "meta-tourism," in which the story of tourism refers back to itself and the representation of tourism adheres to Francoist official ideology, instills a common view of the tourist industry in line with hegemonic power, and invites individuals to play a central role in the tourism project (and hence become an active agent in nation-building) with the promise of economic emancipation.[74] For many scholars, the cinematic meta-discourse to which Crumbaugh refers articulates a very specific message about the "place" of tourism, in which the audiovisual space converges with a narrative space to create a persuasive message about the tourist destination as a product in and of itself as an overt strategy to foment place branding through a carefully curated mise en scéne. Rafael Gómez Alonso in "El turismo no es un gran invento" asserts that the mise en scéne of the so-called "comedias desarrollistas" of many Spanish films from the 1960s posits the coasts as places of possibility, simulacra, that he describes as a "juego de apariencias entre lo que uno es y lo le gustaría ser" (a game of illusions between what one is and what one would like to be).[75] Other scholars have studied how architecture, especially what Juan Antonio Ramírez and Diego Santos called the "estilo del relax" along the Costa del Sol, is re-presented and interpreted through visual mass media, especially film, to mutate into a form of mass media in and of itself whose linguistic code (i.e. its architectural style) is deciphered, decoded, recoded, and converted into a symbol of well-being and consumerist values.[76] Images of this architectural style in film is perceived by some scholars to create a visual archive that that preserves Spanish cultural heritage to present ethnographic survey of modern society, preserve a documentary testimony, and construct a cognitive map of tourist spaces from the 1960s and 1970s through the representation of banal tourist objects like bars, pubs, and hotels as well as souvenirs and postcards.[77]

For my purposes here, I do not examine the hotel in Spanish film from the 1960s and 1970s as simply a backdrop or mise en scéne, nor as a piece of the cultural heritage of coastal tourism, nor in terms of aesthetic design imbued with a linguistic code. Rather, I approach the representation of the hotel in two films directed by Pedro Lazaga, *El turismo es un gran invento* and *El abominable hombre de la Costa del Sol*, as the epitome of Edward Soja's concept of Thirdspace in which the urban environment is comprised of physical, mental, and social spaces that engage and interact in a trialectic process.[78] In *Thirdspace: Journeys to Los Angeles and Other Real-and-Imagined Places*, Soja engages in an alternative reading of Henri Lefebvre's *The Production of Space*, a seminal text that first established the historicality-sociality-spatiality trialectic.[79] Soja is specifically interested in urban spaces he describes as a "city-without-cityness" that he denominates an "exopolis," a hyperreal simulacra of "manufactured landscapes" that turns the city inside-out and outside-in simultaneously, melting the division between the real and the imaginary, the true and the false, the signifier and signified in a spectacular confusion that blurs all familiar categories of knowledge.[80] For Soja, Firstspace aligns with Lefebvre's understanding of Spatial Practice where a physical, visible, material built environment, a perceived space, can be measured empirically and objectively; their linguistic codes, as mentioned earlier, read as a text whose details and design are readily available. By contrast, Secondspace maps onto Lefebvre's idea of Representations of Space and offers an explanatory model that contemplates the ideation and projection of a conceived, rather than perceived, space often at the hands of a creative architect who envisions and re-presents imagined cities and urban spaces. While Firstspace and Secondspace mirror the binary dualities that have historically characterized epistemological interpretative models for understanding urban environments, Thirdspace represents a radical ontological restructuring by conceptualizing Lefebvre's Spaces of Representation as a lived, social space that is infused with historicality and filled with politics, capitalism, and daily social struggles. Comparing it to Borges's Aleph, Soja's understanding of Thirdspace underscores the subject's constant movement between the ontological and epistemological planes, aware of the simultaneous interaction between history, society, and space but also open to the infinite possibilities to remember, recover, or rethink spaces that have been lost or never before considered.[81]

Soja describes Thirdspace as "vitally filled with politics and ideology, with the real and the imagined intertwined, and with capitalism, racism, patriarchy, and other material spatial practices that concretize social relations or production, reproduction, exploitation, domination, and subjection."[82]

The fetishized spaces of the Spanish coasts offer a prime example of the exopolis and its carefully curated and manufactured design that Soja describes. The symbolic linguistic codes of the building's aesthetic design may indeed convey ideas and values associated with the ludic atmosphere of leisure and pleasure of coastal tourism, but it is the subject's interaction with the real, physical spaces and the negotiation with the ideas and inherent contradictions they embody that continually shift the individual between epistemology and ontology. The hotels, apartments, bars, restaurants, discos, casinos, commercial centers, and souvenir shops along the Spanish coasts impose a spatial language that is notably divorced from local identity, cultural context, and social history to rewrite the physical space as an alienated (and alienating) urban palimpsest that is redefined through capitalist initiatives, land speculation, and the desire to attract the tourist's gaze. The urban fabric that ties communities together becomes a fabrication of space into a theme-park, a "paradigmatic reflection" that invades, overtakes, and informs lived, social space to re-present reality something transcendental where "everything is possible and nothing is real."[83] While some Spanish films from the 1960s and 1970s such as *En un lugar de la Manga* (1970) may offer a contemplation on the physical transformation of the natural environments along the coasts into ahistorical, acultural urbanized destinations where personal memory and local identity are literally bulldozed, my purpose here is to examine the representation of the hotel, specifically the Don Pepe Gran Meliá in Marbella designed by architect Eleuterio Población Knappe, in two Pedro Lazaga films through the lens of Soja's Thirdspace. In *El turismo es un gran invento* and *El abominable hombre de la Costa del Sol* the hotel Don Pepe Gran Meliá, the first five-star hotel in the Costa del Sol that opened in 1964, serves as what Soja would call an "iconic emplacement" in which the subject experiences a postmodern confusion of time and space where the physical transformations of the coasts, and the consumerist ideology that drives them, impel ontological transformations on an individual and collective level.[84] Moreover, both films absorb the viewer into the narrative space of the film through a subtle manipulation of the camera's eye at specific moments that assimilates the viewer's gaze by breaking the fourth wall through a first-person point-of-view shot. The use of this technique turns the films "outside-in" by converting the viewer from spectator into participant in the action almost as if it were one of those theme park rides that allows the viewer a first-person thrill, a momentary sensation of leisure and luxury in the shoes of the film's characters.

El turismo es un gran invento opens with a close up of the British, French, German, and Spanish flags and pulls back to a panoramic shot of some undetermined tourist locale where a line of cars arrive to a "Puerta de España" (Port of Spain) and "Aduana" (Customs). A montage of images follow that define this destination as a ludic space defined by capital and leisure—beaches with throngs of sunbathers and swimmers, high rise hotels along the coastline, speedboats with waterskiers, people playing tennis, cranes looming over hotels, and signs directing tourists to money exchanges and restaurants. As the images flow over the viewer in a series of quick cuts, a pop song offers this "place" ironically as somewhere people go to lose themselves, "Me gusta hacer turismo / es algo estimulante / es una emocionante manera de viajar / Olvide sus problemas / no piense en los negocios / y déjele a su socio / el deber y el haber / Relájese en la arena / consígase un flirteo / y sienta el cosquilleo / del sol sobre su piel. / Y luego por la noche / con un whisky delante / descanse en el sedante sillón de un buen hotel" (I like to do tourism / it is something very stimulating / it is an exciting way to travel. / Forget your problems / don't think about work / and let your colleagues / take care of business. / Relax in the sand / Flirt a little bit / Feel the caress / of the sun on your skin / and later at night / with a whiskey in hand / lounge in the comfortable armchair of a high-class hotel). As the song concludes and cedes to a fast-talking voiceover, the viewer is left with an image of the skeleton of a hotel under construction with a large crane looming over the coastline, "Turismo, turismo, turismo" (Tourism, Tourism, Tourism) booms the narrator, "Una palabra mágica que está en boca de todo el mundo. Y que ayer, aunque estaba en el diccionario, nadie sabía lo que significaba" (A magic word that is on everyone's lips. And that yesterday, although it was in the dictionary, nobody knew what it meant.) The rhythm of the narrator's voice coupled with the rapid succession of images evokes the sense of vibrancy and vitality tourism is perceived to inject into Spanish society. He urges, "¡Viajar, viajar, viajar! En coche, en avión, en barco, como sea, a pie si es necesario. Conocer cosas nuevas, comer paella" (Travel, travel, travel! By car, by plane, by ship, however, by foot if necessary. Get to know new things and eat paella!). The Costa del Sol, a geographic location for tourists and a metaphorical destination for Spanish modernity, offers leisure and culture as equally valued commodities subsumed by and consumed within the logic of global capitalism. This opening scene concludes with a montage of quick-cut still shots of signs for money exchanges, parking lots, and restaurants that finish with close-ups of hotels that quickly zoom out and

cut from one to another, producing a sense of velocity and vertigo conveying the dizzying and disorienting effects of capital. At the end of the opening credits, the viewer reads that the montage is composed of images from
coastal cities from throughout Spain, "Los exteriores de esta película se han
rodado en Madrid—Marbella— Torremolinos—Torrelaguna—Valdemoro—
Talamanca—Torremocha—Aigua Blava—Benidorm—Salou—La Junquera—
Mazarrón—Tossa—Bagur—Tarragona—Barcelona—Alicante." That these
locations are interchangeable emphasizes the commonality of the tourist
experiences there as spaces defined by capital and leisure where one goes to
lose oneself. A close-up on car license plates from other European countries
through another series of quick edits celebrates a new Spain whose porous
borders invite foreign consumption—in sharp contrast with the autarquic
policies of the first half of the Franco dictatorship. Torremolinos, then exemplifies Spain's incursion into mass media global capitalism as what Tatjana
Pavlovic has called a "mobile nation" in which the modern values of mobility,
technology, and capital have supplanted the previous patriarchal, conservative, traditional values now considered backward.[85]

The ludic, Dionysian disorientation of the opening scene shifts to a quiet,
empty field in Aragón where a group of men survey the area, and the mayor
(Paco Martínez Soria) argues that the pueblo Valdemorillo needs to embrace
the economic model set by the Costa del Sol in order to revitalize the life of
the town.[86] The alcalde exemplifies Harvey's urbanization of consciousness
as he fully assimilates the ideology behind the narrative of development,
"Estamos olvidados. Y lo que es peor, atrasados. Lo que hay que hacer es
cambiarlo todo, ponerse al día, y hacer aquí la Costa de Valdemorillo" (We
are forgotten. And even worse, we are behind the times. What we need to
do is to change everything, get with the times, and create here a Costa de
Valdemorillo). As they walk the town, he points out the need for modernization and the town assessor (José Luis López Vázquez) takes notes. Local
customs must be redefined within the logic of global flows of capital and
the demands of international tourism he asserts. The stream where women
wash clothes should be converted to a coastline, the decaying seventeenth-
century fonda replaced with a parador, a "supermercado" constructed where
townspeople can sell their "melocotones" (peaches) and "higos" (figs), and
finally, Spanish customs perceived to be inconsistent with a modern identity must be eliminated, "Hay que acabar con el dominó, con el tute, y con el
mus. Es un atraso. Hay que echarlo todo abajo" (We need to get rid of domi-
nos, tute and mus. It is backward. We need to get rid of it all). Nevertheless,
one major obstacle stands in the way of their desire to attract tourists and,

more importantly, the capital they would bring to the town. When the assessor informs the mayor that to undertake such a large-scale urban renewal project would require a huge infusion of cash ("un dineral"), the mayor's response announces the kind of public/private collusion that undergirds the development of the coasts as well as the prioritization of urban design over urban planning to construct ludic spaces along the coast in the interest of economic advancement. At the local bank, after an employee denies the mayor the funds he requests and instead tells him to take out a line of credit, the mayor replies indignantly, "¿Para qué si es para el beneficio del pueblo? ¿O quieres que todo siga igual? Aquí la gente o se muere de aburrimiento o se muere de hambre" (What for if it is for the benefit of the town? Or do you want everything to stay the same? Here either people die from boredom or they die from hunger). The mayor later solves this problem by establishing a "suscripción popular" (public quota) in the town that is both "voluntaria y obligatoria" (voluntary and obligatory) to raise the funds needed to travel to the Costa del Sol and begin the cycle of what Harvey calls "flexible accumulation," or using capital to earn capital.[87]

Once in the Costa del Sol, the mayor and the once reticent assessor become enthralled with the luxury of high-rise hotels like the Don Pepe Gran Meliá, the leisurely lifestyle on the beach, and the open sexuality of scantily clad Scandinavian women, especially a Swedish dancing group named "Las Buby-Girls" whom they later invite to Valdemorillo. When the men first enter the hotel, the perspective of the viewer shifts from observing them approaching the entrance to a first-person point of view. As the doorman opens the door, the viewer becomes ironically aware of their own gaze and the means through which the consumerist ideology of the hotel is assimilated visually through the illusion of luxury and the promise of escape from the mundane activities of everyday life. Glass doors epitomize Lefebvre's illusion of transparency as a long marble floor hall extends before the viewer and the sunlight in the distance promises a world of pleasure and leisure. The lobby itself offers the characters a transitional space both physically, ideologically, and ontologically as they explore the unfamiliar modern trappings of various spaces in the hotel including their room, the restaurant, the pool, the night club (named Whisky a go gó like the famous eponymous locations in Paris and Los Angeles), multiple bars, and the outdoor dining area. The characters' ontological shift is manifested in the transformation of the outward trappings of their life in the pueblo, specifically their suits, in favor of the loud mismatched shorts and shirts prevalent along the beaches. Their inability to forgo the boína (and dark shoes) reveals not an abrupt shift in

FIGURE 1.1. Night view of Hotel Melia Don Pepe, Marbella, Costa del Sol, date unknown

social values but a progressive interpenetration of traditional and modern identities in a culture of contradictions. The mayor and the town assessor have not only read the hotel's spatial discourse, but they have more importantly assimilated the ideology of its spatial representation and the allure of its symbolic power by integrating the spatial practices therein. Throughout the film, the Don Pepe looms over the mayor and town assessor (as well as the other vacationers at the hotel), as a physical, almost anthropomorphic, manifestation of capital that keeps a vigilant eye over the guests. More than simply product placement, the Don Pepe Gran Meliá epitomizes the transformation that Manuel Vázquez Montalbán described where the political repression of "el Gran Hermano" (Big Brother) becomes the social control of "el Gran Consumidor" (Big Consumer) through the constant surveillance of the panopticon (as we saw earlier in Palomino's *Torremolinos Gran Hotel*).

Yet, as their money dwindles, they convince the town to send more funds not with the promise of progress for the town but by tantalizing them with the fulfillment of their individual desires for prestige, power, and sexual prowess. The mayor and town assessor reproduce the ontological trialectic of the Don Pepe Gran Meliá by sending postcards that convey, or better yet market, visions of how their lives might improve. The mayor and the assessor entice the gaze of the residents in the pueblo, particularly the men, through postcards that not only portray the impressive modern built environment of the Costa del Sol, but engage them on an ideological level. The camera's eye shifts from observing the characters as they contemplate the postcards to a first-person point of view that assimilates the gaze of the townspeople with ironic awareness of the symbolic power of the representation of space. The point of view shifts again as each character transports themselves to an imagined scene in the space of the Don Pepe represented in the postcard they hold, where they envision their desires become realized. Through the shifting points of view, the spectator experiences the destabilizing effects of capital as one's gaze is assimilated spatially and ideologically through postcards that act as dream generators. Don Marcial, the local landowner who has bankrolled the trip, contemplates a postcard at an empty table in the hotel restaurant next to a large window that overlooks cypress trees alongside the garden area. He envisions himself in the space along with the mayor and other men from the town, dressed in suits, who indulge in the pleasures typical of powerful men by smoking cigars and drinking whiskey as if they were titans of industry. A postcard of five women posing in bikinis inspires the meek Alejo to dream of bikini-clad blonde women who pursue him poolside with aggressive sexual desire and lift him up with ecstatic, orgiastic laughter, a celebration of his irresistible masculinity as the hotel filling the screen behind the women seems to look on approvingly. Yet, it is the owner of the town's only inn who articulates the ideological power of the visual representations of the hotel spaces as he contemplates an alternative life as the doorman at the Don Pepe and exclaims, "Daría todo que tengo para tener un hotel como éste en el pueblo." (I would give everything I have to have a hotel like this one in the village.) If the postcard generates the dream, then the hotel itself offers the space for that dream to come true.

The visual representations of the hotel's built spaces engages the unconscious desires of the townspeople in *El turismo es un gran invento* and fosters an imagined or conceived space, what Soja would refer to as Secondspace, whose ideological force manufactures Debordian "pseudo needs."[88] Spectacle subverts the tangibility of what is real, Debord argues, by transforming the consumption of products into the consumption of illusions, where desire is reified through the physical spaces of the hotel itself. Later, when the mayor and tax assessor travel to Madrid with don Marcial in hopes of meeting with the Minister of Tourism, they unwittingly signal the economic, political, and ideological transformations of Spain in the 1960s. The imposing brutalist concrete façade of the Ministerio de Información y Turismo, a typical staple of monumental fascist architecture, clearly communicates the building as a space of power and dominance, access to which is prohibited for the likes of simple peasants like those from Valdemorillo. Yet, while the gray tones of the building's exterior and an overcast Madrid contrast with the exuberant brightness of the Costa del Sol, bubblegum pop music plays as the camera pans to a large billboard that reads "España es diferente" to connect the seemingly divergent worlds of an austere Madrid and a libertine Marbella through the common economic enterprise of tourism. That the men wait outside with several large baskets of figs and peaches, physical products from the agricultural heritage of their town that they intend to offer as gifts to the Minister of Tourism if granted audience, suggests they have not fully learned the lessons of theTorremolinos imaginary from their trip to the Costa del Sol. A quick cut to an interior lobby of the hotel of presents the viewer with a close-up of a painting depicting a rural scene of men on horseback herding cattle, which contrasts the authentic lived rural identity of the inhabitants of Valdemorillo with one-dimensional representations that appropriate that identity as cultural patrimony within the context of tourism. This juxtaposition between the real and its representation calls to mind Magritte's famous 1929 painting The Treachery of Images and captures Baudrillard's distinction between the "weight, opacity, and substance" of the object and the "abstract, formal (lightness)" of the commodity whose "visible essence" is always manifest and readable through its price.[89] Likewise, tourism posters that reproduce images of people, places, and things associated with Spanish culture, history, and gastronomy line the walls of the lobby and redefine Spain's cultural patrimony into commodities whose perceived value has been simplified within the consumerist logic of tourism. Advertising, concludes Baudrillard, invades everything with what he calls the obscenity of the all-too-visible, where there are no secrets any more and everything has dissolved into one-dimensional information: "all functions abolished in a single dimension, that of communication. . . . All secrets, spaces and scenes abolished in a single dimension of information."[90] After the Minister refuses to meet with them, a cut to the exterior shows the men sitting dejectedly at the corner of a busy intersection of the Castellana surrounded by the figs and peaches they had brought, literally contemplating the lost fruits of their labor. The volume and velocity of the cars behind them evoke Spain's movement into a (post)modernity in which the men (and their agricultural products) are not only out of place but left behind.

At the conclusion of *El turismo es un gran invento*, Lazaga ironically underscores the fleeting flexibility behind "flexible accumulation" when the town celebrates a letter received from the Ministry of the Interior granting the mayor a hearing within four months. Under a billboard boasting the upcoming inauguration of the Parador de Turismo de Valdemorillo (despite the fact that no plans for construction exist or have even been approved), townspeople dance a traditional Aragonese jota.[91] Not only does the dance contrast with the sexualized spectacle offered by "Las Bubygirls," when they perform in the town, but it leaves the viewer with lingering doubts about the survival of authentic local customs as they are reconstructed and reconfigured within the capitalist framework of global tourism. While the mayor had originally wanted to replicate the Firstspace physical trappings of the Costa del Sol in Valdemorillo with a literal coastline, he and the others appear to have learned from Marbella, to borrow from Venturi, by assuming its underlying logic and applying it to their town through the construction of a Parador hotel. Maite Méndez Baiges describes the Disneyfication of Spanish cultural heritage that underlies such hotels and calls them a "parque temático de lo nacional, rescatando las pasadas glorias de su entorno rural" (theme park of national identity, retrieving past glories from their rural environs).[92] Far from the modern art deco–inspired design associated with the "estilo del relax" along the Costa del Sol, the system of state-run Parador hotels, originally established in 1928 by King Alfonso XIII, blend and blur history, culture, and consumption by adopting and adapting monumental spaces like palaces, castles, fortresses, convents, and monasteries into hotels around which rural tourism can be constructed and expanded. That the leaders of Valdemorillo hope to incorporate a Parador as the impetus for tourism there indicates their awareness of the ideological and economic impact of the hotel and announces their assimilation into Thirdspace.

In *El abominable hombre de la Costa del Sol*, Don Federico, marquis de Urbión, undergoes similar ontological and epistemological transformation as the mayor and other townspeople in *El turismo es un gran invento* through his experiences at the Don Pepe Gran Meliá in Marbella. The film offers a kind of coming-of-age Bildungsroman story that follows the evolution of don Federico (Juanjo Menéndez) from a timid clumsy child-like naif into a confident composed well-respected Director of Public Relations at the most luxurious hotel in the Costa del Sol. Don Federico's transformation parallels the shifts in Spanish society during the years of *desarrollismo* in the 1960s when the closed hierarchical system of social classes connoted by don Federico's noble title shifts to an open free-market capitalist society where upward mobility seems to be achieved through unbridled consumption. This shift is communicated visually in the film through the juxtaposition of enclosed physical spaces, namely the austerity of the monastery in the opening scene as well as the interior design of the home belonging to the Duke of Puentelarra (Jorge Rigaud), don Federico's father, with the bright, sunlit openness of the Don Pepe Gran Meliá. The ascetic atmosphere of the monastery, where don Federico had been preparing to enter the priesthood, contrasts deeply with the hedonistic lifestyle that the protagonist encounters in the Costa del Sol at the Don Pepe. Similarly, tapestry-covered walls, the abundance of antique vases, and the hyperbolic number of crossed swords and prominently displayed dueling pistols throughout the Duke's house evoke the decadence of Golden Age Habsburg Spain. But the sleek, modern façade of the Don Pepe and interior spaces are designed to be airy and sophisticated, conveying the cultural values of the *aperturismo* era in Spain where the economic miracle appeared to open access to an elite lifestyle through consumption. That the monastery's abbot and the Duke of Puentelarra both chastise don Federico, the former for his lack of religious conviction and the latter for his perceived unmanly mannerisms, suggests an identity crisis in the protagonist who has literally and figuratively not found his "place" in society. The Duke, an arrogant status-driven womanizer, is especially critical of his son and believes intellectual prowess in the areas of philosophy and literature have done little to prepare his son for the "real world," confining him to the space of books. By pulling strings to arrange for his son to travel to the Costa del Sol to work as the Director of Public Relations, the Duke hopes the experience of true work will endow don Federico with the masculine sense of self that agrees with his own patriarchal mindset. Yet, while the Duke is operating within a Firstspace imaginary, that the physical dislocation of his son will provoke an existential transformation, what don Federico encounters is the social, lived space of the Don Pepe, in which constant ideological negotiations within Thirdspace redefine his sense of self within the discourse of tourism and leisure.

While the mayor and tax assessor in *El turismo es un gran invento* travel by bus to arrive at Marbella, a mode of transportation that emphasizes their "paleto" outsider status within Spanish modernity, don Federico's social entitlement allows him the luxury to travel by plane to the Costa del Sol and arrive at the Don Pepe on one of the hotel's private shuttles, a small van branded with the hotel's name in a stylized font. Nevertheless, despite their differences in social class, don Federico travels along the coast with the same wide-eyed wonder as the characters in *El turismo es un gran invento* as if he had entered some undiscovered and previously unimaginable foreign territory. The camera focuses on don Federico as he stares out the window of the shuttle with his mouth agape and traces his route along a map, but subtle cuts transition the camera's perspective so that the viewer assumes don Federico's point of view and, consequently, his fascination with the Mediterranean landscape and culture. Signposts that point toward "Torremolinos" identify and define place as do iconic landmarks such as the famous discotheque Tiffany's, yet blonde women in bikinis and sweeping views of the sea along with souvenir shops and hilltop medieval castles frame the destination's space as one of ludic consumption. The shift in camera point-of-view positions the viewer alongside don Federico and aligns their consciousness with his as he discovers the foreign world of the Costa del Sol, assimilates the ideological space of the hotel, and undergoes an ontological transformation within that space. Don Federico's naïve understanding not only about the workings of the hotel's operations and physical space but, more importantly, the ideological underpinnings of the space are clearly demonstrated in his first interaction with the Don Pepe's director. While don Federico cites definitions of public relations and its importance in hospitality from a book he carries with him, the physical, slapstick humor of his bumbling around the director's office mocks such intellectual understanding of his role at the hotel. That the hotel director's office is decorated with a panoramic image of the Alhambra, the famous Moorish fortress in Granada, alongside an aerial photo of the hotel Don Pepe subsumes the cultural history of the former into the capitalist logic of the latter by converting it from object into commodity, as Baudrillard would say. The Alhambra, then, becomes a space of consumption within the logic of tourism through the visual association in the juxtaposition of the two photographs. A kind of mise en abyme, the presence of a photo of the Don Pepe within the hotel itself ironically deconstructs the ideological underpinnings of the space through distanced self-awareness by engaging and exposing the consumptive gaze of the spectator. Throughout the film, subtle place-branding tactics offer a similar type of ironic self-awareness where the name and logo of the hotel literally inscribe spaces, from the airport shuttle to the jackets of the waitstaff in the hotel restaurant, as ones of advertising and marketing for the tourist experience.

While he unpacks his suitcases in his suite in the Don Pepe Gran Meliá, the "camarera" (chambermaid) Flora (Rafaela Aparicio) sews Federico's jacket, which was ripped after it was caught in the door of the airport shuttle. Although the logic of late capitalism permeates the hotel and infuses its spaces with the atemporal non-permanence that typifies non-places, Flora serves as a kind of informant in the anthropological sense whose institutional memory bears witness to actions and activities of the hotel, specifically of the previous Director of Public Relations. When Federico asserts that he does not drink, smoke, or womanize, Flora quite accurately predicts that he, like the Directors of Public Relations who preceded him, will embrace the hedonistic behaviors so intimately connected with the ludic atmosphere of the hotel and coastal tourism in general. In various scenes when Federico is engaging in the activities that he swore to Flora he would avoid, the camera pans to the chambermaid watching from a hotel window above, shaking her head in judgmental condemnation of his transformation. Like Federico's father, the Duke of Puentelarra, Flora epitomizes a more traditional way of thinking in which labor is visible through the results of the service rendered, such as her sewing, or a specific product that is manufactured or harvested, as in the case of the figs and peaches delivered from Valdemorillo in *El turismo es un gran invento*. Federico, already assimilating the ideology of the hotel, explains to her that a Director of Public Relations plays a crucial role in the hotel's success by helping the client feel at home but "sin ninguna de las incomodidades" (without any of the inconveniences). That Federico repeats this phrase several times along with famous capitalist dictums like "The customer is always right" not only signal his existential transformation and his assimilation of the cultural logic of capitalism, but also establish his role as the proxy for the hotel itself, its interlocutor that frames, articulates, and promotes the discourse of leisure. Similar to the buildings in Palomino's novel *Torremolinos Gran Hotel* and various scenes in Lazaga's *El turismo es un gran invento*, the physical structure of the hotel looms over Federico as a kind of panopticon whose god-like omniscience surveils both employees and visitors to perpetuate adherence to the market through the ludic, Dionysian atmosphere of all spaces within the Don Pepe whether exterior or interior from the pool and tennis courts to the restaurant and night club to the lobby and even the guest's rooms themselves. The use of a "tele-tracer" not only asserts the advanced technological modernity Spain's aperturist economic policies have brought, if only for select areas and select populations of the country, but it also underscores the hotel's omniscience and control in its ability to locate Federico at any moment and to call him into service day or night.

Federico proves himself to be quite adept as the Director of Public Relations and his progressive shift from the meek bookworm at the beginning of the film to a self-confident man of the world demonstrates the malleability of identity under the pressure of the hotel's ideological forces. The protagonist himself ironically recognizes his ontological transformation when he states, "Empiezo a ser otro" (I am becoming someone else), and when his father visits his son in the Costa del Sol he remarks, "Estás muy cambiado" (You have changed quite a bit). Within the space of the hotel "all that is solid melts into air," to paraphrase Marshall Berman's now classic examination of the social and economic forces that frame the experience of modernity. The hotel is a transcultural space as evidenced by guests who visit the Don Pepe from all over the world—including an British businessman and a Middle East oil tycoon, but especially the women who pursue Federico, namely a famous Chilean singer, a Greek heiress, and a wealthy American widow—yet the Don Pepe, and by extension all hotels, is also an a-cultural non-place where identity is molded according to the ludic ideals of consumption that typify coastal tourism. The disorienting effects of capital are visualized during a scene in the hotel's night club where a Latin American singer performs the Afro-Latino Panamanian salsa song "Guararé" that the viewer original heard during the film's opening credits. That the viewer recognizes the song from the beginning of the film creates a sense of dramatic irony and pierces the fourth wall by privileging those outside the diegetic frame of the film with a deeper awareness of the song's symbolic relevance. As the performer's energy fosters a frenzied atmosphere, the lyrics invite an understood "you" to learn from the song, apply its moral, and head to Guararé: "Guararé, Guararé, Guararé / Everybody para Guararé /Aprendan de esta cancion / Apliquen la moraleja." A town in Panamá, Guararé in the context of the song is less a physical destination and more a state of mind. The didactic tone of the song further breaks down the barrier between the film and the viewer by educating the "listener" about the alternative meaning of Guararé that awakens a sudden and uncontrollable masculine sexual desire for a woman: "El que no tenga pareja / que duerma con camisón" (He who doesn't find a mate / should sleep with a nightgown alone). The sexualized hedonistic atmosphere of the nightclub provokes a dizzying effect that is communicated visually through the first-person point-of-view in which the viewer experiences Federico's double vision as the singer and then others in the club multiply and spin. Yet, in an ironic shift, when the viewer sees multiple images of Federico himself spinning, the film signals the fourth wall's disintegration and the viewer's ironic assimilation of the delirious effects of the hotel's ludic Thirdspace ideology.

Throughout Lazaga's *El abominable hombre de la Costa del Sol* cultural models anchor the characters to counteract the disorienting effects of capital within the a-cultural space of the Don Pepe hotel. In his book *The Condition of Postmodernity*, David Harvey notes that the transition to flexible accumulation, facilitated by new organizational forms and innovations in technologies of production, not only accelerated turnover time in production, improved flows of communication, and expanded the circulation of commodities but also altered the nature of consumption away from goods and into services,

in particular spectacles, happenings, and distractions.[93] Among the consequences of this shift are an increased volatility and ephemerality of products
and services as well as ideas, ideologies, and values such that individuals
revert to "images of a lost past (. . .) and excessive simplification (either in
the presentation of self or in the interpretation of events).[94] This tendency to
seek ideological stability in an oversimplified notion of the past to protect
oneself from the fragmenting effects of capital and consumption is evident
in several moments throughout the film. For example, when the emir, a bil-
lionaire oil tycoon, arrives to the hotel, Federico and the hotel staff stage an
elaborate spectacle to welcome their VIP guest replete with flags, flowers,
gifts, and a large photograph of the emir himself. Yet, the next morning the
emir's request for camel's milk, his habitual beverage for breakfast, suggests
a yearning for cultural authenticity that resists the allure of the simulacra.
At other moments, cultural references from Western history and literature
offer models for behavior and identity to which characters turn for a simplified understanding of their self and their situation. In moments of emotional
or situational confusion, Federico and his main love interest, Cecilia, enter
a kind of dream sequence in the film to assume the roles of such figures as
Christopher Columbus, Don Quixote and Dulcinea, Don Juan Tenorio and
Doña Inés, Romeo and Juliet, Cleopatra and Mark Anthony, and Othello and
Desdemona. By playing a role, Federico and Cecilia seek stability in familiar
models as a way, ironically, to preserve their "authentic" sense of self within
the hedonistic atmosphere of the Costa del Sol. The structure of the film
itself likewise emulates past cultural models with an abrupt conclusion that
ends with Federico and Cecilia's wedding as if it were a Golden Age comedia.
A stark contrast with the libertine attitudes exhibited by guests at the Don
Pepe, Lazaga's implementation of the wedding within the film's narrative
structure serves as a kind of deus ex machina that rescues the characters from
the pernicious effects of capital and saves the sanctity of traditional Spanish
culture through its religious institutions. The austere convent and the Duke's
archaic home at the beginning of the film and the religious ceremony at the
end serve as bookends that underscore the portrayal of the Don Pepe hotel's
Thirdspace ideology, where the delirious effects of capital subvert the perceived stability of individual and collective identity.

CHAPTER 2

Scenes from Paradise

Postcards, the Tourist's Gaze, and the Generation of Dreams

Washed by the Mediterranean Sea, the Costa del Sol extends along more than 150 kilometres of coastline in the province of Málaga, in the southern Iberian Peninsula. Its name, the "Coast of the Sun," is not due to mere chance: with over 325 sunny days a year and a benevolent climate, this is a paradisiacal place with beaches to suit all tastes.

Each beach has its own charms. Some are livelier, others are quieter and more solitary; some are absolutely untouched and others have the most modern services. You will surely find your own personal paradise on the Costa del Sol.

~ HTTPS://WWW.ANDALUCIA.ORG/EN/SUN-AND-BEACHES/COSTA-DEL-SOL

In *Travelling Light*, Peter Osborne asserts, "Tourism exchanges all worldly denominations for the currencies of paradise." [1] Tourism's iconographies promise restoration if not salvation through a visual rhetoric that reinforces myths of the South by projecting a culturally authentic and existentially peaceful space where the modern individual may escape the tedium of modern life. Osborne states that such mythology is perpetuated through brochures, posters, postcards, and other promotional media that stock the traveler's "visual combinatorium" and frame how individuals should see the world, desire it, and weigh its cultural meaning. [2] Through intense colors, alluring composition, and their ubiquitous presence, tourism promotional materials seek an emotional connection with the viewer by communicating the transcendent power of the utopian destination that awaits. [3] Osborne continues that the world of the tourist is always "over there," framed through its visual

[67]

representations as "exotic-ordinary," endowing the subject with a pre-existing knowledge of the "site" by informing the "sight" of the tourist.[4] Tourism imagery and iconography, then, collapse the space between "the promotion and the promotion's object" such that "the advertisement has become its own commodity."[5] Images associated with tourism propaganda ironically subvert the cultural authenticity that the traveler seeks by commodifying local identity and transforming cities and towns into deterritorialized sites of consumption offered as ludic, paradisaical spectacles that promise restoration and rejuvenation through pleasure.

Of all the forms of visual tourism propaganda, nothing is more iconic or ubiquitous of tourism than the postcard; and nothing epitomizes the collapse between the promotion and promotion's object than the postcard; and lastly, nothing exemplifies more how advertisements become their own commodities than the postcard. Tourist postcards offer a very promising burgeoning field that expands the study of photography through the examination of images that are intentionally designed to be circulated within a capitalist framework. In Spain, such images present a discourse of consumption that "constructs" an imaginary of the Mediterranean coast (as well as the cultural identity to be found there through), but they are unique from other types of photography because postcards are meant to be purchased and shared, often transnationally, thus implicating the tourists themselves in the distribution of images that market tourist cities. In this way, postcards may be studied both for the latent ideology of the visual representation as well as examples of material culture that directly connects with consumerist tenets of tourism to complement the ideological impact of the image itself. Postcards from the early days of Spanish tourism sought to attract and engage the foreigner's gaze with the promise of a Spain that was folkloric, rustic, and exotic yet also luxurious, modern, and sexualized. Postcards (as well as other tourist souvenirs) offer the first instance of spectacle that assimilates contradictions into a Marcusian "one dimension," which promises to fulfill one's desires through the logic of late capitalism by projecting the Spanish coasts as a utopian escape from the pressures of a modern society. Moreover, that websites like delcampe.net, a kind of eBay for collectors, offers tens of thousands of postcards not only attests to a widespread industry that published these materials and promoted their distribution as a core aspect of the tourist experience, but also points to an evolution of the tourist enterprise that actively engages nostalgia through the fetishization of these objects that are bought and sold alongside more traditional types of collectibles like coins and stamps.

Ironically, postcards are perhaps the most ubiquitous element of tourism yet also the most vastly understudied.[6] Images of idyllic beaches, high-rise

luxury hotels, and bikini-clad women posit a sense of permanence that promises escape from the mundane stresses of modern life by enticing the consumptive gaze of the tourist with the promise of leisure, rejuvenation, and
self-discovery. The purposeful physical construction of cities like Torremolinos and Benidorm in the 1960s as fetishized urban spaces designed to attract
tourism capital is reinforced through the ideological construction of postcard
images that engage the gaze of the tourist to assert the beaches and hotels as
culturally constructed ludic "non-places." So, while postcards have received
scant scholarly attention compared to other forms of visual and material culture, they offer a very nuanced and rich view into the past as cultural artifacts
that offer clues about a shared imagery that fomented a sense of collective
identity, as Dotterer and Cranz affirm, through the "creation of a national
urban culture" projected inwardly as well as outwardly.[7] More than simply
photography, the mass production of these objects attests to the social significance of souvenirs like postcards and the overt awareness of the viewer's
consumptive gaze and the intentional desire to mold and direct it. In *The
Tourist*, Dean MacCannell refers to souvenirs such as postcards as the "minutiae of material culture" yet recognizes that their ubiquitous presence in consumer culture also endows them with symbolic significance that conveys the
status and social power of the tourist.[8] If a photograph, as Barthes outlines
Camera Lucida: Reflections on Photography, is "always invisible" and serves as a
"prosthesis" that "offers an immediate presence to the world" both politically and metaphysically, then the postcard is quite the opposite.[9] The postcard, in contrast, is ontologically self-aware of its own design to attract the
consumptive gaze of the tourist both as part of a nostalgic enterprise to reify
and distill past travels in a single object and to communicate social and
cultural hegemony through the symbolic power of travel.[10] While Barthes
asserts that a photograph possesses an "evidentiary force" whose "power
of authentication exceeds the power of representation," postcards normal-
ize and naturalize a vision of everyday life by mystifying and fetishizing the
tourist destination, especially in the case of beach locales.[11] If Lefebvre's
assertion in *The Production of Space* that urbanized regions along the beach,
most notably on the Mediterranean Sea, are a "space of dream," then the
postcard is the dream generator; it instills the tourist with the nostalgic
desire to return to that place and other future travelers with the consumptive desire to discover it.[12]

As Verena Winiwarter, Jonas Larsen, and more notably John Urry have
detailed, the rise of tourism as a billion-dollar global industry parallels the
transition from a culture reliant on the printed word and text to one permeated with images, still and moving. Larsen even goes so far as to say that

tourism and photography are "modern twins" that benefitted from technological advances in the nineteenth century such as the steamship and the railroad that made the world more accessible geographically (though only for those social classes that could afford to travel) and the camera that made the world more accessible visually.[13] Moreover, photography is deeply intertwined with the contemporary tourist experience and the marketing of so-called destination tourism that frames cultural myths through carefully constructed images of places that literally sell an experience to the potential traveler through the representation of place. Yet, in the case of postcards, the image, although commercially contracted and mass produced, is complemented with the written message of the tourist who literally inscribes and thus calcifies the implicit ideology that is communicated visually about the place visited and the tourist experience there. The agency asserted by the tourist in the selection and purchase of one tourist postcard over another impels what Larsen calls a "vicious hermeneutic circle" in which the tourist experience and how they relate it and remember it is framed by the visual images they have consumed and even replicated in their own personal photography.[14] The message of a postcard, then, along with its underlying ideology is composed of two complementary parts, the recto and the verso as Derrida calls it, in which the image and the written note compound each other in such a way as to exert power without coercion through pleasure.[15] In her study of postcards from Paris at the turn of the twentieth century, Naomi Schor notes the power of pleasure in images that reduce the complex reality of the city to discrete units that "can be easily manipulated and readily consumed."[16] She adds that the side of the postcard with the written note records exchanges that often explicitly refer to the choice of image. Moreover, that the written message of a postcard be publicly visible, a dramatic cultural shift from the traditional privileged private epistles of the past, situates anyone who encounters the postcard in a position of voyeur whose gaze likewise assimilates the myths about everyday life latent in the postcard. In *The Tourist Gaze,* Urry coincides with MacCannell in his understanding of the tourist experience as a search for the real and the authentic in other places and other times distant from the everyday life of the traveler.[17] But for Urry, the creation of what MacCanell has called "pseudo-events" or a "staged authenticity" represents an intentional attempt to direct and construct the traveler's gaze with signs—those tourist objects and attractions—that the tourist collects to affirm the narrative that had been constructed originally for their gaze.[18] What is more, the same gaze becomes legitimized through material objects like photographs, postcards, films, or souvenirs that allow the gaze (and the consumption of signs) to reproduce themselves ad infinitum in a kind of mise en abyme. The gaze of the traveler, then, does not only consume objects, places, attractions, and experiences but rather the "mechanical reproduction" as Walter Benjamin would call it, offers a simulacrum of the real and the authentic that the tourist seeks and that ironically affirms the narrative of that sought out authenticity. This reproduction of the gaze, moreover, underscores the values of consumption that constitute and inform the tourist gaze itself.

With the exception of Jordi Puig's 2017 artistic curation of postcards from the 1960s and 1970s titled *Costa Brava: Postals, Postales, Cartes Postales, Postcards* and, to a lesser extent, Alicia Fuentes Vega's *Bienvenido, Mr. Turismo: Cultura visual del boom en España,* no scholarly attention has been given to the cultural impact of postcards in Spain and the normalizing effect they have had on the massification of leisure and tourism in Spanish society and the fabrication of a visual narrative about Spanish identity projected globally.[19] The study of tourist postcards in Spain is certainly an area rich for exploration for scholars in Iberian studies that explore cultural production as it relates to development and modernization in Spain over the last half century. For example, one could undertake a taxonomic examination of postcards to identify, classify, and categorize the types of images that recur and how the objects of the everyday are presented whether buildings, people, street scenes, nature, interior spaces, events, and more. Moreover, because postcards have so long been considered trivial, banal, and insignificant, there are no library collections where scholars could examine postcards. Rather, tens of thousands of postcards exist in the world and are only obtainable through websites such as Delcampe (https://www.delcampe.net/en_US/collectibles/), a marketplace for collectors where postcards may be bought and sold alongside more traditional collectible items such as stamps or coins as well as vinyl records, rare books, photographs and even old paper. As a memento, a postcard by definition is imbued with nostalgia and evokes Nora's notion of a "lieux de mémoire" that bridges both individual and collective memory. But for scholars who focus on memory studies, the passage of the postcard into the realm of "collectible" endows it with additional concentric levels of nostalgia with possible ideological implications that literally objectify the past and render it obtainable through discrete materials as if they were synchronic vivisections of a moment in time. If one were to take a more diachronic approach to postcards, an analysis of images over time could offer a kind of visual narrative of modernization in Spain and the liberalization of Spanish society; for example, one may track the urban development along the coasts from the 1960s to today or detect the opening of sexual mores as bodily representations become more gratuitous if not exploitative, especially during the years after Franco's death during the so-called Destape (literally meaning "Uncovering"). Another potential area for scholarly examination is the actual material mass production of postcards during the Franco regime where commercial processes, economic policies, and political ideology overlap. Who published the postcards? Who photographed the images? Who authorized those images? Were images censored? Lastly, a focus on postcards could contribute greatly to a digital humanities project that could combine all of these aspects into a kind of visual archive that also offers a dashboard where one could track the geographies of tourists who visited Spain, what areas they concentrated in based on nation of origin, where they sent the postcards, and even what were perhaps the most popular images they sent. Clearly, the sheer numbers of postcards dispersed around the world makes any of these possible initiatives challenging, but the research opportunities are potentially as numerous as the postcards themselves.

Norman Stevens attests to the research opportunities the study of postcards offers in the title of his book *Postcards in the Library: Invaluable Visual Resource,* in which he notes that postcards contain a great deal of information about a society at a given moment, but they may also serve a historical purpose as the only visual image of a certain building, monument, person, place, or other object at a specific time.[20] Moreover, he continues, because they were produced as items for mass consumption with no intentional literary or social purpose, they offer a "true reflection" of society, the attitudes and cultural values it seeks to project, and offer a window into the world as it was viewed.[21] Stevens doesn't seem to consider that many if not most postcards, especially those related to tourism (and coastal tourism in particular), are produced with a commercial purpose in mind in which the image literally "sells" a place to the viewer. In this sense, perhaps the postcard is not a mimetic reflection of society, but certainly may be understood to communicate a carefully designed visual image that conveys the way in which a given society would like to be perceived. As Schor indicated, the power of the image resides in the pleasure it evokes rather than the coercion it exerts. For our purposes here, I examine images of hotels in postcards related to coastal tourism in Spain during the 1960s and 1970s that underscore the hotel itself as an icon that "sells" the Spanish coast as a constructed space of consumption where the tourist, through capital, may both escape yet also rediscover themselves. More than a mere backdrop for various tourism activities, the hotel often acts as a protagonist that moves people, economies, and even ideology by simultaneously crystallizing and instilling the values of consumer capitalism. Yet, the individual inscription and the movement across borders of the postcard itself contradict the idea of a common experience of these places through the personal impressions the tourist offers by literally and figuratively inscribing him or herself into the landscape of the coasts. A central paradox of postcards, and of tourism in general, is that while postcards represent the material culture as mementos purchased within the context of mass tourism that seemingly mold consciousness in a Marcusian sense with consumerist values, there is also a notable Gramscian notion in which one possesses a certain level of agency to interact with cultural products on their own terms and the handwritten message may often assert and capture the individual experience of the tourist at the hotel but also consent to the ideology of its discourse.

As one peruses the collections of postcards available at collectibles sites online, it becomes clear that the vast majority offer photographs of hotels. That the hotels often commissioned photographers and contracted publishers to print postcards as part of an overt marketing strategy to promote its brand abroad offers one possible explanation about the overwhelming percentage of postcards that feature a hotel. If, as Lefebvre stated, coastal tourism is the space of dreams, and the postcard is the generator of that dream, then the visual discourse of the images present the spectator with a modern earthly paradise that offers leisure and hedonistic pleasure as the core values of modern life. The hotel, then, is not merely the backdrop for the tourist experience, not simply the mise en scéne upon which the action occurs. It is the protagonist that frames and defines the tourist's experiences, reifies and distills the core consumerist values of that experience, and catalyzes the economy through the colonization of surrounding urban spaces.

It should be no surprise then, that picture postcards connected to coastal tourism in Spain appeal to the global tourist's gaze through images of hotels that communicate visually more than any tourist brochure could with narrative text. The names of the hotels often brand the front of the postcard in a clear marketing strategy that identifies the (non) place and fixes its location as a ludic space and a destination to be desired. In some postcards, the hotel, and thus the space, is not named such that the mysterious locale invites the curiosity of the postcard recipient (assuming the sender knows the location because they have spent their vacation there) to engage as an active participant in the construction of the postcard's meaning by seeking the name and location on the back side of the postcard. Such an action may seem minute, but that the viewer feels even the slightest engagement in the signifying process could have a profound emotional and ideological impact. The hotel names themselves communicate a not so tacit promise to the tourist that what this non-place offers is an escape from modernity and its mundane minutiae to a mythical space where the tourist is pampered with luxury and leisure. Such names as Hotel Edén, Hotel California, Hotel Paradis, Hotel Tahiti, Hotel Hawai, Hotel Copacabana, and Hotel Oasis Park evoke a kind of tropical earthly paradise that is green and lush but that are also intertwined with deep cultural and sentimental myths about utopic destinations and self-discovery.[22] Other hotels evoke more classical myths with names of Greek and Roman deities related to the sea like Neptuno, Tritón, Calypso, or others like Helios (the personification of the sun), Venus (the goddess of beauty and love), or the similarly named Hotel Olympus Place, Hotel Olympic, and the Hotel Olympic Park (including the iconic five rings that symbolize the Olympic Games) located in Tarragona, the Costa Maresme north of Barcelona, and Lloret de Mar in nearby Costa Brava, respectively. Names like Centurión and Augustus as well as the Presidente, Príncipe Sol, the Carlos I or the Jaime I, the Almirante, or the Salou Princess communicate a level of stature and authority that set an expected level of service befitting royalty. Still other hotels capitalize on the natural surroundings by evoking the flora and fauna of the Mediterranean coast with names like Palmasol, Nautilus, los Pelícanos, Aguamarina or simply Marina, the Coral, Montemar, the Riviera, Joya, Playamar, Delfín Park, the Hotel Brisa, or the famous Pez Espada. Lastly, other hotels embrace an overt ludic identity and promise pleasure without pretension with names like Fiesta Park Hotel, Hotel Playa Capricho (meaning "caprice" or "whim"), Holiday Club del Sol, Hotel La Piscina, Casino Gran Hotel, Hotel Don Juan (a reference to the famous Spanish literary archetype and model for the stereotypical "latin lover"), and Hotel Las Vegas that conjures the libertine atmosphere of so-called "Sin City" more than fertile meadows (the literal translation of "vega" in its plural form).[23]

While the name of the hotel may evoke deeper connotations if not solicit a deeper ideological meaning, the photographic images on the postcard amplify the "traveler's paradox" described by Minca and Oakes with a series of concentric contradictions that both offer a unifying discourse of pleasure at the same time they point to the complexity of the tourist experience. On one hand, the image with its identifying information in the photograph of the hotel itself or on the reverse side of the postcard fix location with specific and identifiable references that suggest the location of place and a destination to which the tourist has or will arrive. Yet, on the other hand, the hotel as a transitory, transactional, and temporary non-place epitomizes the notion of deterritorialization described by Deleuze and Guattari in which local iden-tity is subsumed, subjugated, and alienated by the seeming objectivity of real estate speculation within capitalism. Similarly, the mass production of postcards epitomizes the packaged massification of so-called charter tour-ism yet the individual selection, purchase, and inscription on the postcard suggests a level of agency to endow the tourist experiences with some level of tailored uniqueness. At the same time, however, while the written message may assert the tourist's agency in scripting the narrative of their individual experience, many times their message bolsters the underlying ideology of the photographic image and, by extension, the ludic discourse of coastal tourism more broadly. Some postcards offer what is called a "multi-view" in which three to four images offer a mosaic designed to communicate, if not market, the many opportunities for distraction and diversion available. Often, the image of the hotel is juxtaposed (as we will see in a moment) with street scenes of a commercial zone for shopping, an aerial view of the hotel's proximity to the beach, the exterior of a "typical Spanish" restaurant, or oftentimes a woman in traditional flamenco dress. Thus, while the hotel projects an expected level of leisure facilitated through modern construction and aesthetically pleasing postmodern design, the inclusion of a flamenco dancer seems to intimate a level of cultural authenticity that would also be accessible to tourists. However, that the dancers in postcards are often staged exposes the falsification of cultural identity and the othering exotification of Spanish culture within the capitalist structures of global tourism[24]. Repre-sentations of local culture, then, are subverted of authenticity which is sup-pressed in order to yield visual space to the discourse of pleasure, escape, and consumption offered by tourism.

These paradoxes expand into the types of postcards themselves. The series of paradoxes that surround postcards attest to their status as quite a unique piece of material culture. Moreover, such paradoxes erect obstacles for research beyond the sheer number of artifacts to study. Though many images of postcards are available on social media platforms like Pinterest, websites like Torremolinoschic.com, and on auction marketplaces like delcampe. net or hippostcard.com, such images would not be considered fair use if a researcher sought to reproduce the images in a book or an article. Little information is known about the photographers who produced the images, and many of the publishers that produced the physical postcards in Spain in the 1960s and 1970s no longer exist. Those that do continue to operate most likely do not hold the copyright since the work was often commissioned by a hotel or a city/region's tourism offices. Additionally, often the same photographic image is used by various publishers with differing composition in its presentation. One such image simply titled "Escena típica andaluza" (Typical Andalusian Scene) appears on postcards published by Mane, Baena, Edisol, and others almost as if it were a stock image. The question of who holds the rights becomes all the more poignant given these circumstances. The Ministry of Tourism's digital collection of tourism posters and brochures does not include postcards, and no known museum collection of postcards seems to exist from whom one could solicit the rights for reproduction of the image. What I have done is to follow the examples of other academic publications in which postcards that are not part of a specific collection but that the author has acquired are cited as part of their personal collection. While they were (and continue to be) mass produced and many of the styles in which the layout of the image or images mirror each other regardless of locale—whether the Costa del Sol or the Costa Blanca or the Costa Brava—there is at the same time quite a bit of variation in the composition of the image itself. Such considerations as camera angles, lighting, distance, interior or exterior, positioning and perspective reveal a complex mosaic of the "types" of images, and varying levels of aesthetic innovation, in how the urban environment of the Spanish coasts, specifically the hotel, is portrayed. Not meant to be an exhaustive taxonomy (that may be better suited for another book project), it is relevant to contemplate the many strategies in which the so-called "real estate" on the front of the postcard may be organized visually yet with a singular objective in mind that is to instill desire in the viewer. For example, the multi-view mentioned earlier divides the space on the front of the postcard into four quadrants that offer diverse but complementary perspectives on the tourist offerings in a coastal town (as we will see further). An aerial view of the hotel with the sea behind it may be aligned next to a streetscape photograph of the shopping district or a restaurant while another section may show the exterior, especially the pool area, or the interior, especially the luxurious lobby, and the last quadrant may evoke some suggestion of Spanish culture designed for consumption, perhaps a burro or a flamenco dancer Other postcards may offer a single wide shot of the hotel at a straight angle that is meant to capture the dimension and size of the physical structure to communicate the modern luxuries and the leisurely escape that awaits the tourist. Other postcards present the hotel in a low-angle shot looking upward toward the building that occupies most of the frame and seemingly looms over the viewer to assert its iconic status. High-angle shots often present the hotel from the land with the deep blue Mediterranean Sea in the background to communicate the atmosphere of leisure and pleasure that envelop the locale. Others, however, offer aerial views from the sea looking toward land in a way that communicates clearly the site's proximity to the vast expanse of pristine beaches along the Spanish coast. Still other postcards may include some blurred element of nature, say a tree or a rose bush, in the foreground with the hotel in focus behind it or with some rustic element of traditional Spanish culture, in particular a fishing boat that evokes the coastal lifestyle before mass tourism, against the modern hotel as the backdrop. Some postcards present night views of the hotel illuminated that portray a calm, serene atmosphere of relaxation and sophistication. Other postcards include images of bedrooms and other interior rooms like lobbies, bars, or restaurants that may or may not have people yet provide a blank canvas onto which the viewer may imagine themselves enjoying the luxury of the hotel's modern installations. Many of the postcards feature the pool prominently, with men and women lounging outside sunbathing, often receiving drinks from waiters, in a mise en scène that epitomizes the leisure of Spain's coasts and onto which the viewer may project themselves and dream of one day experiencing the scene before them. No matter the angle, the composition, or the lighting, tourist postcards coincide in generating dreams of leisure along the Spanish coasts where the hotel is a utopic earthly paradise that is both a metaphoric emblem of coastal tourism as well as synecdochic catalyst of the consumerist machinery of Spain's seaside tourism industry.

Set against the backdrop of the mountain range in Marbella (misspelled on the back of the postcard as Mabella), the Hotel Don Miguel looms as a beacon of modern luxury whose expansive pool invites the viewer to imagine themselves lounging leisurely alongside other tourists. The lush greenery around the hotel and the pool area connote an edenic peace distant from the stresses of everyday life. The viewer's gaze from behind the sedentary tourists mimics their own as they look upon the pool's cool blue water from egg-shaped, space age designed chairs that line the perimeter of the water.[25] That the gaze of the tourists seems focused on the same object suggests their assimilation of the consumerist ideology of ludic coastal tourism. The fact that the viewer's gaze folds into that of the tourists in the image as if we were already part of the scene implies a subconscious invitation to join the ludic atmosphere and assume the same ideology of leisure and consumption. Moreover, with the absence of any geographical markers, the Hotel Don Miguel seems to exist in seeming isolation from any local culture or population and offers itself as a destination in and of itself, completely deterritorialized within the cultural logic of the tourism industry.

FIGURE 2.1. Postcard of Hotel Don Miguel, Club Mediterranee, date unknown. Ediciones Baena

On the reverse side of the postcard, the sender affirms the image's discourse of pleasure and leisure by offering personal testimony about the "magnificent hotel" and its environs that are a lush, green "enchanting" paradise. That atmosphere of relaxation the viewer encounters in the image is reinforced in the sender's inscription who shares that their daily activities alternate between sports and "siesta." Moreover, the consumption of wine, specifically "rosé," is deemed an "indispensable" component of the tourist experience that seemingly evokes other modes of consumerism and invites the receiver of the postcard to drink in all that the Costa del Sol has to offer, literally and figuratively. Lastly, the reference to the quasi-Olympic physical shape of young people not only echoes the image of beautiful bodies on the front of the postcard through a reference to the athleticism of young people, but it also invokes classical notions of beauty and corporal perfection.

Next, the multi-view postcard guides the viewer's gaze in a seemingly cinematic fashion in which each photo not only draws our focus progressively closer to the destination, in the case the Hotel Marina in Benidorm (which is clearly branded in the center of the postcard), but also constructs a visual narrative about the tourist's arrival to their final destination and the pleasure

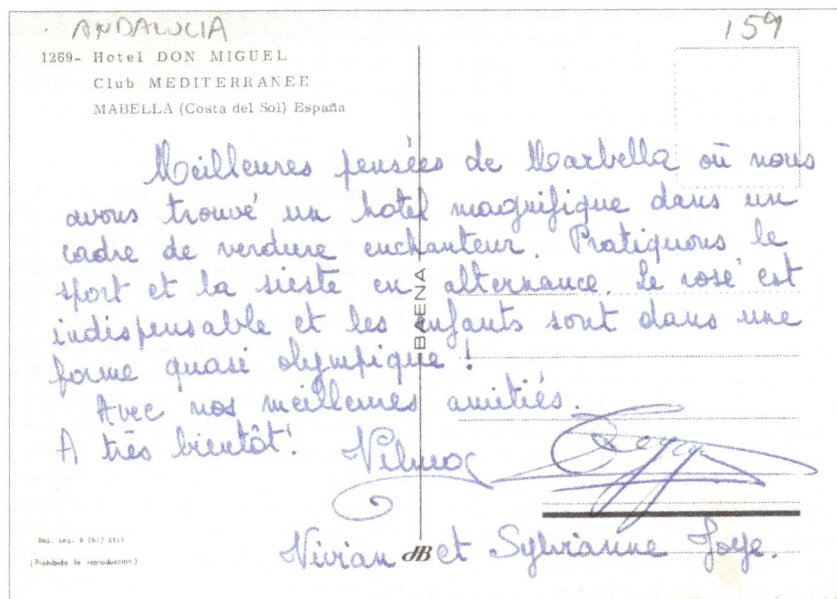

FIGURE 2.2. Reverse side of postcard of Hotel Don Miguel

that awaits them there. The photo in the lower right quadrant offers a panoramic view of Benidorm, labelled moreover as it would be in a film, as if we were arriving after a long journey and the city appears before us as a welcoming oasis, nestled in a lush green valley alongside the sea, that we peer through the trees as we come over the last hill. In the upper left quadrant, the visual field presents an establishing shot of the hotel's exterior at dusk with palm trees and the pool in clear view, anticipating the next day's activities, as lights illuminate the entrance. The image in the upper right of the postcard suggests a tracking shot in which the viewer can imagine themselves moving up the tiled stairs through the sequence of sleek arches with the curated hanging gardens, reminiscent of the mythic tiered gardens of Babylon, which adorn the walkway. Lastly, while the lower-left image denotes the traveler's arrival to their destination, the buffet display surrounded by sharply dressed waitstaff, chefs, and a maître d' suggest that the hotel will cater to the tourist's needs for leisure and pleasure. Moreover, that the paella is prominently displayed as it is delivered from the kitchen suggests the consumption of culture through the gastronomic markers stereotypically associated with Spanish identity. Curiously, the sequence of images does not follow a traditional

FIGURE 2.3. Hotel Marina, Benidorm 1987. Ediciones Hermanos Galiano

Western textual pattern that might start with the panoramic shot in the upper left and progress clockwise around the center of the postcard to simulate the viewer's approach to their destination by starting with the panoramic shot of Benidorm and culminating with the interior shot in the lower quadrant. That this progression appears out of order, so to speak, requires the viewer's active participation in the construction of the visual narrative by reordering the images mentally into a logical sequence. Thus, the viewer assumes the role of protagonist in a story that is told, moreover, through a first-person point of view where the eye of the camera and the viewer's perspective collapse into each other. The simple message in French on the reverse side, "Greetings from Benidorm" both reaffirms the journey narrative of the images but more importantly accepts the iconic importance of the hotel as destiny and destination. Announcing their arrival to Benidorm while the visual narrative posits and promotes the destination as the Hotel Marina equates the two to suggest that the hotel itself is Benidorm in a way that epitomizes Harvey's "urbanization of consciousness." There is no space, literally or figuratively, to include local identity except as an exotic culinary experience that has been assimilated into the ideology of consumption.

From the early years of coastal tourism in Spain, a dual discourse marketed the modern hotel installations that promised luxury and leisure while also

FIGURE 2.4. Hotel Pez Espada, Torremolinos 1961. Ediciones Domínguez

promoting traditional Spanish culture as a primitive exotic other. Walking the line between that which is modern and that which is primitive attracted tourists, especially those from cold cloudy northern Europe, with an escape that is at once geographical, metrological, cultural, corporal, and emotional. The postcard I analyze next (Figure 2.4), from Torremolinos in 1961, follows the same visual tropes as other postcards in which the newly erected modern Pez Espada exists in seeming deterritorialized isolation from any town or local population. Although the sea is behind the viewer, the bright cloudless sky that sets the backdrop to the hotel and stretch of beach that reaches the doors of the Pez Espada promise the sun and sand the tourist who visits the Costa del Sol desires. The juxtaposition of a traditional fishing boat with the towering (at the time) hotel points to the economic transition along the Spanish coasts away from traditional and authentic modes of labor such as fishing to a service industry dominated by hotels, restaurants, stores, and bars. That two toddlers pose patiently for a photograph alongside the fishing boat suggest a similar shift in the relationship with the Mediterranean Sea from one defined by work to one defined by pleasure; yet both represent in different ways the economic livelihood and sustenance of coastal Spain. However, the fact that two young boys in bathing suits holding their inflated floaties waiting to swim pose alongside the boat subverts the boat's original cultural significance by converting it into an empty signifier and assimilating it into the logic of late capitalism by transforming it into a prop for tourist photo opportunities. The sender's message on the back, again in French, confirms the heat of the Costa del Sol that is suggested in the image but also emphasizes the ludic, libertine atmosphere of the coast where they dine every night in their bikini. More importantly, the sender's exclamation "quelle différence" reinforces the consumption of Spain's exotic otherness as a selling point for tourists from Northern Europe.

The juxtaposition of modern amenities and exotic otherness in Spanish tourism postcards is most evident in the representation of flamenco and Romani culture in which bodies, male and female (but mostly female), are dressed, positioned, and staged as cultural commodities to entice the tourist gaze. Flamenco (along with bullfighting) becomes a monolithic cultural referent that synthesizes Spain's national identity marketed to a foreign demographic by erasing the complexities of Spanish history and culture. The images associated with flamenco culture that are incorporated into postcards, brochures, and other forms of tourist propaganda elide the violence, inequity, marginalization, and poverty that have plagued Romani communities for hundreds of years. Rather, the State appropriates flamenco culture and presents a romanticized, sanitized version of it that reduces Spanish identity to figures of men in a stereotypical cordobés hat and women in polka dot dresses.[26] The consumption of visual images that portray individuals dressed in stereotypical flamenco attire not only informs the viewer with cultural information, however simplified and falsified, about Spain but connects flamenco culture to the tourist destination in a second level of misinformation. In this way, the images set the tourist's expectations for kinds of cultural spectacles they might hope to consume while on vacation. As sites of consumption, coastal cities like Benidorm and Torremolinos anticipate the neoliberal age where the markers of local culture lose their meaning within the logic of global capital. The staged authenticity of flamenco culture in postcards mirrors the stage performance spectacle tourists will view on their visit but also offers a materialization of that vision that reifies, reinforces, and re-presents the exotic, orientalist, kitschy falsified authenticity of the other.

As the next postcard demonstrates, the so-called "panoramic view" acquires a double meaning that not only describes the camera perspective that captures Benidorm from a distance. With the two photos of people dressed in flamenco attire, it also conveys the cultural context a tourist may expect to encounter in this landscape. In the center of the postcard, the

Benidorm's crest, with a wavy "Benidorm" and "España" on either side as if they were banners, seemingly legitimizes the images with the stamp of heraldic approval that situates the viewer within official visual discourse. Ironically, the presence of the crest, the two photos of people adorned in flamenco garb, and the panoramic view of Benidorm invite the viewer into a complex meaning-making exercise by challenging them to discern the relationship between the various images. Certainly, a possible option for the viewer is to take each image separately, as a world of signification unto itself, yet the composition of the postcard places the images in relation to one another through an intentional juxtaposition that begs the viewer to seek associations that endow the mosaic with a singular understanding of the represented space. The black spaces on the front of the postcard evoke the gaps that the viewer must fill to draw connections among the distinct images to create meaning.[27] Yet, a more discerning examination exposes a fragmented visual discourse whose discordant readings produce a disorienting effect in the viewer that is both caused by and resolved by the cultural logic of capitalism. First, the city's crest itself presents the viewer an image where a Roman tower on a golden beach faces a bay, composed of wavy blue and white stripes to connote the tide, and is flanked by two other towers in the distance. The boat and Roman towers assert Benidorm's maritime heritage as a coastal city, while a diamond-shaped "royal senyera" (the traditional flag of the Valencian Community) with vertical red and yellow stripes looms over the central Roman tower as if it were the sun and asserts the region's contemporary national identity. The crown looming atop evokes the history of royalty, alluding to the medieval origins of many such crests that emerged as kingdoms united within the Iberian peninsula in the wake of the Christian victories over the Moors.[28]

If the crest in the center of the postcard offers a visual focal point for the viewer that anchors the viewer's understanding by delineating local geographical identity, then the question becomes: What is the role of local cultural identity in the other photographs on the front of this postcard? In the panoramic view of Benidorm's bay, the high-rise hotels seem to have replaced the Roman towers whose purpose was to protect seafarers and local populations from marauding invaders and thus ensure the area's physical and economic security. The hotels, it would seem, serve as a beacon that draws the foreigner to its beaches precisely by erecting themselves on the ruins of the past with modern ahistorical amenities. Moreover, the two photos on the lower half of the postcard confuse the viewer's understanding of the local cultural context even further. By literally framing the scenes of men and women in flamenco dress underneath the image of the Benidorm coastline, the postcard similarly frames the viewer's cultural expectations. Three women dressed in vibrantly colored dresses—one blue, one yellow, and one pink—pose with two men in traditional flamenco campero suits—one black and one tan—with a typical cordobés hat. They are situated on the stairs surrounded by the shrubbery of a park the viewer is led to believe is some location of Benidorm, a microcosm of sorts of the macrocosm panoramic view. In the image on the left, the fact that the men stand stiffly and awkwardly while the women perch precariously on a railing creates a visual (and thus dramatic) tension in the photo's composition. The man in the tan suit gazes downward toward the woman in pink as she looks upward at him; yet the others in the photo cast their gaze in different directions such that the artificiality of the image is noticeable. Similarly, in the photo on the right, the men stand while the women sit on the top step of a landing with legs crossed, a projection of a kind of patriarchal portrait that is gendered in its staged construction. The specificity of place through both the historical and symbolic importance of the city's crest and the panoramic view of Benidorm clash with the cultural mismatch of flamenco in Valencia. A musical art form associated with Andalucía, the presence of flamenco on the front of the postcard epitomizes the fabricated pastiche and "loss of history" Jameson associates with a postmodern aesthetic whose superficiality and lack of local cultural context typify the "cultural logic of late capitalism" and the "postmodern hyperspace" that transforms local and regional identity into commodity. That the inscription on the back reads "Very sunny greetings from Benidorm" in French signals the over-arching identity of coastal spaces as one of leisure, articulates the fusion of the local and global that occurs in that space, and hints at the superficiality of the tourist experience even when seeking "authentic" cultural encounters.

A similar postcard from Torremolinos includes the image of a woman in a red flamenco dress with a long train and the typical "tacones" (heels) worn by women for flamenco dancing. With a large abañico (fan) on the wall and a guitar carefully placed on a chair below, the woman strikes a familiar flamenco pose with her hands behind her and her head slightly tilted as she faces the camera almost defiantly. The whitewashed walls and the décor of the empty *tablao* (flamenco stage) serve as the backdrop for the flamenco dancer, and all these elements coalesce to offer the viewer markers of perceived cultural authenticity. The staged authenticity of the image is underscored by the fact that the woman is literally on a stage and suggests the performative aspect that underlies not only the flamenco spectacle but the way in with flamenco is packaged for tourist consumption. That this image appears as one of four on a postcard much like the one discussed earlier (for the Hotel Marina in

FIGURE 2.5. Panoramic view of Benidorm. Hermanos Galiana Fotografía

Fig. 2.3), divided into four quadrants, posits flamenco among the elements in the Costa del Sol designed to enhance the visitor's leisure. While the postcard from Benidorm marks place with an official crest and a decorative serif font often used to communicate tradition and grandeur, the postcard below fixes the geographical location with a centrally placed "Torremolinos" in a whimsical, almost comic sans font that conveys fun and frivolity. Behind "Torremolinos," the light blue background with random white dots evokes the seaside locale while the hollow lettering invokes MacCannell's understanding of such coastal resort towns as "empty meeting grounds" that tourists fill with meaning through consumption. Each photo depicts a social space within Torremolinos that entices the tourist gaze with the anticipation of distinct experiences within each space. Each experience, however different, connects leisure with consumption to inform, in an almost prescriptive manner, the kinds of experiences a tourist may anticipate in Torremolinos. Whether strolling through a shopping district to buy souvenirs, lounging on the beach walking distance from the hotel, exploring the coast's nightlife, or attending a flamenco show, the activities that define the Lefebvrian social space of Torremolinos revolve around consumption, transaction, leisure, and pleasure. Any marker of local

FIGURE 2.6. Torremolinos, Costa del Sol. Ediciones Beascoa

cultural identity visible in this postcard—whitewashed buildings, clay roof tiles, fishing boats, the guitar, and even the flamenco dancer herself—are carefully and intentionally constructed signifiers that convert Torremolinos into a paradisiacal, non-place by falsifying Andalusian culture into an economically driven set of commodities within the machinery of global tourism. The erasure of authenticity and identity is underscored by the fact that the unnamed flamenco dancer in the photo is the famous "bailaora" (dancer) María Guardia Gómez, better known as Mariquilla, and the tablao where she is located is the equally famous Tablao Flamenco El Jaleo (today the Taberna Flamenca Pepe López) in Torremolinos.[29] That neither Mariquilla nor El Jaleo were identified reduces both person and place to images, visual empty signifiers, that may be appropriated for marketing propaganda to promote Spanish coastal tourism. In *Kitsch y Flamenco*, Luis Clemente explores objects such as postcards whose cheap materiality endows flamenco culture with a "mimesis falsificadora" (falsified mimesis) that draws it into the realm of kitsch where simulacra trumps authenticity.[30] What is important, he asserts, is the imitation, not that which is authentic, and what it insinuates about "la visión real" (the real vision). With the materialization of a fiction, Clemente asserts, the viewer's gaze assigns a value that was not part of the original meaning, but which separates history and class from any contextual significance the object or the representation may have held. Postcards as well as tourist souvenirs like castanets, keychains, cheap plastic statuettes, coffee mugs, coasters, and abañicos (hand-held fans), exemplify the low-quality reproductions that extol indiscriminate consumerism, a willful penchant for bad taste, the industrial over the artisanal, and the exaltation of appearance over authenticity. Clemente argues that through this material culture fomented by tourism and consumer capitalism, flamenco enters the realm of kitsch where objects are characterized by their banal uselessness.

As I mentioned earlier in this chapter, many of these images appeared repeatedly on different postcards from different printers in vastly different formats. Sometimes they were stand-alone images, other times alongside a panoramic view or specific locations on the coast, or at times in a mosaic of three or four images. Such is the case with the image in the upper right quadrant of the Torremolinos postcard (Fig. 2.6). However, while many of the images repeat across various postcards, different printers keep the original photo intact but either position it alongside other images and/or adjust the size of the image. The postcard simply titled "Mariquilla, Costa del Sol" (Fig. 2.7) separates and isolates the image of the flamenco dancer from the original photo, enlarges her image, flips the original image in a mirror reflection, and super-imposes her on an aerial view of the Costa del Sol. Overlooking the Playa de la Roca and the Playa Bajondillo with the iconic high-rise apartment towers of Playamar in the distance, the mismatched size and perspective of the gigantic Mariquilla confuse and disorient the viewer.[31] While the recognizable spatial markers, specifically the Playamar towers, situate place, the line of parasols, sunbathers, and beachgoers indicate the activities, behaviors, and even relationships that define the space in view.[32] If the image were only of the coast, the tourists, and the towers, the connotation would be clear, but the image of the oversized flamenco dancer disrupts the landscape and distracts the viewer. While the name Mariquilla suggests the identity of the flamenco dancer (something not included in Fig. 2.5), the lack of context (specifically the environs of the tablao in the original photo) and the obviously manufactured image that includes an oddly placed palm leaf ironically reveal a level of self-awareness of the falsified representation on the postcard's front. The pretense of authenticity absent, the artificial juxtaposition of this constructed (and manipulated) image of the Costa del Sol seems to indicate a reflection of the artificial construction of the coast itself. The spectacle associated with the flamenco dancer, stripped of even the simulacra of authenticity, communicates the imposed atmosphere of inauthenticity designed to attract tourists with the fabricated authenticity of the flamenco show. This postcard reveals a double deterritorialization that strips the dancer from the tablao (itself a

FIGURE 2.7. Mariquilla, Costa del Sol. Ediciones Beascoa

staged representation of flamenco culture and music) but also disrupts the perceived integrity of the coastline with the presence of an enormous fla-menco dancer. The visual disruption provoked by the juxtaposition of radi-cally mismatched images on this postcard ironically signals the fact that the construction of high-rise apartment buildings like those of Playamar and the intrusion of mass tourism itself represent a disruption along the coastline both geographically and culturally.

The presence of a woman in the foreground of a postcard, whether she is a flamenco dancer or a sunbather, is a common visual trope that seems to seek a heteronormative gaze by framing the Spanish coasts as gendered spaces where staged authenticity, sexual pleasure, and leisure intertwine and inform the cultural myths associated with these tourist spaces. Often the sexual myths and cultural stereotypes meld in the images of the postcard in ways that underscore the intimate ties between the ludic atmosphere of coastal spaces and the promises of exotic cultural otherness. For example, the visual composition of the next postcard (Fig. 2.8) plays on a number of cultural myths recognizable to the Western eye, specifically those of Adam and Eve in the Garden of Eden, that convey the sense of an earthly para-dise. Yet, at the same time, the name of the hotel across at the bottom of

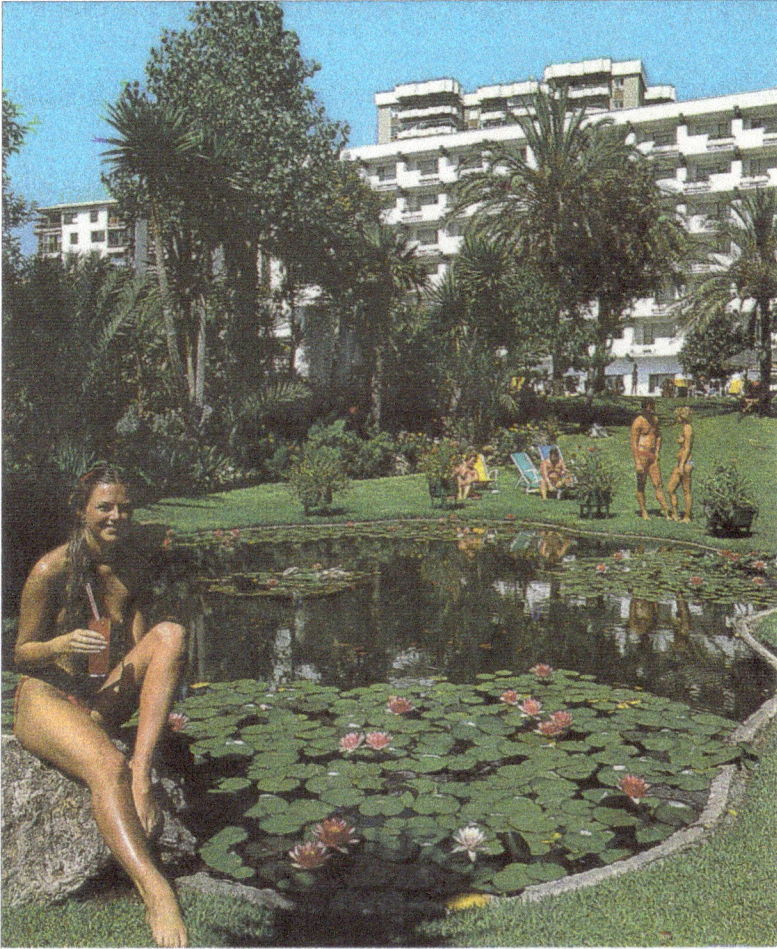

FIGURE 2.8. Hotel Al-Andalus, Torremolinos, Spain. Ediciones Foto Antonio

FIGURE 2.9. Hotel Club Playa del Sol, Estepona, Costa del Sol. Ediciones Domínguez.

the image, Hotel Al-Andalus, invokes the mythic identity of southern Spain during the Arabic presence in Spain from 711 to 1492. That Spanish history becomes a marketable commodity noticeable in the name of the hotel hints at the burgeoning area of cultural tourism and the future explosion of museums along the coast, especially in Málaga, that package the past as consumable narratives within the tourist experience. The lush green environs along with a lily-pad covered pond (rather than a swimming pool) stage nature to emphasize the mythic paradisiacal imaginary of the place represented in the postcard. Two couples in the distance on the other side of the pond endow the image with a sense of perspective and visual depth at the same time their presence suggests a heteronormative understanding of the space in view.[33] In the foreground of the image, on the side of the pond nearest the viewer, a blond woman in a bikini poses on a boulder, holding a beverage as she smiles invitingly. By breaking the fourth wall with her gaze and smile, the woman implicates the viewer in the scene and essentially invites them onto the "stage" and the imaginary of the space that is represented there. The postcard itself, then, becomes a kind of gateway whose space extends to, and includes the viewer inviting them to step into the earthly paradise before them. The hotel, obscured behind palm trees and other greenery, embodies

FIGURE 2.10. Hotel Anabel, Costa Brava, Spain. Gráficas Coll.

the consumerist ideology and ulterior motives that underlie the construction of the image and its illusion of transparency.

Where hotels both serve as iconic monuments that appeal to the tourist gaze and epitomize a non-place, bodies at the beach—especially female bodies—become synonymous with the deterritorialized, inauthentic landscapes of coastal tourism. The female body may be understood as an empty signifier, again invoking MacCannell's understanding of the "empty meeting ground," who acquires meaning in postcards through specific clothing (whether bikini or a flamenco dress), posing and positioning, and location. The female body itself, then, becomes a deterritorialized space that is designed to appeal to the heteronormative tourist gaze as a consumable commodity, "exported" and redefined within the transactional exchanges of a global market during the expansion of Spain's tourism industry and its integration of democratic ideals.[34] The female body, much like Torremolinos or Benidorm themselves, becomes a fetishized space where identity is subsumed through a commodified (and commodifying) gaze and transformed into spectacle, a performative space in and of itself. In postcards such as Figures 2.9 and 2.10, women lounging poolside pose in ways that make it seem they are unaware that they are being photographed. Not only does such inauthentic staging perpetuate the sense of leisure associated with tourist spaces, but the photo creates a predatory-like tone that ironically sets the viewer as an unwitting voyeur accomplice to the discourse of consumption.

As represented in postcards, then, the tanned bodies of tourists comprise the physical, material, built environment as much as the hotels themselves or the commercial and leisure spaces surrounding the hotel like restaurants, night clubs, and shopping districts. The representation of people in postcards transforms the physical places into social spaces and sets the viewer's expectations for behaviors, activities, relationships, and interactions. The places viewed on the front of the postcard offer an escape, then, that is as much emotional, moral, and social as it is a physical teleportation to an exotic, foreign locale. Not only do the images indicate the kinds of tourist activities one might anticipate in a tourist resort in Torremolinos or Benidorm, but they inform the viewer about the acceptable ways in which one may behave, dress, speak, or interact with others. Free from the moral strictures or social expectations of "civilized" society, the ludic spaces of coastal tourism encourage tourists to engage their hedonistic, voyeuristic, Dionysian impulses through leisure and consumption. Panoramic images of the coastline, then, inevitably include images of people (white European people) with tanned, athletic bodies lounging, walking, swimming, and more at the beach in the idyllic space of paradise.[35] Seemingly a snapshot of tourists in their natural habitat, the scene in Figure 2.11 presents the viewer with a dynamic array of beach activities where people both see and are seen within the spectacle atmosphere of the coast. A pair of women stroll along the coastline toward the camera (and thus the viewer), one casting her gaze downward while the other looks at her in what appears to be conversation. A solitary shirtless man walks several paces behind the women and looks ahead toward the woman in his path who is laying on the sand sunbathing. A couple of men also seem to notice her as they head perpendicular to the others toward the water. Another shirtless man in bathing trunks stands still and looks out into the water while a couple next to him appear to be in conversation. Colorful beach umbrellas extend into the distance, other beachgoers walk along the water in the opposite direction away from the viewer, and others swim. The high-rise hotels that make Benidorm so recognizable curve along the bay, hugging the beachside as they stretch into the distance. The scene seems to capture a natural and authentic moment in time, a veritable snapshot of the tourist experience, that depicts the diverse vectors along which individuals may venture and invites the viewer to imagine and dream about their own experience there, imagining and inserting themselves in the scene before them. The perception

FIGURE 2.11. View of Eastern Beach, Benidorm. Ediciones Hermanos Galiana

that this scene is an authentic moment, however, normalizes the predatory capitalism that underlies both the physical construction of the built environment, most noticeable in the surrounding hotels and restaurants, and the social imaginary that defines the alienated (and alienating) experience of individuals surrounded by others, yet who do not form a collective or feel a sense of belonging.

For Marc Augé in *Non-places: An Introduction to Supermodernity*, one of the key characteristics of supermodernity is that a series of accelerated transformations in time, space, and ego have generated a crisis of meaning through a disorienting excess of images and information. Especially in the area of space, rapid means of transportation developed in the second half of the twentieth century have radically transformed the scale of space making global travel radically more accessible, while satellite technology for mass communication have made images and information about events around the world available instantaneously. Spatial overabundance, Augé asserts, acts as a "decoy" that minimizes authentic local culture and ethnology and fosters fictional "symbolic universes" that depend on the recognition of cultural markers—not the knowledge of them.[36] Visual signs and codes perpetuate invented cosmologies to fabricate an accepted understanding of spaces and existence that elides diversity, identity, and conflict and perpetuate a homogeneous world view in the interest of publicity and marketing. Parallel to the physical transformations of urban areas—most noticeable for Augé in the proliferation of installations needed for the accelerated circulation of passengers and goods, commercial centers, and even refugee camps—visual references and cues foment an imaginary space that implies an ideological transformation in both individual and collective understanding of space. Augé is thinking of mass communication and televised images on screens, but even now, well into the Internet age, picture postcards are still intimately associated with the tourist experience and hold a unique status among the objects that evoke the commodities of tourism. The picture postcard reifies the tourist experience through a material relic that offers a "lieux de mémoire" where a nostalgic, idyllic re-collection of the past may be deposited and accessed, individually as well as collectively. The open public discourse of such objects, both in the image on the front as well as the written message on the back, coalesce to generate dreams of paradise through the creation of "symbolic universes" that encode coastal spaces with an imaginary that promises existential salvation through leisure, pleasure, and consumption. That images are overtly "massaged" (to borrow from Marshall McLuhan) underscores the emptiness of the authenticity that is re-presented on the front of the postcard. By manipulating the visual signifiers, such postcards become spectacles in and of themselves that entice the tourist gaze to offer an imagined space, constructed ideologically as much as physically, that promises paradise.

CHAPTER 3

Empty Tourist Spaces

Paradise, Satire, and the Photography of
Martin Parr and Carlos Pérez Siquier

I like to explore the chasm between representation and reality.

MARTIN PARR

The immensely popular British sit-com *Benidorm* (airing for ten seasons from 2007 to 2018 on ITV) dispels the dreams of paradise generated by postcards and tourism propaganda through its satirical portrayal of a diverse set of characters on holiday at the all-inclusive Solana Resort. By day, overweight Brits in Speedos lounge poolside eating, drinking, smoking, and reading never leaving the confines of the resort and its promise of "free" amenities included in the cost of the resort. A steady flow of pizza, hot dogs, burgers, ice cream, baked potatoes, and sausages sates the tourists' desire for consumption with no regard for cultural authenticity or, at the least, a discerning palate. In the evenings, the holiday-makers transition from the pool to Neptune's Bar where they consume spectacle as much as they do food and drink. Decorated as if it were the interior of an old pirate ship, replete with barrels and helms as well as costumed waitstaff to further the ambience, vacationers enjoy singing performances, karaoke, trivia quiz nights, and more as a part of their holiday experience in Benidorm. The comedic tension of the series derives from the discrepancy between the paradise that is projected through postcards, brochures, and other forms of tourist propaganda and the crass inauthentic (and inescapable) consumerist reality that visitors find there. The Solana Resort offers middle-class Brits a safe, if empty, simulacrum composed of sunbeds, palm trees, and traditional English breakfasts that shields them from the harsh realities of the outside world. As a non-place, the Solana Resort provokes disorienting effects that lead to humorous situations when visitors attempt to leave the resort grounds in search of the beach or some culturally authentic experience. Inevitably, their search for meaning is thwarted and the gravitational pull of the resort's simulacrum draws residents back to its safe, unchallenging environment. In season 2, for example, a young couple from the first season returns to Benidorm for holiday and intentionally seek the cultural authenticity of an outlying neighborhood distant from the crowded pool of the resort, the loud thumping of music late into the night, and the overpriced plastic souvenirs in the commercial districts. After a reservation error at the small hotel, the manager instructs his son to escort the couple to their "sister hotel." The couple express horror as the car pulls up to the Solana Resort and another tourist leans into the window and yells unironically, "Welcome to paradise!" With its montage of images in the opening credits guided by peppy ska-like trumpet, *Benidorm* demonstrates an ironic self-awareness of the role visual culture has played in marketing the coasts as a hedonistic paradise. Throughout the series, *Benidorm* embraces irony and satire by engaging with the viewer's visual literacy of and familiarity with the images of well-being that have endowed the Spanish coasts with the promise of a paradisiacal escape from a mundane reality and the possibility of emotional, if not spiritual, renewal through leisure.

The story of well-being marketed visually to Northern Europeans through brochures, postcards, posters, guidebooks, and other promotional media constitute what Peter Osborne called the "traveller's visual combinatorium."[1] Tourism, he states, specializes in visual goods and services that traffic in the non-material symbolic language of spectacle, simulation, experiences, sensations, and desires. In *Modernity and the Hegemony of Vision*, Daniel Michael Levin analyzes the domination of the visual on everyday life through what he calls an "ocularcentric paradigm" that began with the ancient Greeks.[2] For Levin, a "vision-generated, vision-centered" interpretation of knowledge, truth, and reality not only privilege sight but lead to questions of ontology, power, and ethics and conditions of totalization, normalization, and domination.[3] He states clearly that the power to see is the power to make visible, and the power to make visible is the power to control. Moreover, that vision sits at the intersection of material and ideological realms intimately ties the physical environment with individual and collective dreams. If vision is the primary sense for understanding the everyday experiences of our environments, then any kind of symbolic representation from landscape paintings to maps impact what Paul Rodaway calls our "visual geography" in *Sensuous Geographies: Body, Sense, and Place*.[4] For Rodaway the abstraction of the visual reduces the visual experience exclusively to visual symbols and detaches the representation of visual worlds from the actual visible world.[5] He continues that the landscapes of film, television, and photography may derive from actual environments but when experienced by the viewer they become a type of "virtual geography."[6] This kind of simulation of the real visible world into images presented to a spectator provokes two results according to Rodaway. First, the visual experience is directed by the camera (and the intention of the producer) such that the viewer's presence becomes invisible, their participation in the geographical environment is rendered passive, and seeing morphs into a strictly consumer activity.[7] Secondly, such reduction of the visual image generates a de-politicized fantasy of the "real" that is detached from the everyday experiences of the viewer and that foments a hedonistic consumption of images that subverts critical thought. The treachery of images, to borrow from Magritte, lies in their hegemonic ability to erase conflict and contradiction by obscuring the ugliness of capital and consumption.[8] If leisure areas along the Spanish coasts offer Northern European tourists utopian-esque sites of consumption, then the images of tourist propaganda extol a visual geography based on a fantasy experience of a paradise where emotional and economic pressures cease to exist.[9]

Moreover, as Jonas Larsen points out in "(Dis)connecting tourism and photography: corporeal travel and imaginative travel," tourists do not visit places for their "immanent attributes" but because the fantasy experience and the resulting visual geography to which Rodaway refers weave stories and narratives that people assemble in the construction of their social identity.[10] From the beginning of the tourist industry in the nineteenth century, especially with the emergence of figures like Thomas Cook and packaged travel experiences, the realism of photographic images seduced individuals with the desire to travel. Larsen asserts that contemporary tourism is "increasingly media-mediated" and envelopes people in a world of "texts and images" from books and magazines to paintings and postcards to movies, video games, and music videos that entice our gaze and inform our understanding of place and our experience of it.[11] For Larsen, commercial touristic photography—especially postcards, guidebooks, and brochures—plays a twofold role in that they mobilize individual desires for travel as much as they prescribe destinations with a "desirable imaginative geography."[12] Tourism advertising, he adds, stokes individual desires through "staged geographies," akin to Mac-Cannell's notion of staged authenticity, that are infused with a "therapeutic ethos" that exploits modern anxieties and offers the promise of well-being, restoration, and happiness through consumption.[13] What Larsen calls the "palpable visual grammar" of postcards, guidebooks, and brochures invites the viewer to project their dreams of fulfillment into the imagined, fantasy destination as an "empty" meeting place that acquires meaning through the tourist's gaze, their consumption of images, and the re-presentation of their desires for pleasure.[14]

Urban theorists like John Urry ponder the impact on the social composition of spaces defined by tourism when "real-space relations" are replaced by "imaginary-space relations" in environments that individuals experience as a simulacrum.[15] In *The Tourist Gaze*, Urry signals the deep schism between the social composition of fellow tourists and the social composition of those living in the places visited where tourist practices involve moving into and through various sorts of public space surrounded by others yet completely isolated and alienated.[16] He asserts that the gaze defines social interaction in tourist public spaces like theme parks, shopping malls, beaches, restaurants, hotels, pump rooms, promenades, airports, swimming pools, and squares. Where Lefebvre understands urban space as a complex web of social relations and history, Urry sees the public spaces associated with tourism as alienated simulacra where people "both gaze and are gazed upon by others (and are photographed as they photograph others")[17] Urry points to "themed environments" such as shopping malls that exude a specific aesthetic such as the "Antique Village" or the "Mediterranean Village" or the "Roman Forum." The 1992 Worlds Fair in Seville epitomized what Urry called the "growing intrusion of leisure, tourism and the aesthetic into the urban landscape."[18] Increasingly, he asserts, individuals experience the world's geography vicariously as a simulacrum that is dominated by powerful images, symbols, and icons yet infused with international capital. In the substitution of "real-space relations" with "imaginary-space relations," the social composition of tourists overcomes the social composition of those living in the places visited.[19] Tourists become actors in this staged authenticity through their omnivorous consumption of places within a global culture whose core components are "the hotel buffet, the pool, the cocktail, the beach, and the bronzed tan."[20]

In the introduction to *The Tourist Image: Myth and Myth Making in Tourism*, Thomas Selwyn builds on the theories of MacCannell and Urry to analyze the relationship between the local and the global, the center and the peripheries, in the fabrication of myths of authenticity behind the tourism industry.[21] Selwyn points out that neither centers nor peripheries are immutable locations that are fixed in a geographical or historical sense, but the structural relationships that bind them, especially through labor, often serve to sustain the mythical images that attract tourists (and consequently catalyze the economy). Underlying the economic impulses of this center-periphery dichotomy, Selwyn states, is the commoditization of local "authentic" culture and its fetishization through myth-making images found in tourist brochures, posters, and other sorts of propaganda that project paradise. Ironically, by associating the paradise myth with the periphery, cultures that occupy the so-called "center" (or locations of power), replicate anterior colonial relationships and reproduce the social control associated with them. Visual culture, then, not only informs the tourist with what Crouch and Lübbren call "place-myths" through advertising images, but also influences behavior and practices of being a tourist.[22] In *Visual Culture and Tourism*, Crouch and Lübbren assert that tourists become entrapped in the "discourse of the scopic regime" in which people practice and perform a self-constructed identity of being a tourist that is intimately tied to the constructed "places" of tourism, especially as they are visually constituted.[23] If space is inscribed with significance through visual culture, especially in the depictions of human bodies that occupy those spaces whether the hotel or the beach or the pool, then bodies are also signified in relation to place through their performative actions and behaviors, in particular their gaze. Crouch and Lübbren assert that the tourist does not merely occupy space but resides in relation to it, even if those spaces are alienated simulacra as Urry states, such that the understanding of self and place reconfigure and reinforce each other in a process of "encounter and performance" mediated by visual culture.[24] Tourists, they conclude, not only consume space but also play an active role in producing, constructing, and signifying it.

In his classic study *The Practice of Everyday Life*, Michel de Certeau offers a distinction between "place" and "space" in which the former represents an "instantaneous configuration of positions" and the latter an "intersection of mobile elements."[25] Place, he asserts, refers to the location of elements distributed in relationships of coexistence and thus excludes the possibility of two things being in the same location at the same time. Rather, each element occupy a location next to another and each is situated in its own "'proper' and distinct location" that it defines" and which implies stability.[26] Space, he continues, is in constant transformation and flux because of the "vectors of direction, velocities, and time variables" that characterize its existence.[27] Space is produced, in a very Lefebvrian sense, by the operations that "orient it, situate it, temporalize it, and make it function" through the "ambiguity of actualization."[28] Space, then, is a "practiced place" dependent on different social conventions, situated as actions in a given present, and whose context is modified by transformations across time. The shift from fishing to tourism as the predominant economic activity along the Spanish coasts epitomizes De Certeau's understanding of space: the transformations of its existence across time, the operations that orient it, and the daily practices that define it. De Certeau adds that the opposition between "place" and "space" centers on two types of determinations in "stories" in which the first is told through the objects associated with place and the other related to the operations and "actions of historical subjects" around and within those objects.[29] He concludes by stating that stories, and the performative indications associated with them, catalyze the transformation of places into spaces or spaces into places. In the case of Spain, the story of the coasts as a place for utopic escape, physical well-being, spiritual and emotional restoration, and unrepentant unbridled consumerism permeate the sites located there such as hotels and restaurants as well as the objects associated with them like postcards, souvenirs, guidebooks, and brochures. The actions of the tourist (along with those of many others attached to the tourist industry like waiters, hotel concierges, tour guides, etc.) reinforce the story attached to place through practices and performances that exude leisure, pleasure, and consumption.

Through satire and self-awareness, photographers like Martin Parr from England and Carlos Pérez Siquier (often referred to as the Spanish Martin Parr) dismantle both the story of "place" and that of "space" by engaging the visual stereotypes (most visible in postcards and tourism propaganda) that frame the representation of urban coastal spaces in Spain. This chapter's title evokes Dean MacCannell's *Empty Meeting Grounds: The Tourist Papers* and examines how photographers like Parr and Siquier demystify the tourist gaze to lay bare the underlying values of leisure and consumption associated with global tourism, especially at coastal resorts. By appropriating the "visual grammar" of tourist propaganda, Parr and Pérez Siquier mimic yet undermine the photographic language of tourism and ironically underscore Lefebvre's idea of "social space" where people, relations, history, and material space all intertwine to create meaning and myth. In *A Dream of England: Landscape, Photography and the Tourist's Imagination*, John Taylor denominates these kinds of artists as "oppositional photographers" who "break the rules of composition, subject matter and captioning."[30] While normal tourist imagery is meant to generate dreams, Taylor argues that oppositional photographers seek to disrupt the comfort those images instill to make the problematics of touring evident, rather than transparent, to expose the "historic complexities of race, class and gender" that are repressed within the tourist entertainment industry. Taylor furthermore states that their opposition does not depend on them segregating themselves from the reassuring images of so-called normal tourism but seeks to "rework the language of tourism and play with its appearance and concerns."[31] They take part, he says, in a constant dialogue with the everyday practices and the standard imagery of tourism. Where the tourist photograph presents a beautiful, luminous world free of contradictions, the oppositional photographer depends upon satire to indicate the impossibility of coherence and seek instead irony and confrontation.

While tourism propaganda often hides the tourist or obscures them amid the masses at a beach or pool, Parr and Pérez Siquier subvert and invert the tourist gaze so the individual tourist become the site to see. Through images of obese or undesirable bodies and idiosyncratic moments, these photographers question the over-arching story of well-being through the tourist who occupies the "places" of Spanish coastal tourism and capture the daily practices that define that "space." In this chapter, I examine images from the Spanish beaches in Parr's *Small World*, *Common Sense* and *Benidorm: About the World*.[32] From Pérez Siquier, I will examine his images of tourists along the beaches of La Chanca in Almería with particular attention to his book *La Playa:1972–1996* and the retrospective exhibit simply titled *Pérez Siquier* organized by the Fundación Mapfre Barcelona in 2020.[33] Especially in Pérez Siquier's case, this collection of photos, many previously unpublished, ironically chronicles the urban transformations of the coastal areas in Almería not through photographs of the built environment but through images of tourists themselves who began to arrive to the area of Almería known as La Chanca in the early 1970s after the inauguration of the airport there and the start of the first tourist charter flights. In the case of Pérez Siquier, his photography articulates an internal opposition in which his more satirical images oppose his earlier photography that was featured in tourist propaganda during the 1960s for publications like Everest. In an interview with Laura Terré in 2020 that is featured in the catalog for the exhibit organized by the Fundación MAPFRE, Pérez Siquier laments what he perceives as his contribution to the "creative destruction" of the Mediterranean Coasts in Spain.

Ahora muchas veces lamento toda la publicidad que hice de esas bellezas recónditas. Ese pasado está yendo en mi contra. El paisaje y el ambiente fueron invadidos por una masa de turistas que rompió el paisaje y la esencia de lo que yo había vivido. Con el tiempo, desde un punto de vista romántico, siento que con la promoción que hice de aquel paraíso influí para que desapareciera. Yo contribuí a la llegada de esa masa de gente que acabó por modificar la belleza, la naturalidad. Todo ha quedado marchitado por esa turba.[34]

Now I really regret all the publicity that I did of those hidden treasures. The past is working against me. The landscape and the environment were invaded by a mass of tourists that destroyed the landscape and the essence of what I had lived. With time, from a romantic point of view, I feel that the promotion that I did of that paradise played a role in its disappearance. I contributed to the arrival of that mass of people that ended up altering its natural beauty. It has all withered and died because of that mob.

Lastly, I also study more recent photography of contemporary visual artists such as María Moldes (especially in her Instagram collaborations with the model Miss Beige) and Roberto Alcaraz who have carried on the legacy of Parr and Pérez Siquier. Like Parr and Pérez Siquier, Moldes's photographs similarly question the accepted narrative of Spanish tourism and the ideological constructions that undergird the discourse of spectacle, leisure, and female identity latent in the physical, built environment of the coasts. Photographer Roberto Alcaraz shares oneiric images of buildings in Benidorm that are devoid of people (and thus humanity) and highlight the city as an ornamental if otherworldly backdrop that has been fabricated for tourism and lacks its own identity where there is an atmosphere that is both anonymous and deceptively amiable.

If postcards inspire a sense of *pathos* in the viewer through longing for physical and emotional wholeness and evoke the possibility for fulfilling some sense of cultural authenticity in a fragmented world, then the visual artists I study here expose the paradox of a paradise that is an inauthentic manufactured spectacle. By making the tourist the object of the gaze, these artists capture the alienation of global tourism through a sense of play and irony that transform the emotional impact of postcards, their pathos, into *bathos* by engaging the often absurd behaviors of tourists. If the destination is "staged," then the tourists may be considered performers whose social interaction is as determined and defined by their performance and spectacle as the falsified and fabricated milieu that surrounds them at the hotel, in shopping districts, and especially at the beach. As Peter Osborne points out in *Traveling Light: Photography, Travel, and Visual Culture* tourist spaces are public and global yet they are at the same time private and individual.[35] What Parr, Pérez Siquier, Moldes, and Alcaraz recognize is that the beach is as much a theme park as Disneyland, an artificial environment that sells a utopic imaginary by marketing nature and displacing local residents. For the artists I will study here, the tourist does not merely occupy a space but they actively engage the myths that have informed their understanding of that space and reinforce such myths through their idiosyncratic behavior and actions. Most notably, these artists dismantle the tourist gaze that underlies such social spaces as the beach or the hotel pool where tourists both see and are seen, where they are both alone yet surrounded by masses of people. Through candid shots, often close ups, these artists—especially Parr, Pérez Siquier, and Moldes—separate the individual from the wider surroundings in ways that underscore the isolation and alienation that characterize the social composition of public tourist spaces. Such candid shots offer a counter discourse to the images that populate postcards where people pose to evoke an emotion of pleasure and leisure and a desire in the spectator to immerse themselves in that atmosphere. By converting the tourist from subject into object, these visual artists interrogate and dismantle the what Crouch and Lübbren's notion of "place myths" where stereotypes and clichés attached to particular locations circulate and spread through advertising and reproduce themselves through the consumerist practices of the tourist. Crouch and Lübbren assert that bodies, as well as space, become inscribed with significance and both are deployed powerfully in tourism's visual culture. The visual depiction of the body magnifies the signification of space by demonstrating "what to do" such as lying at the beach or lounging poolside at the hotel. The discourse of the "scopic regime" I mentioned earlier not only entraps individuals but also informs the practices that underlie a tourist's self-construction. More than "being" a tourist, Crouch and Lübbren see the individual in a constant process of becoming where the "self and the object are refigured in the process of encounter and performance."[36] They conclude that a tourist does not simply inhabit space and does not simply consume place but is an active agent in its production and meaning.[37] Through an almost anthropological sensibility, these visual artists capture the global tourist in their "natural" habitat such that the viewer imagines the landscape that surrounds the tourist, contemplates the ecological impact of mass tourism on the native flora and fauna, and visualizes the urban and cultural transformations of the coasts through the influx of foreign tourists who have displaced local residents. Moreover, the composition of the photographs infuses the images with an ironic self-awareness that draws our attention to the making of meaning through the "visual grammar" of tourist propaganda and pries open the utopic imaginary attached to global tourism to question spaces framed by spectacle and consumption.

Place, Space, and the Banality of Tourism
in Martin Parr's Benidorm

Throughout his work, Martin Parr has demystified the power of the published image, what he calls propaganda, by "using and abusing" the visual
mechanisms of tourism photography, especially those of postcards, to offer
a critique of the modern age through humor and play. Images saturated with
color, especially primary colors, Parr's photography mirrors the texture, composition, and visual feel of postcards from the 1960s and 1970s with a deep
sense of irony. As Thomas Weski asserts in the Magnum Photography profile,
Martin Parr counters the power and propaganda of images with "his own chosen weapons: criticism, seduction and humor." Parr first explored the beach
and the cathartic effects of its artificial inauthenticity on the tourist in *The
Last Resort* that explored class and leisure in the popular beach spot of New
Brighton and chronicled the contradictions of British life in the mid-1980s.[38]
Subsequently, in *Small World: A Global Photographic Project*, Parr evokes the
tradition of photographers like Francis Frith who would travel with Thomas
Cook's Grand Tour to exotic destinations around the world in the 1850s. While
Frith's photographs stoke Western curiosities about the mysterious allure of
the eastern Mediterranean through photos of iconic sites like the pyramids
in Egypt, Parr captures the ubiquity of travel and the banality of the tourist
in the age of jets, cheap tour packages, and crass consumerism that blends
and blurs global travel with local cultures.[39] In his introduction to the 2007
edition of *Small World*, Geoff Dyer asserts that Parr's work presents a self-
awareness that both engages the "contradictory history" of travel photography
that sought to capture the exotic otherness of "the orient" and captures the
ironies and idiosyncrasies of tourism in the jet age when travel has become
affordable and accessible beyond the aristocratic classes.[40] Dyer notes that as
the tourist attempts to escape modernity and "the tentacles of this homogenizing 'civilization'" by venturing to more remote and distant locations, they
inevitably and paradoxically "drag those tentacles" after themselves.[41] With a
sense of play, Parr challenges elitist assumptions and hierarchies associated
with photographic journalism through snapshots of absurd tourist behaviors.
Not a biting critique nor a moralistic finger-wagging, Parr's photographs offer
a radiography of the modern world where one can find a kitschy kind of beauty
in the banal and travel exemplifies society's insatiable appetite for consumption. The local and the global, the South and the North, do not clash in Parr's
work but are inseparably intertwined as evidenced in the trinkets, souvenirs,

and clothing that adorn tourists as well as his photographs of individuals being photographed, taking photos, or carrying their cameras as if a weapon slung over their shoulder. Both place and person, the local resident as well as the tourist, find themselves ironically reduced to playing a role in staging the authenticity of the destination, producing and reproducing its meaning through consumption. The meta-awareness of such photographs creates a mise en abyme that dismantles the image's borders by calling attention to the gaze, disintegrates the distance between the viewer and the image, and leaves the viewer with a poignant reflection of their own position within a globalized, consumer culture. What Parr's photographs depict, Dyer states, is not immanence or transcendence or salvation through travel but the "form and state of modern, faithless pilgrimage."[42]

From the leaning tower of Pisa to the Venetian Hotel in Las Vegas and from the Sphinx in Giza, Egypt to the pyramids at Chichén Itzá, the photos in *Small World* establish a series of interlaced themes about global tourism that recur throughout Parr's work and that say something about the so-called age of globalization by exploring the tourist's experience of place and space. The title of the book itself signals the collapse and dislocation of once distant spaces with the advent of jet travel and now, more recently, the internet age and the explosion of mass communication that projects images across the globe within seconds. Clothing in Parr's photos offer signs of cultural dislocation where a tourist at Gaudi's unfinished Sagrada Familia wears a yellow t-shirt that reads Bali, a man in Florence wanders in a brightly colored Hawaiian shirt, and another contemplates Notre Dame cathedral in his NY Yankees baseball cap. Not only is the world rendered smaller but the individual experience of it is mediated, first through cameras, video recorders, and other forms of visual technology and secondly (and perhaps more profoundly) as a consumer who futilely seeks access to the real through its simulacra. In a now famous photo, Parr depicts the other side of MacCannell's "staged authenticity" through tourists in absurd poses acting as if they are holding up the leaning tower of Pisa. Subconsciously, their behavior mimics other photos that prescribe the stereotypical experience of this particular space by imagining and staging the photo they are taking. In other photos, tourists pose for or point their cameras in various directions away from the sight they are supposedly there to see in a way that dissolves the borders of the image to suggest more that lies beyond the limits of the narrative eye that frames the image and calls our attention to our own mediated existence. In other photos, statues offer miniature replicas of the tourist attraction itself, a woman at a beach wears a t-shirt that depicts a woman at the beach, a woman holds a postcard of a golden temple that is directly behind her, vendors trail tourists in Gambia with authentically inauthentic necklaces and trinkets, and a large Polynesian-themed indoor water park with a retractable roof and a horizon projected on a huge screen envelopes the tourist in a beach simulacra. The layers of mediated, meta-discourse in *Small World* obfuscate the viewer's search for meaning in the image at the same time they simulate the same search for meaning and authenticity undertaken by the tourist themselves and expose the myths of tourism propaganda. Yet, the interpenetration of global and local in Parr's photos expose discrepancies in economic power and the inequalities of globalization. The relations between "visitor" and "host" are conditioned by conspicuous consumption in ways that exemplify García Canclini's notion of hybridization where local identity finds the need to commodify itself as a viable strategy to "enter" modernity.[43]

Small World concludes with a series of beach scenes that include images from Río, Mallorca, and Tenerife and capture the silliness of tourist behavior that is impelled by unbridled consumption and falsified authenticity. Parr follows *Small World* with *Common Sense*, a collection of 350 photos he accumulated between 1995 and 1999 that explore global consumerism and disposable culture in the developed world and include his first photos from Benidorm. While the beach epitomizes the tourist experience for Parr, Benidorm offers the photographer a place that is constructed on the foundation of unabashed inauthenticity and crass consumerism where lights, colors, and architecture along with tourist behaviors present opportunities for singular, iconic photographic moments. Similar to the title of his previous book, *Common Sense* offers an ironic double meaning that suggests a level-headed sensibility noticeably lacking in many of the photographs while also hinting that the absence of "common sense" has indeed become a cultural value globally that has replaced emotional intelligence, empathy, and decency with consumerism, simulacra, waste, and tourism. The arbitrary selection of images stream at the viewer, page after page in a series of disjointed images that exemplify the experiences of the modern tourist who consumes culture without context or memory. Moreover, that Parr employs a macro lens with a ring flash endows the images with a hyper-real, up-close quality that unveils the lurid, vulgar side of tourism and contradicts the projected image of beauty and paradise seen in postcards and tourist propaganda. Images are so close to the subjects—the back of a man's head wearing a blue baseball cap with the Nike tag visible, a gold crucifix laying on the bronzed chest of a sunbather, cigarette butts poking out of the sand, etc.—that their tight cropping disorients the viewer, disjointing them from spatial or historical context, in a way that captures the aesthetic and the affect of a fragmented world. The deep saturated colors evoke the technicolor of 1950s and 1960s postcards at the same time they mimic the garish plastic minutiae ubiquitous in a global consumer society. In their collection of Parr photos from *Common Sense* (acquired in 2000), the Tate Museum asserts that Parr's pictures paradoxically "reinforce national stereotypes" at the same time they "demonstrate how consumer culture has made international boundaries more indistinguishable." Scenes of accumulation and waste convey an overwhelming sense of banality that permeates the consumer experience, especially through tourism, that Parr approaches with an attitude of curiosity and play that oscillates between yet another paradox according to the Tate: a "hedonistic celebration" and a "cloying sense of disgust for what may be seen as the more debased aspects of contemporary culture."[44]

Parr's first images from Benidorm, in particular the now-iconic image of a woman sunbathing with blue eye covers, appear in *Common Sense*. For Parr, Benidorm epitomizes the modern tourist destination, exemplifying the distinction, tension, and interdependence of place and space that de Certeau described. As a place, Benidorm offers a purposeful and intentional simulacra that actively suppresses cultural authenticity in favor of a colorful hedonistic paradise. And as a space, individuals build social relations built on transaction, consumption, and leisure without the weight of history, politics, or conflict. Of all the locations that Parr has visited and photographed he has returned to Benidorm time and again, and it is the only location that has received its own stand-alone exhibition of photos (numerous times) along with catalogs and books focused solely on images Parr has taken there. In "Fleshpots of Catalonia: Martin Parr's Benidorm," the introduction to *Benidorm: About the World*, Gerry Badger states that Parr's photos from Benidorm are a "singular manifestation" of a theme that has permeated the photographer's work throughout his career: the phenomenon of the seaside resort.[45] Parr, he asserts, finds amusement in and applies his ironic bent to the artificial theatre that has developed in the last fifty to sixty years. Badger, however, does not view Parr as a misanthropic, disaffected satirist but more so a self-deprecating humorist who delights in the whimsy of his subjects and their situations at the same time he critiques the values of a consumerist society. Parr's entire "modus operandi,' he states, depends upon slipping adroitly between photographic worlds in ways that question the role off the photographer, the status of the photographic image at our culture's core, and the very nature of that culture itself at the turn of the millennium. The

Benidorm series, Badger asserts, is a "case in point." Parr, Badger concludes, depicts a "hell rather than a paradise," but ironically it is a traditional vision of hell in that it entails broiled flesh.

A place that Parr himself has described as "crazy photogenic," Benidorm is the only city among the many global locations Parr has visited to be the singular subject of a photography exhibit or publication.[46] Everything about Benidorm intersects with the aesthetic and intellectual purpose of Parr's so-called new European color expressionism: The vibrant tones of the tourists' clothing (and flesh itself) and the kitschy trinkets, the intense Mediterranean sunlight, the falsified resort atmosphere that induces tourist performativity, the vertical built environment that offers an imposing backdrop and frames the tourist experience, and the mass consumerist ideology that permeates the space, drives its existence, and epitomizes the culture of late capitalism. With a 50mm macro lens with a ring flash, Parr's images present up close, hyper-real technicolor (if not psychedelic) images similar to what he created in *Small World* and *Common Sense* that subvert the traditional discourse of portrait photography and interrogate the composition and constitution of social documentary photography. Throughout *Benidorm: About the World*, people appear with their backs turned to the camera or lounging seemingly unconscious, often with their mouths agape in mid-snore, in the sun, unaware of Parr's proximity with their bodies in quasi-sexual poses. In photos where the subject appears aware of the camera, the individual poses yet appears dis-embodied where the focus centers on some aspect of their face or body (brightly colored toenails, a tall glass of Coca-Cola in front of them, a hand-held electric fan that cools their sunburned flesh, a cheap soccer ball held against a portly stomach, or the long ash of a lit cigarette in a hand). Parr embeds global brands like Coca-Cola or a paddle-ball handle that displays a cheeky portrait of the Spice Girls in ways that anticipated current day product placement and the insidious infiltration of consumer capitalism into all aspects of daily modern life. Moreover, Parr includes close-up images of food—an overcooked egg in plain white toast, a large bowl of vanilla ice cream covered in soggy strawberries, insipid stewed brussels sprouts and green beans, and stacks of greasy fried ham—that point to a gastronomic devaluation as local culinary traditions cede to global fast-food trends devoid of flavor, cultural context, or visual appeal.

With a Magritte-like sense of ironic play, Parr exposes concentric layers of gaze that frame the tourist's experience of place and space and interrogates the underlying ideology of resort cities like Benidorm as sites of consumption. In Figure 3.1, the viewer's gaze is drawn to the bright red cap in the

FIGURE 3.1. SPAIN. Benidorm, 1999. © Martin Parr / Magnum Photos

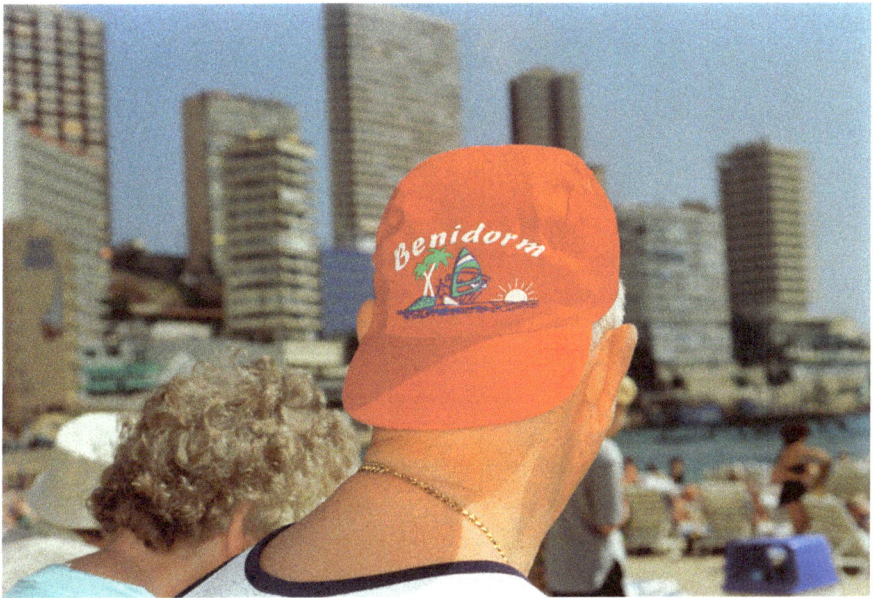

FIGURE 3.2. SPAIN. Benidorm, 1997. From "Common Sense." © Martin Parr / Magnum Photos

FIGURE 3.3. SPAIN. Benidorm. Commission for Spanish *Vogue*, 2019. © Martin Parr / Magnum Photos

center of the frame that ironically identifies the location of the built, urban environment in the distance with clear white lettering that reads "Benidorm." That the cap also includes a scene of a windsurfer, palm trees, and the setting sun portrays the leisure activities associated with a ludic tourist space yet also dismantle the viewer's gaze with a scene within a scene. The cartoonish representation of tourist performativity on the cap exists within the wider frame of the tourist scene in Parr's photograph, and the fact that we are contemplating a tourist who seems to be contemplating the scene before him, especially the urban skyline, calls attention to the ideological impact of representation. That the cap itself is a tourist souvenir poignantly underscores the resort city as a site of consumption inscribed, literally and visually, in the tourist experience of the built environment.

If Parr had been appropriating the visual grammar of postcards to mimic their look, feel, and colors as well as the poses of the people who appear in them, then his inclusion of a photograph of a postcard among the images from Benidorm more overtly questions the ideological impact of this ubiquitous piece of tourism material culture. Again, with Magritte-like irony, Parr's photo of a postcard presents concentric gazes that draw the viewer's attention to the visual construction and composition of the image and how it frames our understanding, awareness, and expectations of the place represented there. Moreover, that the front of the postcard is stamped with a bright red price tag that reads 225 pesetas pierces the illusion of transparency and identifies the resort city as a site of consumption. By rupturing the representation of paradise, Parr literally reframes Benidorm (and other resort coastal cities) as spaces of alienation rather than physical rejuvenation or spiritual salvation. Absent a sense of collective solidarity, tourists engage the space as individuals who perform according to the expectations established through the visual consumption of images in postcards, brochures, and other forms of tourism propaganda.

Throughout the 2000s, Parr returned to Benidorm multiple times and last visited in 2018 to shoot photos for a layout in *Vogue España* that appeared in June 2019 titled "I Love Benidorm."[47] That the photos form part of a shoot for a highly recognized fashion magazine does not diminish the sense of play, whimsy, and irony that have characterized Parr's photography throughout his career. Rather, as McLuhan would say, the medium is the message. Since its purpose is the visual consumption of images, publishing his photos in *Vogue España* offers Parr a space in which to dismantle the viewer's gaze in innovative and provocative ways. Not only do the brilliant colors of the Benidorm landscape complement the style and flair of fashion and offer an enticing visual backdrop for this particular photo layout, but the consumerist nature of the images to promote both the fashion and publishing industry inadvertently interlaces with the construction of Benidorm as a site of consumption to promote the tourism industry for over a half century. In Figure 3.3, the model dons a cheap tourist t-shirt that mirrors the title of the layout while snapping a selfie of herself with the bay and Benidorm skyline behind her. That she focuses her attention on her smartphone rather than Parr seems an ironic acknowledgement of a new era of photography and the proliferation of non-professional images via social media. The telescope next to her signals an obsolete way of seeing and its contrast with the cell phone underscores the advent of digital age in which seeing and being seen happens digitally through carefully curated "stories" on social media platforms. Curiously, this photo seems to harken another iconic Parr photo I mentioned earlier in which tourists posed as if supporting the leaning tower of Pisa. While the model in the photo is not striking an ironic pose stereotypical of a famous tourist location, there is a certain level of performativity that typifies the gestures, poses, and facial expressions produced, consumed, and reproduced in selfies on social media platforms. Ironically, Parr's surreptitious snapshot of the model in mid-selfie hints at another aspect of smartphone photography, and one that photographers like María Moldes exploit, which is the omnipresence of cameras in daily life, a constant and continuous surveillance, and the resulting dissolution of divisions between private and public spaces. While the concentric levels of gaze overlap—the viewer who observes Parr who photographs the model who contemplates her image in the smartphone—the resort city looms in the background as if to remind us that the beach itself is a space defined by the gaze, by private consumption and public exhibition.

The Price of Paradise in the Photography of Carlos Pérez Siquier

It is ironic that Carlos Pérez Siquier (1930–2021) is often referred to as the Spanish Martin Parr considering he is twenty years older than Parr and that he was snapping photos of tourists along the Spanish coasts in his home province of Almería in the 1970s well before Parr "discovered" Benidorm. Pérez Siquier has received numerous awards for his photography, and in 2003 he became the only Andalusian photographer in Spain to be awarded the coveted National Photography Award from the Spanish Ministry of Culture. In 2018, Carlos Pérez Siquier earned the Medalla de Oro al Mérito en las Bellas Artes (Gold Medal of Merit in the Fine Arts) from the Ministry of Culture. Previous recipients of this award include Salvador Dalí, Luis Buñuel, Joan Miró, Plácido Domingo, and Pedro Almodóvar. He co-founded the Agrupación Fotográfica Almeriense (AFAL) and its journal that lead the vanguard of Spanish documentary photography in the 1960s by bringing together photographers from all over Spain such as Ramón Masats, Ricard Terré, Gabriel Gualladó, Francisco Ontañón, Xavier Mierachs, Paco Gómez, Alberto Schommer, and Oriol Maspons.[48] Even though Pérez Siquier published his photos internationally in such venues as Harper's, his work did not gain widespread global attention until 2007 when Martin Parr curated an exhibit of photos in New York for the Hasted Hunt gallery titled "Colour before Color." This exhibit featured the work of Carlos Pérez Siquier's *La Playa* series alongside the works of five other

European photographers that Parr considered the pioneers of color photography: Luigi Ghirri from Italy, Keld Helmer-Petersen from Denmark, Peter Mitchell from the United Kingdom, Ed van der Elsken from the Netherlands, and John Hinde from the United Kingdom. And although the theme and visual language of Parr's and Pérez Siquier's beach photography coincide in unique and unexpected ways—syncopated colors, close-ups that obscure or distort the body, unusual geometric combinations, absurd tourist behaviors, obese or grotesque forms that defy accepted notions of beauty—the socio-cultural circumstances and historical context that frame their respective photographic work offer distinct yet complementary points of entry through which to consider the phenomenon of global tourism and its impact on local cultures.

Martin Parr is often considered a "post-tourist" photographer, one who observes the habits and behaviors of tourists from a privileged self-aware outsider position with the purpose of dismantling the consumerist practices and attitudes that frame contemporary tourist experiences.[49] In the 1950s, Carlos Pérez Siquier established himself as a social documentarian photographer whose black and white photos of La Chanca, an impoverished area of Almería in southern Spain, adhered to an Italian neorealist aesthetic to offer a psychological portrait of a place and a space at the periphery, forgotten and abandoned by both Spain and modernity. Through his spontaneous photos of the people on the street and the geography of La Chanca, Pérez Siquier sought to capture the quiet dignity and persevering character of individuals in their everyday life who had been stigmatized as culturally backward and relegated to oblivion. Himself a native of Almería, Pérez Siquier is decidedly not a "post-tourist" and understands his camera as a mirror that reflects the stark realities of a desolate landscape at the periphery in southern Spain and the inhabitants who live there. Pérez Siquier instills his black and white photos (as well as later color images) of La Chanca with a poetic sensibility that captures the spirit of the town by juxtaposing light and shadow, utilizing the white walls of the Andalusian buildings to frame subjects and create geometrical designs, capture individuals in motion to offer the viewer a sense of the dynamic spirit of the community and to find the authentic reality lived there through the unposed and spontaneous gestures and facial expressions of children and adults alike. Some photos offer a perspective from a distance—like those of the inhabited caves or the rooftops of the low whitewashed buildings—that capture the living conditions of the population who survive extreme poverty.[50] Others portray residents in their everyday activities like sweeping the dirt road in front of their home, carrying large jugs of water back from the small river, hanging laundry to dry in the harsh sun of

FIGURE 3.4. 1958 in La Chanca 1956–1965. © 2022 Artists Rights Society (ARS), New York / VEGAP, Madrid

FIGURE 3.5. 1962 in La Chanca 1956–1965. © 2022 Artists Rights Society (ARS), New York / VEGAP, Madrid

southern Spain, or a bride and groom smiling as they walk through a crowd of people after their wedding ceremony. And many photos present subjects, mostly children, who look directly into the camera and convey to the viewer a deep sense of pride and even a kind of happiness within the context of their physical surroundings and economic conditions.

With the collection of images in *La Playa* series, Pérez Siquier does not abandon his dedication to the social documentarian purpose of photography but sharpens its critical edge by capturing the radical transformation of La Chanca as it becomes unrecognizable both physically and demographically when high-rise hotels and vacation resorts replace the white-washed Andalusian village and Northern European tourists supplant local residents and their culture. Curiously, Pérez Siquier's photos from *La Playa* do not offer images of the physical transformations of the built environment along the coast such as hotels or other structures associated with the profound economic changes that catalyzed the *desarrollismo* policies of the 1960s. Rather, his lens focuses on the dramatic shift in the people who occupy the "place" and who have reshaped its "space" by redefining social relations there within the context of tourism, leisure, and pleasure. The evolution of Carlos Pérez Siquier's photography, from the black and white photos of La Chanca in the 1950s to the vibrant color images of tourists in the 1970s, offers a visual testimony of the "traveler's paradox" described by Minca and Oakes in which the local culture is marginalized and commodified in order to meet the demands of global tourism. That the archetypical whitewashed buildings figured so prominently in his photos from the 1950s yet images from *La Playa* omit long, panoramic shots of the coastline or distant angles of the hotels, restaurants, night clubs, and casinos erected there suggests an intentional decision to allow the viewer to imagine what has been erased from the landscape of Almería with the influx of tourists from Northern Europe and the mutation of La Chanca from oblivion to tourist destination. Ironically, the global transmission of visual images first generated worldwide attention on the area of Almería in the wake of the Palomares incident in 1966, when a United States B-52 bomber collided with a tanker aircraft during refueling and four hydrogen bombs fell into the sea near the fishing village Palomares after the planes exploded. In an effort to quell fears about radioactive contamination, the Spanish Minister of Information and Tourism, Manuel Fraga Iribarne, and the United States Ambassador, Angier Biddle Duke, swam on nearby beaches at Mojácar in front of newspaper photographers and television cameras. The now famous image of Fraga and Duke emerging from the sea, their smiling faces attesting to the ludic experiences of the coast, offered an enticing glimpse of the pristine beaches, sunny climate, and calm welcoming water of Almería's coasts to people around the world.

With the photographs and televised images of Fraga and Duke to market an illusion of well-being, Almería's coasts are plucked from oblivion and plunged directly into the realm of the hyperreal. The image, and its transmission through global mass media networks, becomes the battleground over truth where Carlos Pérez Siquier counters the myths of tourism propaganda with irony, satire, and self-awareness while also maintaining his focus on the social documentary capacity of photography. Moreover, no other photographer in Spain was more acutely aware of the myths generated by tourism publications. During the 1960s, Carlos Pérez Siquier acquired a poignant understanding of the role images play in forging and propagating a mythic sense of place and space by working as a photographer for the Ministry of Information and Tourism. His photographs of Spanish landscapes appeared in state publications as well as private ones like Everest Publishing's collection, dedicated to the provinces in Spain.[51] His work with the Ministry of Information and Tourism offered Carlos Pérez Siquier the opportunity to witness first-hand the physical, social, and cultural transformation happening across Spain and the impact of tourism and its propaganda in those transformations. At the press conference for the publication of *La playa* in 2019, Pérez Siquier noted the inauguration of the airport in Almería in 1968 as the watershed moment that converted the solitary beaches of Almería into an explosion of "color y cuerpos exuberantes" (color and exuberant bodies).[52] Within the framework of Spain's desarrollismo (developmentalism) led by technocratic politicians like Manuel Fraga Iribarne, the visual image becomes an ideological battleground for the control of information. The thematic and technical evolution of Carlos Pérez Siquier's photography not only captures the culture shock between local residents and new waves of invading foreigners who descend upon Almería's coasts. Rather, the physical mutation of the places along the Mediterranean beaches in the photos of Carlos Pérez Siquier lay bare the deep paradoxes of the social transformations throughout the country as Spain "sells" its natural resources to foreign interests and adopts the cultural values associated with consumer capitalism to achieve a sense or status of well-being.

In his introduction, simply titled "La playa," Rafael Doctor Roncero notes the paradoxical postmodern turn in which that paradisiacal natural resources of Spain's coasts—almost constant sun and near perfect climate—were exploited not in the interest of manufacturing goods but in the service of simulacra. A new landscape that marketed a new conception of paradise framed

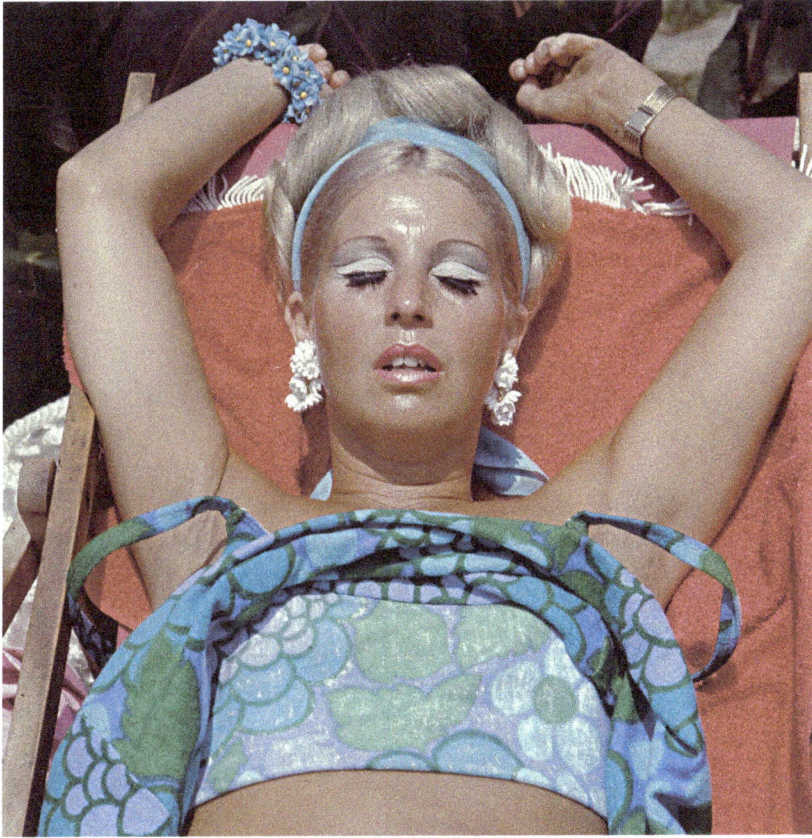

FIGURE 3.6. Marbella (1974), La playa 1972–1996. © 2022 Artists Rights Society (ARS), New York / VEGAP, Madrid

by consumption and capitalist norms imposed itself on this place and redefined its space, "Se instaló, sin obstáculo alguno, un nuevo paisaje, un nuevo modo de vida y aparecieron por doquier miles y miles de cuerpos que de una manera entre jocosa y grotesca invadían lo que hasta ahora había sido, a pesar de tanta violación constante, un lugar paradisiaco" (Without any obstacles at all, a new landscape installed itself with a new way of life and thousands and thousands of bodies appeared everywhere that invaded, laughably and grotesquely, what had been until now, in spite of constant violations, a paradisiacal place).[53] If tourism and photography emerged together in the modern world at the dawn of the Industrial Age in the nineteenth century, then the modernization of Spain through the physical mutation of the coasts is likewise accompanied by innovations in photography through the work of Carlos Pérez Siquier. Moreover, that Spain's economic miracle is driven by the periphery is ironically paralleled by photographers, concentrated in Almería, that abandon traditional black and white images, considered high art, for those in color that had previously been associated with commercial prints and therefore deemed of low artistic value. Martin Parr himself wrote about Pérez Siquier for the first issue of *Impresiones*, a digital journal dedicated to Spanish photography that first appeared in 2013. To offer some historical context through which we might understand the revolutionary impact of Carlos Pérez Siquier in the world of photography, Parr explains that during the early 1970s black and white photography was the chosen medium of any serious photographer, while color was considered the domain of the commercial world or personal snapshot photography.[54] The avalanche of color that befalls the Spanish coasts—bronzed flesh, vibrant bikinis with exotic prints, hip décor with neon glow—offers Carlos Pérez Siquier a symbiotic opportunity to expand his experimentation with color photography that evokes a pop art aesthetic, while also inverting the institutional prejudices against the use of color in the early 1970s to redefine social documentary photography and criticize the cultural impact of crass consumerism.

The transition of the physical environment along the coasts, then, is most clearly understood through the shift in the kinds of bodies that occupy that place and transform it into a space of spectacle. Pérez Siquier himself would engage in a certain level of performance by intentionally unnerving tourists with close-up shots that he would take not with a telephoto lens (like Martin Parr) but by physically invading their space on the beach. In the images of the *La Playa* series, individuals would be facing away from the camera or only a portion of their body was in view, or a person would appear headless. In other scenes, tourists were caught lounging in uncomfortable and often unflattering positions that suggested a kind of amoral (in)sensibility that underlied tourist behavior at the beach if not a complete disregard for local culture (now a common complaint throughout cities in Spain where neighborhoods contend with rude tourist behaviors). Moreover, images of mud-covered legs and buttocks (similar to the images from María Moldes's Bloop series), close-ups of plastic dolls and other toys on the sand, and discarded plastic garbage bags announce the advent of plastics in everyday life and demonstrate a prescient awareness of the ecological impact of tourism on the Spanish coasts, where waste is understood as a necessary by-product of the culture of consumption promoted there. By making the body itself the protagonist of his photos, Carlos Pérez Siquier invites the viewer to reconsider

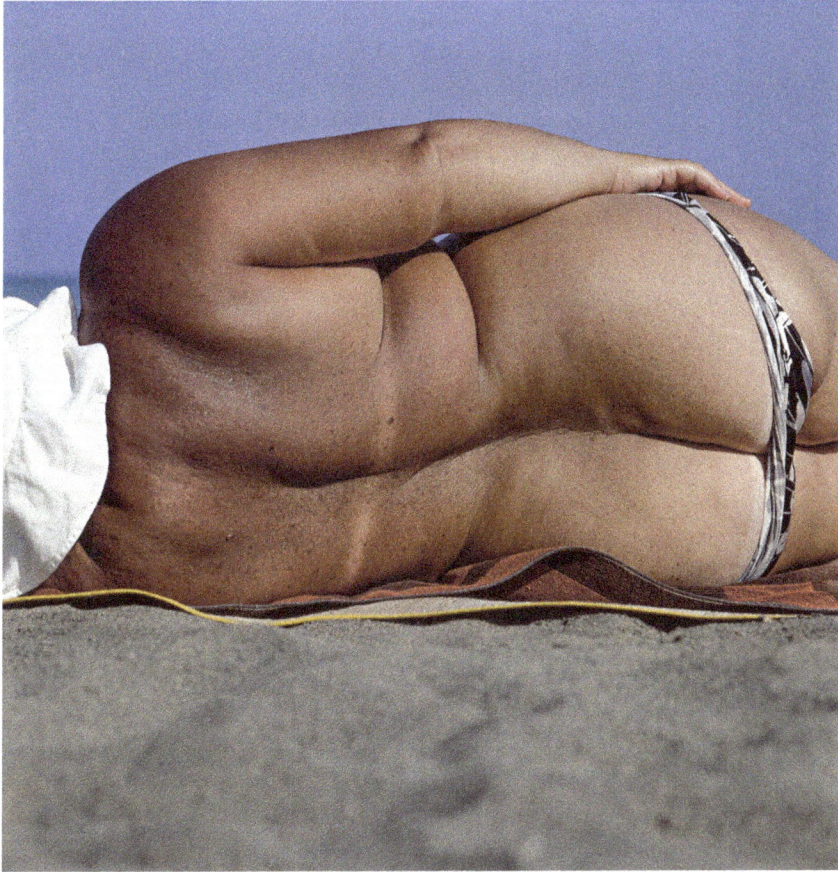

FIGURE 3.7. Aguadulce (1980), La playa 1972–1996. © 2022 Artists Rights Society (ARS), New York / VEGAP, Madrid

their understanding of the elements that constitute a portrait and instead interrogate the ways in which the geometry and geography of the tourist body mirrors the material and social transformations occurring around them. While postcards often included (and continue to include) idealized female bodies that entice the male gaze and exude an atmosphere of leisure and well-being, Pérez Siquier's photos subvert the heteronormative gendered erotization of leisure spaces on the beach by focusing on garish makeup, moles and stretch marks, body and pubic hair, varicose veins, rolls of flesh, cellulitis, pot bellies, scars, and even prosthetic limbs. Images of obese, grotesque bodies contrast with the scenes of poverty and hunger witnessed in Pérez Siquier's photos of La Chanca in the 1950s and signal the comfortable sedentary lifestyle of northern Europe's middle class and modern Western society more broadly. In some photos, Pérez Siquier captures images of beach towels, yet more ubiquitous products associated with coastal tourism, that themselves offer representations of topless women at the beach. Such ironic self-awareness invites the viewer to dismantle the underlying discourse of sex, leisure, and hedonism that frames the construction, both material and ideological, of the towel, the image it offers for consumption, and the social space surrounding it.

Laughable and grotesque, as Doctor Roncero mentioned, Pérez Siquier's collection of images often presents the bodies at odd angles and a level of abstraction that Carlos Gollonet asserts infuses them with satire and irony inherited from Valle-Inclán's *esperpentos*.[55] In his contribution to the Fundación Mapfre's catalog from the retrospective exhibit titled simply *Pérez Siquier* (at the Fundación Mapfre Barcelona from February 14 through May 17, 2020), Gollonet notes that the deformed bodies evoke Goya's dark paintings by opening themselves to humor, satire, and ambiguity and expose the moral deformities of modern society. What is truly grotesque and painful, he asserts in "Pérez Siquier, pionero del color," is to contrast the "imágenes paradisiacas" (paradisiacal images) of the Almería coasts that appeared in the Everest tourism guides in the 1960s and see what they have transformed into today, "Eran idílicos pero pobres, y resultó imposible frenar aquella avalanche sin planificación ninguna que incluso hoy sigue suponiendo una extraordinaria presión en torno del cabo de Gata, milagrosamente protegido y aun así ocupado paso a paso" (They were idyllic but poor, and it turned out impossible to impede that avalanche without any urban planning that even today continues to grow and imposes extraordinary pressure around the area of Cabo de Gata, miraculously protected but encroached upon little by little).[56]

Radioactive Images in the Urban Photography of María Moldes and the Era of Instagram

The same interpenetration of deformation, irony, kitsch, whimsy, and social critique that appear as themes in the photographs of Martin Parr and Carlos Pérez Siquier also manifest in the work of contemporary photographers like María Moldes and Roberto Alcaraz. Though both Moldes and Alcaraz participate in traditional photo exhibits in physical "brick-and-mortar" galleries, the primary mode through which they promote their work is virtually through social media platforms, in particular Instagram. By distributing their work through Instagram, Moldes and Alcaraz are not only able to connect with viewers more widely and more directly in ways that subvert the limits (both spatial and temporal) of traditional photo exhibits but also signal the influence of mass media technology in the construction of a utopic coastal imaginary. In "Instagram City: New Media, and the Social Perception of Public Spaces," Patricia Toscano asserts that the advances in communication technologies in the last twenty years have created a paradox. On one hand, dependence on digital connectivity has wrought the erosion of social relations and "the depletion of contemporary public space."[57] On the other hand, although social interaction may occur primarily through the Internet, Toscano recognizes that such connections may offer opportunities to develop new forms and practices of urban regeneration. She refers to a new culture of "cosmopolitan localism" that has blurred the distinction between real and virtual by redefining physical places with a newly acquired a digital identity that offers a less rigid paradigm to describe contemporary reality.[58] Social media plays a critical role in the perception and representation of public spaces by offering a democratic platform through which citizens may resist stereotypical images associated with urban spaces, especially those seen in tourism accounts on Instagram, and may create a collective narrative of their everyday lives through photos, videos, and stories they post.[59] While the photography of both Moldes and Alcaraz, much like that of Parr and Pérez Siquier, employs irony to unveil the latent contradictions within the visual imagery of tourism, their chosen delivery technology offers an especially poignant commentary on the construction of public images in what Joan Fontcuberta calls the "post-photography era."[60] In the "post-photography era," Fontcuberta argues, the quantity and immediacy of visual images through digital technologies outweighs their quality and their composition, thus creating a pollution of icons that contaminates the visual ecology. While the "post" prefix in Fontcuberta's term may suggest that some new media has supplanted an older one, Moldes and Alcaraz's use of Instagram epitomizes what Henry Jenkins refers to as "convergence culture" where "old and new media collide, where grassroots and corporate media intersect, where power of the media producer and the power of the media consumer interact in unpredictable ways."[61] The ways in which visual images, public space, and tourism inform and influence each other is not necessarily new, but the creation of a virtual public space with a digital visual identity in which individuals are able to produce and consume photos simultaneously carries deep transformations within cultural systems. In the age of the "selfie," Instagram "users" construct their identity through images they share but also assist in the construction of the public image of their surroundings—buildings, streets, monuments, people, landscapes, etc.—and guide the narrative of the visual imagery through hashtags that frame their experience and entice followers to engage with and participate in that experience as well.[62] Official Instagram accounts like @spain (with over 750,000 followers) as well as regional or municipal tourism office accounts (@viveandalucia, @visitcostadelsol, @visitvalencia, @malagaturismo, and many others) engage in essentially the same kind of destination building enterprise as Francis Firth did over a century ago or tourism guidebooks more recently. That this visual storytelling about place and space occurs in such an interactive digital format blurs the distinction between the local and the global even more and adds a virtual dimension to their status as non-places. Not only are they fabricated, ludic sites of consumption but the transmission of their images through digital networks endows them with an irreality because the sites only exist on our screens.

With "Escenas de una vida radioactiva," María Moldes erupted onto the photography scene in Spain in 2014 with an innovative approach to the subject of Benidorm. The title of this "intervención urbana" (urban intervention, as Moldes refers to it on her c.v.) evokes the irreality of late capitalism in the era of mass media and digital technologies mentioned above and prepare the viewer to enter a world that seems in Moldes's words "ciencia ficción" (science fiction).[63] On one hand, the images themselves evoke another world saturated with kitschy colors, dominated by absurd alien behaviors, and characterized by a futuresque cityscape that extends upward under the ultraviolet radiation of an unforgiving sun. On the other hand, her decision to use an iPhone 5 to photograph rather than a traditional camera, even a digital one, offers insights about the impact of technology on everyday life and her decision to distribute her photos through Instagram invites the viewer to contemplate the inundation of visual virtual media in the postmodern world.[64] In her classic book *On Photography*, Susan Sontag wrote that there was something "predatory" about photography that turns people into objects that can be "symbolically possessed" by "seeing them as they can never see themselves."[65] Moldes epitomizes this predatory aspect of photography that Sontag describes where her use of the iPhone allows her to move unseen among the masses of the beach seemingly hunting people who become objectified as fixtures of the coastal landscape alongside the skyscraper hotels. Moldes states that she prefers the iPhone over a camera because it offers her the ability to experiment with lighting, angles, composition, and framing more than a classic hand-held camera, but even more she feels that using an iPhone

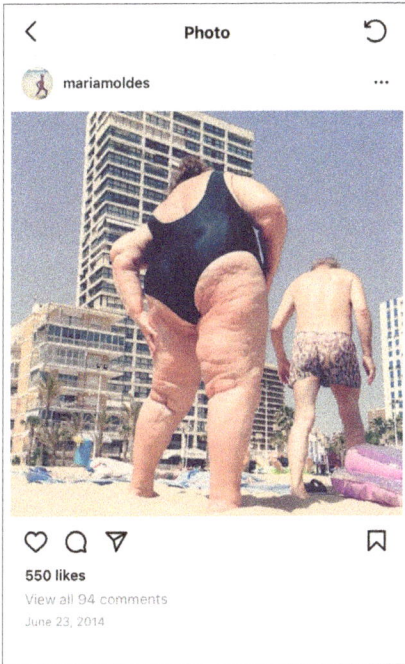

FIGURE 3.8. María Moldes, Instagram: @mariamoldes

FIGURE 3.9. María Moldes, Instagram: @mariamoldes

situates her images within the current social and historical moment. Not professionally trained in photography, Moldes studied psychology in Galicia and considers herself an auto-didact who found inspiration in other urban photographers such as Alex Prager, Ricardo Cases, Viviane Sassen, Joan Fontcuberta, and Bruce Gliden. Moreover, the democratic aspects of social media offer her a platform to maintain direct communication with people who follow her work, and she was included as part of the first Instagram photobook *Out of the Phone*, a collection of exclusively mobile photography submitted using the hashtag #outofthephone in 2014 that allowed photographers to share, connect, and learn from each other.

Elements of photos from "Escenas de una vida radioactiva" echo the techniques and the tone of images from Parr and Pérez Siquier to offer a viewer a message that is as much critical and ironic as it is melancholy and innocent. She captures unflattering angles of bodies at the beach, impromptu scenarios of ridiculous behavior, random images of hands with freakishly long nails or sun-toasted flesh or gaping mouths of tourists, and random detritus like plastic bottles or abandoned bags of food or even someone's dentures floating in the shallow waters. If, as Sontag suggested in 1973, that photography's primary motivation is to convert experience into an image through an ongoing search for the photogenic, then Moldes (like Parr and Pérez Siquier before her) purposefully and intentionally seeks the un-photogenic. She both critiques the excesses of tourism and consumer capitalism at the same time she discovers beauty in the absurd and delights in serendipitous moments of unexpected photo opportunities while also asserting an acute self-awareness of a highly mediatized reality that surrounds us and questions the discourse of leisure in tourist propaganda.

Moldes's collaborations with "Miss Beige" in a series of photos that form part of the "Escenas de una vida radioactiva" counter the spontaneous shots of impromptu tourist behavior on the beaches of Benidorm, with intentionally staged scenes through a deeply self-reflexive kind of performance art. Miss Beige, the name of a character invented by model Ana Esmith, defies feminine stereotypes and the heteronormative fetishization of the female body in mass media. She is a middle-aged woman who dons a drab monochrome beige dresses buttoned to the neck, clutches her purse and a hammer with old-fashioned gloves, walks about in beige shoes with a low thick heel, encounters others with unkempt and unwashed hair parted down the middle, and looks through her square glasses toward the camera with a sour unsmiling face. Declaring herself the "anti-selfie" on her Instagram profile (@miss_beige), Miss Beige's laconic gaze toward the camera asserts an ironic awareness of the viewer and herself as she moves through daily life in modern society and encounters a broad range of circumstances and situations in locations throughout Spain. Through this sense of irony and play, Miss Beige presents herself as both subject and object and offers a reflection on the fine line that separates who we are from the image we project ourselves to be. Miss Beige not only undermines the falsified construction of mass media images, but also subverts cultural myths that undergird Spanish national identity especially as they relate to questions of gender identity, sexual norms, patriotism, sports, and much more. On her Instagram profile, she hints that her purpose relates to the dismantling of those cultural myths that frame our consciousness through our everyday interaction in public spaces. She states, "Miss Beige, taking the streets" with a hammer emoji after it. Yet,

FIGURE 3.10. María Moldes, Instagram: @mariamoldes

her awareness of what exactly constitutes "public space" acquires a level of nuance in the next line that reads, "Through play and with her gaze turns the spectator into the spectacle." Through her "performance" in different settings Miss Beige astutely deconstructs the fabricated identities that populate social media platforms and demystifies the image as purely spectacle. Yet, she also lays bare the daily spectacles that constitute everyday life in the physical world and the cultural myths that inform our awareness and our behaviors. As tourists frolic in the water or toast in the sun, Miss Beige's dour gaze pierces the illusion of transparency that has normalized places like Benidorm as sites of consumption. Her plain appearance contrasts with the vibrant colors and kitschy aesthetic of coastal tourism and her conservative wardrobe likewise diverges from the exposed flesh of bare-chested men and bikini-clad women that characterize the beach. The absurdity of wearing a dress with gloves and heels to the beach is accentuated in Figure 3.10, as she wades waist deep into the water without much enjoyment. She visually posits doubt about the freedom promised through leisure and dismantles the myth of paradise with her scowl.

Paradise Kitsch and Benidorm as a Dreamspace in Roberto Alcaraz's Photography

While María Moldes's Benidorm is otherworldly in its playful "radioactive" depiction of alien behaviors that typify the tourist spaces along the coasts, Roberto Alcaraz's photos offer the viewer a Benidorm that is ethereal and empty, silent and harmonious. Devoid of any human presence, Alcaraz chooses not to focus his lens on stereotypical lobster-red tourists or the chaotic atmosphere of leisure spaces along the beaches or the crass, wasteful consumerism as does Moldes. Rather, Alcaraz adopts the techniques of architectural design photography with an ironic awareness to explore the contradictions of Benidorm through its buildings. Inspired by Lewis Baltz's New Topographic movement, which explored man-altered urban and suburban landscapes through minimalist approaches to photography, as well as Martin Parr's sense of ironic play, Alcaraz's photographs find beauty in the banal through a style that Kluid Magazine calls "paraíso kitsch" (paradise kitsch).[66] Alcaraz transforms the brutalist architecture of buildings constructed to accommodate the influx of mass tourism into delicate, dreamy structures that seem to offer the viewer an alternate reality from that often associated with the crass consumerism of coastal cities like Benidorm. By playing with colors, especially buildings adorned with pastel hues, as well as geometric designs created by the lines of the buildings and the shadows cast by structures around them, Alcaraz's photos present simple compositions through delicate framing. The juxtaposition of small hotels erected in the 1960s alongside cement behemoths from the age of mass tourism and charters in the 1970s and 1980s and then more recent postmodern constructions creates a kind of aesthetic mosaic in Alcaraz's photographs. In many ways, Alcaraz's photographs share an aesthetic quality with Carlos Pérez Siquier's images from Níjar, both those in black and white and subsequent photos in color where he would frame objects, people, and street scenes with the geometry, colors, and shadows of the buildings themselves in a delicate way. On one hand, the different architectural styles in Alcaraz's photography offer an aesthetic chronology of the built environment in Benidorm and the growth of the urban surroundings as the tourism industry expanded. Yet, on the other hand, the colors, materials, dimensions, and styles of buildings constructed during various moments of Benidorm's history endow Alcaraz's photographs with a depth that belie their minimalist approach and defy the one-dimensional simulacra often associated with coastal tourist cities. In line with the philosophy of the New Topographic photographers, Alcaraz's Instagram profile prepares the viewer's experience by stating, "ordinary places, ordinary things, ordinary pics" (@ benidormdreams). In his interview with Elena Velasco, Alcaraz asserts that his intent is to pierce the illusion of transparency of those spaces, buildings, and other elements of our physical surroundings that we ignore or overlook and thus become "la nada" (nothingness) that characterizes our existence.

Alcaraz explains that his attraction to Benidorm is borne out of the contradictions inherent in the city and the tourism industry that, on one hand, have brought jobs and resources to many yet, on the other, have adhered to an urban development plan that is completely unsustainable. In *Ensayo y error Benidorm*, Alcaraz writes that if his attention on Benidorm derives from the city's contradictions, then so too are his own feelings about the city contradictory.[67] Alcaraz currently resides in Sabadell, outside of Barcelona, but he grew up outside of Benidorm in a small town named Villajoyosa. He understands the assertion urban geographers make that as a vertical city Benidorm is much more intelligent and efficient than many other cities in the world, but Alcaraz also ponders what has been lost on both an individual and collective level, "A veces visito sitios a los que hace años no voy y recuerdo que, donde ahora hay un rascacielos, antes había pinos junto a la playa en la que solía comer con mi familia equipados de sombrillas, colchonetas, neveras portátiles . . ." (At times I visit sites where I have not been in years and remember that, where there is a skyscraper now, there used to be some pine trees right next to the beach where I would eat with my family equipped with beach umbrellas, cushions, and coolers . . .).[68] Not only is Benidorm a non-place dedicated to tourism and constructed of hotels, apartahotels, restaurants, casinos, aquaparks, and other sites of leisure, but culturally the city presents a series of contradictions that intrigue Alcaraz. He notes that the Irish holiday St. Patrick's Day is more celebrated in Benidorm than any local or regional festival, its moderate climate offers such an attractive destination for retirees around the world that among older demographics there is an ethnic heterogeneity one might only expect to find in a capital microcity. Additionally, he continues, Benidorm's contributions to Spanish culture over the last fifty years or more should not be underestimated. Before he catapulted to global stardom, Julio Iglesias began his career in Benidorm and performers like Manolo Escobar, Mari Carmen, María Jesús, and Boney M. spent much of their artistic careers in Benidorm. And, Benidorm also captured the interest and imagination of filmmaker Bigas Luna in *Huevos de oro*. So while he admires the work of photographers like Martin Parr and María Moldes, Alcaraz also feels that their attention to the absurd antics of sunburned tourists perpetuates the common myths and caricatures about

Benidorm and fails to capture the city's contradictions and paradoxes. For this reason, Alcaraz focuses not on people but on buildings and the everyday details that "escapa el plan urbanístico" (escape the urbanization plan) to find patterns that offer a kind of poetry and allows the viewer to imagine an alternate reality by seeing the city with a gaze that is free of prejudice or pre-established ideas.

Alcaraz's photographs invite the viewer to explore the traveler's paradox through images that overtly separate place—the physical environment—from space—the human interactions that frame the political, social, economic, labor, and cultural relations of a given place. Although its tourism model may be unsophisticated—cheap prices, frenetic nightlife, plentiful sun, and clean beaches—Alcaraz seeks to exculpate the city for the excesses of those who visit. His images present the city as backdrop scenery that has been intentionally fabricated to fulfill the desires of millions of tourists and by avoiding the distracting behavior of those tourists one can contemplate the contradictions of Benidorm that is both an "espacio sin identidad, una tierra de nadie" (a space without identity, a no man's land) and "de y para todos" (of and for everyone) that offers an "ambiente anónimo pero ameno, sin pretensiones" (anonymous but pleasant atmosphere, without pretensions) [69]. With titles such as "concrete beach," "Giant tanga," (a tongue-in-cheek reference to the Hotel Bali's thong-like architectural design), "We feel special after all," and "Child's game," Alcaraz not only frames the narrative of the images he shares on Instagram, but also distills the contradictions of Benidorm by ironically questioning the accepted narrative that has endowed the city and its buildings with meaning. Through humor and a sense of play, Alcaraz draws the viewer's attention to invisible, unseen, or otherwise overlooked details of everyday life in the city—whether Benidorm or any other city—to see its urban spaces literally from a new angle and through a different lens. Through this new and unique perspective, the viewer can critique the trajectory of urbanization along the coasts, contemplate its impact on both the collective and individual psyche, and imagine alternate realities where the city's design (and hence its narrative) unfolded differently.

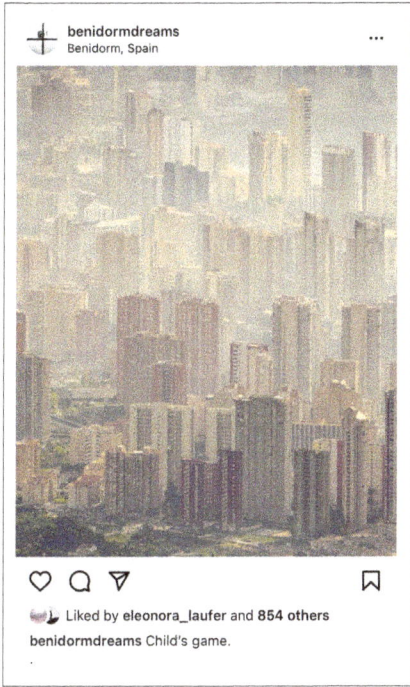

benidormdreams
Benidorm, Spain

Liked by **eleonora_laufer** and **854 others**
benidormdreams Child's game.

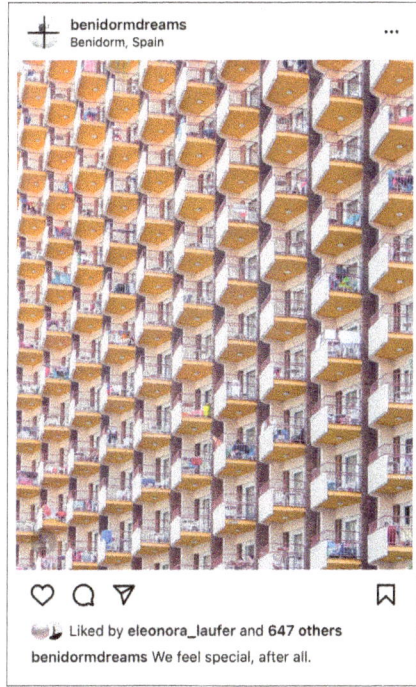

benidormdreams
Benidorm, Spain

Liked by **eleonora_laufer** and **647 others**
benidormdreams We feel special, after all.

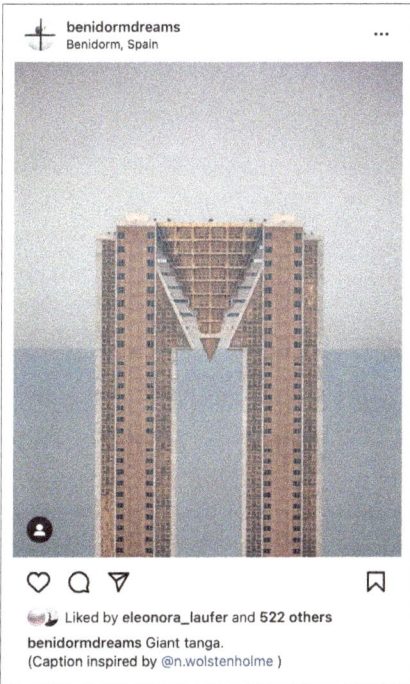

benidormdreams
Benidorm, Spain

Liked by **eleonora_laufer** and **522 others**
benidormdreams Giant tanga.
(Caption inspired by @n.wolstenholme)

FIGURE 3.11. "Child's game," Roberto Alcaraz, Instagram: @benidormdreams

FIGURE 3.12. "We feel special, after all," Roberto Alcaraz, Instagram: @benidormdreams

FIGURE 3.13. "Giant tanga," Roberto Alcaraz, Instagram: @benidormdreams

CHAPTER 4

From Tourist Paradise to "Paraíso Fiscal"

Construction, Corruption and the Legacy of Jesús Gil

"España no es que sea diferente; es que es inverosímil"
(It is not that Spain is different; it's that it is unreal.)

AMANDO DE MIGUEL

Corruption may be considered almost synonymous with construction when contemplating the urban projects that have built the coasts in Spain over the last seventy years. The presence of crime along the Spanish coasts may be understood in two ways that point to the ugly unseen processes beneath the glossy surface of the tourist experience. On one hand, so-called "corrupción urbanística" (urban corruption) has been a common practice in which politicians, mafiosos, lawyers, police, and construction companies curry favors with each other through bribes, price fixing, tax fraud, money laundering, falsification of documents, and more in order to grant licenses, facilitate permits, and award bids for hotels, aquatic parks, golf courses, and recreational sites—all related to the tourism industry. A major corruption scandal centered principally in Marbella exploded along the Costa del Sol in the summer of 2006 and offered a prelude to the impending economic crisis of 2008. Referred to as Operación Malaya, an investigation conducted by the Ministry of the Interior exposed what *El País* called in an editorial the "perfecta simbiosis entre política y construcción" (the perfect symbiosis between politics and construction).[1] This scandal unveiled dozens of other similar enterprises throughout the peninsula and implicated the spectrum of political parties to expose endemic corruption within the fiscal, juridical, and political institutions that guide modernization and urbanization projects in Spain. On the other hand, the same infrastructure that has drawn millions of tourists over the years has also constructed an ideal space to facilitate a lucrative yet violent drug industry of narco gangs from all over the world: An international airport, luxury hotels, and residential neighborhoods where individuals can live anonymously, cash-based enterprises perfect for money laundering, a large port at Algeciras (the fourth biggest in the world that not only receives tourist cruises but large shipments of cocaine), access to the Mediterranean Sea (where Morocco is a mere nine miles away and easily reached for contraband trafficking), proximity to Gibraltar (for offshore investments), and a perfect climate.

Where Mario Gaviria boasts Benidorm as an urban model for sustainable development, Marbella (and the Costa del Sol more broadly) epitomizes more accurately the de facto urbanization practices along the coasts that have married the philosophy of land speculation with rampant corruption. The earthly paradise marketed to tourists in guidebooks, postcards, and other propaganda that promises visitors physical and spiritual rejuvenation through leisure and pleasure, finds in Marbella a "paraíso fiscal" (fiscal paradise), a haven for illegal activity, where money laundering and tax evasion abound in the absence or scarcity of taxes or other applicable financial controls for foreign residents as an incentive to attract foreign capital. Enticed by the promise of millions of euros, especially in the construction industry, the utopia conveyed in tourist brochures quickly morphs into a dystopia driven by money laundering, collusion and favor trafficking, bribery and embezzlement, murder and disappearances, and the widespread presence of mafias from around the world, namely Russia. Progressive deregulation related to urban development has undermined democratic ideals and processes through opaque economic practices and complicit international financial institutions that protect the illegal activities of corrupt parties with impunity. An inversion of Plato's cave, then, in Marbella democracy is a façade where the shadows control reality in what should be considered a logical extension of the scene from Ángel Palomino's *Torremolinos Gran Hotel* where board members extol their abiding philosophy in closed door, back-room meeting, "A forrarse, caballeros" (Let's make a killing, gentlemen).[2]

The confluence of crime and corruption in an urban setting make the coasts an ideal setting for noir fiction and film. Recent novels such as Juan Félix Bayón's *De un mal golpe* (2006), Alberto Llamas's *El asunto Melkano* (2013), and Salvador Rivas's micro-novel *Playa del gato* (2019) explore the prevalence of crime and corruption by embracing the noir genre to unveil the world of mafias, bribes, corruption, and crime—all connected to politics and construction that dominate the Costa del Sol. Born in an era of crisis during the 1920s, noir offers a dark vision of modernity in which crime is endemic to the urban environment and society is deeply corrupt and corruptible, controlled and directed by unseen nefarious networks of power. Such a genre offers an ideal vehicle to examine the criminal underpinnings of tourism in Spain and the corruption at the core of the modernization project of the last few decades. Eduardo Jiménez Urdiales's *Sombras del Poniente* (2019) similarly looks to the early years of the tourism boom as an exploration of the shadows that loomed over the construction industry and its subsequent economic miracle, coloring over Spain's modernization projects of the last fifty years. The Spanish film *La caja 507* (2002), directed by Enrique Urbizu, follows Modesto Pardo (Antonio Resines), a humble bank manager near Marbella, who seeks revenge for his daughter's death seven years earlier in a forest fire. Legal documents he discovers after a robbery of several safe deposit boxes in his bank reveal that the fire was not accidental but intentionally set to clear land for a mega-urbanization tourist project. Recent thrillers including *La isla mínima* (2014), *El niño* (2014), *Toro* (2016), and *The World is Yours* (2018) reveal a vast underworld of drug trafficking, prostitution, gangs, and murder that ironically thrive in the political and economic conditions along the coasts, hidden from "normal" society but aligned with the values of savage capitalism. On television, crime and corruption associated with the coasts have inspired mini-series like *Operación Malaya* (2011) and *Crematorio* (2011, based on the eponymously named novel by Rafael Chirbes). The Telecinco series *Brigada Costa del Sol* (2019), produced by Mediaset España along with Warner Brothers and Netflix, offers a primetime crime drama set in Torremolinos in the late 1970s that traces the origins of Spain's first narcotics unit. Víctor Santos's graphic novel *Intachable: 30 años de corrupción* tells the story of César Gallardo, a rising political star, whose quest for power occurs in the atmosphere of sex, crime, greed, and lies along the Mediterranean Coast.[3] César Gallardo's story is the story of Spain in the era of speculation, construction, and the crisis after the burst of the real estate bubble.

The scope of this chapter, however, is not to analyze noir film and fiction set along the coasts but to examine the politician Jesús Gil y Gil as a cultural icon who is most notable for the corruption on the coasts and may be seen as the model for the representations of corrupt politicians in fictional works. The atmosphere of impunity and corruption associated with construction and tourism along the Costa del Sol offers a distorted vision of modern society that may also be viewed, paradoxically, as the logical extension of the quest for an economic miracle in building an earthly paradise. Also, again paradoxically, the real happenings, incidents, experiences, and attitudes related to politics and corruption along the coasts offers a more unreal and inverosimile vision of society than any work of fiction could hope to produce. In the wake of the 2008 economic meltdown, however, the pervasive corruption in Marbella was anything but isolated to that city of the Costa del Sol and served more appropriately as a proverbial "canary in a coal mine," as many other corruption scandals tied to construction and tourism emerged over the subsequent years throughout the Peninsula. The purpose here, then, is to analyze the emergence of Marbella as a model for corruption from 1995 to the financial crisis of 2008, understand Jesús Gil y Gil as a kind of cultural icon that emblematizes and distills that corruption, and question the impact of his legacy in both the social and physical landscape of the Spanish coasts through the prevalence of so-called "ghost hotels."

In *La séptima potencia: España en el mundo*, Spanish sociologist Mario Gaviria presents a "diagnóstica" (diagnostic) of Spain's evolution since 1960, which he describes as a period of unprecedented economic growth accompanied by political and social advances that the country had never seen before in its history.[4] For Gaviria, Spain is on an upward trajectory despite any dips in the international market that maps the country onto a Scandinavian model of economic welfare (or well-being) that evokes social solidarity through a stable economy and inspires a respectful attitude and a sense of stewardship toward the environment. The title of the book refers to Spain's ranking at the time as the economy with the seventh largest Gross Domestic Product in the world and thus, along with many other data points and rankings by various international organizations, validates the assertion that Spain has abandoned its peripheral status to join the Global North as an industrialized economic power of the so-called First World. Gavira refers to cities and urban spaces as the materialization of the welfare and happiness Spanish society has enjoyed through its expanded economic power since the 1960s.[5] The expansion of the Gross Domestic Product, he explains, has empowered municipal governments to invest in infrastructure, public facilities, parks, highways, high voltage power cables, fiber optic connections, telephone lines, and gas and oil pipelines. The world to come, he states emphatically, is "prioritatriamente urbano" (primarily urban) and Spanish cities especially are constantly improving and ever more livable.[6] If the expansion of cities and the growing urbanization of Spain represents the materialization of welfare of Spanish society, then, Gaviria asserts, the development and urbanization of the Mediterranean coasts in Spain signify the materialization of welfare for Europe's leisure classes. Twenty years after the publication of *España a Go-gó*, Gaviria revisits and assesses his assertions about the tourism industry in *La séptima potencia* and determines that his evaluation of the economic and social impact of tourism and his predictions about the industry's continued importance in Spain were right on the mark. In *España a Go-gó*, Gaviria stated that coastal tourism in Spain would be "*imprescindible y a largo plazo insustituible*" (indispensable and irreplaceable in the long term), a statement he confirms in 1996 and affirms for at least the next ten years (placing that date ironically close to the 2008 financial collapse).[7] He describes coastal tourism as the "cenicienta" (Cinderella) of the Spanish economy that without grandiose strategies or complex planificación has transformed Spain into one of the most economically powerful countries in the world.[8] Gaviria finds it paradoxical that, despite its clear social and economic benefits over the previous thirty-six years, Spaniards should despise the tourism industry so profoundly. While global tourism was expected to grow at 5 percent annually through the end of the 1990s and into the 2000s, Gaviria sees no reason why the expansion of Spain's tourism industry should not exceed that. He states that the coast of Alicante (commonly referred to as the Costa Blanca)—from Dénia to Torrevieja with Benidorm as the center point and the entire Costa del Sol from Marbella to Almería along with the Canary Islands, especially Tenerife, and the Balearic Islands, in particular Mallorca—will continue to drive tourism and ensure Spain's well-being indefinitely. If the future, as Gaviria predicts, will inevitably be urban, then, he advocates, society must embrace and value the new Spanish urban culture, without nostalgia for its rural past. Benidorm exemplifies the model for sustainable urban development and epitomizes the notion of urban well-being that Gaviria believes holds the key to a prosperous future for Spain. Though he does not explicitly refer to Benidorm as a paradise, he certainly sees it as a utopian model—spatially, functionally, and symbolically—to follow throughout Spain, starting at the coasts and the islands.

Gaviria is writing *La séptima potencia*, we should remember, in 1996 at the start of the so-called *hormigón* (cement explosion), also known as the *ladrillazo* (brick boom), when Spanish construction expanded exponentially, especially along the coasts, from the mid-1990s until the financial collapse of 2008. Writing just over a decade later, journalist Íñigo Domínguez Gabiña offers a different perspective of the coasts, urban development, and the promise of prosperity held by the models of such coastal cities as Benidorm in his *Mediterráneo descapotable: Viaje ridículo por aquel país tan feliz*.[9] After working in Italy for seven years as a correspondent for *El Correo* newspaper,

Iñigo Domínguez Gabiña returned to Spain and decided to rent a Peugot 207 to travel along the Spanish coasts in July 2008, mere months before the financial collapse. *Mediterráneo descapotable* is the book-length compilation of articles that Domínguez Gabiña published previously in *El Correo*, in which he chronicled his experiences and impressions through eighteen entries as he ventured from the French border to Tarifa, with stops in cities defined by urban coastal tourism including Marina D'Or, Benidorm, Manga del Mar Menor, Palomares, Nerja, and Marbella among others. In "El cielo enladrillado. Paisajes y figuras de la crisis española (2008–2015). Discursos y narrativas de no ficción actuales," María Angulo Egea refers to chronicles like that of Domínguez Gabiña as "periodismo narrativo" (narrative journalism).[10] Books like Javier López Menacho's *Yo, precario*, Pedro Simón's series "La España del despilfarro" for the newspaper *El Mundo* in 2014 as well as Domínguez Gabiñas *Mediterráneo descapotable* among others recount stories of the "barbarie inmobiliaria" (real estate barbarism) during the development boom of the 1990s and early 2000s that have created the urban ruins of the twenty-first century.[11] Through a blend of discursive techniques, both rhetorical and poetic, Egea asserts that the narrative journalism genre offers a realistic approach to social woes by exploring the personal destruction that the crisis has wrought. In the case of *Mediterráneo descapotable*, Egea likens its satirical road trip through a beastly landscape to Hunter S. Thompson's gonzo journalistic writing in *Fear and Loathing in Las Vegas: A Savage Journey to the Heart of the American Dream* (1971). The book includes an appendix titled "Cómo acabó todo: un pequeño informe" in which the author examines the after-effects of the financial collapse and the exposure of pervasive corruption that underlied the "fiestón inverosímil de avidez, codicia, ignorancia y ansia de poder" (unbelievable orgy of greed, lust, ignorance, and inquenchable thirst for power) during the boom years of construction along the coasts.[12] If Domínguez Gabiña's impressions of macro-urban development along the coasts in 2008 exposed fissures in the foundation of Spanish modernity and the first indications of crisis, then his perspective from the lens of 2015 and the aftermath of bank failures, corruption scandals, prison sentences, the loss of billions of euros, and the mass evictions that plagued Spain affirm the fragility of Spain's modernization project that tied tourism with construction. In his "Nota previa" at the beginning of the book, Domínguez Gabiña reframes his original writings, originally devised as a strategy to fill the newspaper with readable summer material, and now understands his journey along the coast as an "instantánea" (polaroid snapshot) of a "país defectuoso" (defective country) that was about to explode.[13]

Armed with an English-language tourism guide to Spain from 2007, the author quotes a passage to demonstrate ironically that for anyone paying attention the signs of crisis were visible in its description of Spanish society during the first decade of the twenty first century, "La deuda nacional y de las familias está aumentando y gran parte del crecimiento económico se basa en dos fuentes poco de fiar a largo plazo como el turismo y la construcción"(the national debt and household debt is increasing and a large part of Spain's economic growth is based on two sources of income unreliable in the long term that are tourism and construction).[14] Such a frank description of Spain not only resists genre conventions of tourism guidebooks that extol para-disiacal portrayals of the country and its landscape as we saw earlier in the introduction, but also undermines the accepted myth of well-being to which Gaviria referred earlier in this chapter. Domínguez Gabiña at the outset of his journey recognizes inherent contradictions within this image of well-being that Spain projects in which people are earning more money, have better cars, go to the gym, and know about wines yet everything is more expen-sive and "la tortilla de patatas cada vez se hace peor" (Spanish omelet gets worse everyday).[15] Through his journey along the coast, Domínguez Gabiña narrates his experiences in third person referring to himself as "el viajero" (the traveller) and establishes one of the central objectives of *Mediterráneo descapotable*, then, is to dispel the myth of well-being that pervaded the con-struction boom and inculcated the idea that real estate was an investment in which one never lost their money. What he discovers is a landscape of simu-lacra within simulacra in which the coasts have been fabricated into theme parks, literally and figuratively, defined by speculation and consumerism that the author describes as a "monstruosidad de grúas y rascacielos" (construc-tion cranes and skyscrapers).[16] From actual theme parks like Tierra Mítica in Benidorm and Polaris World in Murcia to fantastical vacation cities like Marina D'Or to the vast expanses of golf courses in Andalucía, Domínguez Gabiña contemplates Spain's altered landscape, both physical and moral, and wonders how Spain would have survived had it not "invented" tourism, a clear and ironic reference to Pedro Lazaga's classic 1968 film *El turismo es un gran invento.*[17] The urban abuses, he argues, have not only converted the coasts into a so-called desert of the real that lacks authenticity. Not only is one unable to differentiate a Mediterranean town in Spain from any other, but, Domínguez Gabiña argues, the Spanish model for coastal development has established the canon for urban coastal development in Mediterranean countries like Croatia, Turkey, Tunisia, and even Libya.[18]

In the appendix to *Mediterráneo descapotable*, Domínguez Gabiña details the widespread corruption that impelled the urban development of the boom years, underlied the speculation fervor and uncontrolled conspicuous consumption, and inflated the real-estate bubble to unsustainable proportions through the nineties and the first decade of the twenty-first century. In the appendix, a more serious journalistic tone replaces the jocular, gonzo-esque satire of the chronicles from 2008, and the author pierces the illusion of transparency behind the notion of social and material well-being to which Gaviria pointed earlier by unveiling the web of corruption pervasive in urban development projects along the coasts that came to light in the wake of the 2008 financial crisis. The desire to invest in "ladrillo" (brick), even from the early years of Spanish coastal tourism during Spain's Economic Miracle, epitomizes Fernando Roch's notion of the "ciudad inmobiliaria" (speculation city) in his article "La ciudad inmobiliaria y el precio de la Vivienda."[19] For Roch, the ciudad inmobiliaria mirrors Harvey's notion of monopoly and flexible accumulation from "The Art of Rent," in that urban space is considered a commodity and a vehicle for accumulation through processes that differentiate housing prices and generate capital gains through rent that is collected from properties. That such accumulation appears stable, objective, and scientific is a façade that obscures, he argues, the hegemony of capital and the powerful interests of the elite, in particular construction companies, politicians, and banks. Especially during the construction boom of the 1990s and 2000s the frenetic expansion of what was considered "suelo urbanizable" (developable land) also established a paradigm that promoted widespread money laundering, collusion, bribery, and embezzlement. The interdependence of tourism and construction fostered the perfect condition for a volatile real-estate bubble, which burst in 2008 with dire consequences for Spanish society, families, and individuals. In the wake of a global market meltdown, tourism stagnated and Spain's economy paralized while debt (State and individual) skyrocketed, mass evictions ensued, and the construction fervor froze leaving many urban development projects as unfinished mausoleums. Domínguez Gabiña cites a study from the University of La Laguna de Tenerife in the Canary Islands that compiled the 676 most important corruption cases, most of which were uncovered after 2005 with the first cases appearing in Marbella. He states that more than half the population in Spain has experienced a corruption case in their municipal government. Of the 676 cases, Andalucía and Valencia have the most, and Murcia boasts the largest percentage of local governments affected by corruption.[20] That so many cases emerged in Autonomous Communities along the Mediterranean Coast is no coincidence, and Domínguez Gabiña points to one city in particular that has been notorious for corrupt construction practices since the early 1990s under mayor Jesús Gil y Gil: Marbella. When the Caso Malaya

erupted in 2006 it was (and still is) the largest corruption scandal in the history of Spain and although Jesús Gil had died a year earlier and had not been
mayor of Marbella since 2002, authorities uncovered a "sistema de corrupción generalizada" (system of generalized corruption).[21] Jesús Gil's tenure
as mayor from 1991 to 2002 and the dominance of the GIL political party in
Marbella boasts the dubious distinction of ending in the first dissolution of
a local government in democratic Spain. The Caso Malaya is the direct result
of a system of corruption established during Gil's time as mayor and implicated Juan Antonio Roca, the director of urbanism under Gil, as well as Julián
Muñoz, assistant to the mayor, and Muñoz's wife, famous flamenco singer
Isabel Pantoja. Marisol Yagüe, also of the GIL party, was also sentenced in
connection with the Caso Malaya.

Creating the Conditions for Crime and Corruption on the Mediterranean Coasts of Spain

The prevalence of crime and corruption along the Mediterranean coasts
serves, then, as a core principle that has literally built modern Spain but also
instilled the values that brought about the economic crisis of 2008. In *El modelo inmobliiario español y su culminación en el caso valenciano*, authors José
Manuel Naredo and Antonio Montiel Márquez demystify the notion of social
and material well-being attached to construction and real estate markets,
and assert that the "burbuja especulativa" (speculation bubble) is the result
of a philosophy of "urbanismo salvaje" (savage urbanism) that dates back to
the Franco days.[22] The Franco regime gave a "Copernican turn," they say, to
the real estate model and tied itself to a housing policy that has remained
fundamentally intact to this day. The objective of the book is to understand
the persistence of the "modelo inmobiliario español" (Spanish real estate
model) and its application in the case of Valencia in order to understand the
origins of Spain's current economic (and political) ills, and to devise strategies to overcome them. Urban development in Spain, Naredo argues, has
been governed by the business of real estate speculation that exploits the
possibility of adding tremendous value to land simply by declaring them
"urbanizable" (developable).[23] The authors state that examples of this practice
exist throughout the Iberian Peninsula going back decades, but speculation
practices reached their zenith in the tourist zones along the Mediterranean
coasts with unprecedented economic consequences where the rezoning and

reclassifying of land for the purpose of speculation defied notions of urban planning to favor the powerful and the wealthy. While this practice began under Franco, it continued during the fledgling democracy and still characterizes urban development policies throughout the country. The authors assert that the corruption cases that flourished in Spanish courts during the second decade of the twenty-first century are just the tip of the iceberg and point to extensive bad practices that benefit the elite classes. Especially during Spanish democracy, they argue, certain institutional changes allowed local and regional governments the legal and authorized power to rezone land as they wanted (and often for the benefit of the rich and powerful with complete impunity).

As a result, the institutional framework in Spain fostered two processes that mutually benefited each other. First, new constructions were promoted as a valid and viable strategy to obtain capital gains through the rezoning and reclassifying of lands at the discretion of local authorities, a view supported by the powerful construction-real estate lobby in Spain (its own roots reaching back to the Franco days). Secondly, another process promotes home ownership as an investment goal for families, supported, moreover, by a very well-developed system of mortgage credit. These two complementary processes created the conditions for a real-estate boom that was more intense than anywhere else in Europe and made Spain a leader in the consumption of cement (even above other countries with a greater population). Financing the real estate bubble, though, not only devoured individual family savings but during the last years of the boom depended on external debt to keep the Spanish economy afloat. As is well known by now, the overinflated real-estate bubble burst under the financial strangulation that resulted from the absence of international liquid capital that had previously been so cheap and bountiful—an abundance that left real-estate properties overvalued, underutilized, and in a state of disrepair.[24] What Naredo calls the "patología del crecimiento" (pathology of growth) has not only led to widespread "conurbación difusa" (urban sprawl) but created a "metástasis" where rapid and uncontrolled urban growth act as malignant cells that invade and destroy the healthy fabric of established communities. However, he believes it is erroneous that this fervor for speculation began with democracy after Franco.[25]

During the "años de desarrollo" (years of development) in the 1960s, he argues, the rezoning and reclassifying of lands as "urbanizable" led to great fortunes for the powerful by transgressing any notion of urban planning with the lucrative promise of easy money through the so-called "pelotazos urbanísticos" (urban booms). Many of the large real estate and construction companies that formed part of the Francoist oligarchy consolidated (and continue to today) while other more local enterprises emerged, such as influence trafficking. The "transición democrática" (democratic transition) coincided with certain social and geo-political circumstances that made it seem as if the culture of the "pelotazo" and the practice of "urbanismo salvaje" would die along with the Franco regime. A prolonged decline in real estate markets and the oil crisis of the 1970s paralleled a demographic and migratory decline that seemed to impel a philosophy of urban planning to improve the stability of urban environments.[26] However, Naredo points out three conditions that allowed the Spanish real estate model, which began under Franco and was a cornerstone of the so-called Spanish Economic Miracle, not only to continue but to flourish in the democratic years. First, the political regime of the dictatorship metamorphosized into and overlapped with a new oligarchic manifestation of power. Secondly, a crisis in urban planning at a bureaucratic level led real-estate developers and politicians to undertake development projects outside the official planning processes, especially at the local level, protected with legal impunity and armed with the rhetoric of the economic and political impact of growth. As a result, the urban megaprojects that seemed scandalous during the Franco era multiplied exponentially and dwarfed in their dimension, scope, and cost compared to those undertaken during the democracy. Lastly, after Spain's incorporation into the Eurozone 1999 (comprising countries that use the euro as their currency), the abundant and inexpensive financing available through the EU catalyzed the real-estate bubble and expanded Spain's real estate model even further.[27] The corruption cases that emerged after the 2008 financial crisis, Naredo states, are the tip of the iceberg of many more extensive ills inherited from a half century of Francoist despotism and a political transition that excluded voices critical of the system in order to reaccommodate the power elites under the guise of democracy.[28] If the planning process was considered a paper tiger during the Franco years that the powerful adapted to their interests, then, asserts Naredo, whatever tenuous barriers were in place to protect the legitimacy of the process were almost completely dissolved during the democratic era to facilitate the "edificabilidad" (buildability) at the discretion of municipal governments in accordance with investors and land owners to increase revenues. A neoliberal, market-driven zeitgeist established a new model of "caciquismo" (political bossism) that protected the interests of the elites through laissez faire attitudes and extensive corrupt practices.[29]

If the guiding philosophy of urban development in Spain has its cultural, structural, and institutional roots dating back to the Franco years, then, changes in the administrative, regulatory, fiscal, and legal conditions between 1995 and 2007 making speculation endeavors more permissive exacerbated the issue with devastating political and economic consequences for the country. Fernando Jiménez Sánchez asserts in his article "Boom Urbanístico y Corrupción Política en España" that fundamental changes to laws regulating land speculation fomented a pervasive atmostphere of corruption, especially along the coasts, by allowing municipal governments a high level of discretion in determining their urban policies in the interest of promoting an image of material well-being though tourism. Urban development plans at the municipal level in Spain, he states, are completely free to orient the future development of local territories based on the "vocación turística o industrial" (tourist or industrial vocation).[30] Or, a municipal government may decide to maintain the status quo, extend the city in any direction, or expand it outward or even upward. Such discretion is compounded by an elastic flexibility to modify existing urban plans, introduce rezoning measures, and sign new construction agreements between the local government and private entities.[31] Moreover, he notes that judicial process in Spain is extremely slow which makes it a highly inefficient mechanism to mete out justice and an ineffectual process to combat corruption. Additionally, Jiménez Sánches believes that tolerant societal attitudes in some parts of Spain toward urban corruption make it more difficult to pursue guilty parties.[32] Especially in areas where there exists tension between economic development and environmental protection, Jiménez Sánchez asserts, the resolution tends to favor the former over the latter.

Fernández Durán describes the spectacularly intense process of urbanization and construction that Spain saw between 1995 and 2006 as a "tsunami urbanizador," which exacerbated the structural obstacles to control corruption with economic incentives that propelled land speculation, illegal building projects, and urban expansion, especially along the Spanish coasts. The exponential growth of what Jiménez Sánchez calls "suelo artificial" (artificial surfaces) between 1987 and 2006 has led to the "consolidación de un nuevo modelo de ciudad dispersa o difusa" (the consolidation of a new model of diffuse or dispersed city) that is ecologically unsustainable because it consumes tremendous amounts of land, generates much more atmospheric pollution, creates a much higher dependence on private transportation, and increases the pressure on public services like waste collection, water treatment, health services, and education.[33] Moreover, Jiménez Sánchez notes that the costs of construction have only increased 35 percent between 1997 and 2006, while housing costs have increased 175 percent. He includes other data as well that conveys the extreme fragility of the housing bubble that Spain was manifesting during the years leading up to the financial crisis of 2008. Most notably, the passage of laws that served as an "agente urbanizador" (urbanizing agent) by expanding the definition of what land was allowed to be developed into urban projects led to a spectacular increase in income for local governments, derived directly from the monetization of urban development bureaucratic processes.[34] Jiménez Sánchez states that during the early part of the 1990s it was commonly accepted that the high housing costs were fundamentally due to the scarcity of land on which to build new constructions. The Ley Reguladora de la Actividad Urbanística (LRAU) that was passed in 1994 in Valencia was designed to make the bureaucratic processes related to land speculation and development more "agile." This law served as a model that was integrated in other areas throughout Spain and literally paved the way for the infamous Ley del Suelo in 1998 that facilitated the classification of lands as "urbanizable" (developable) where it would have been illegal to build previously. Jiménez Sánchez asserts that the confluence of these three factors has generated two important public problems: a disordered urbanization and construction process that seeks financial income at the expense of environmental sustainability along with a worrisome increase in political corruption, especially in local governments. He cites the Comisión de Peticiones del Parlamento Europeo that outlines the grave problems that such intense urbanization along the coasts has generated in Spain between 1997 and 2006, where the "'enladrillado' del litoral" has wrought the desctruction of fragile flora and fauna for the massive financial enrichment of a tiny, exclusive minority at the expense of the majority of the population.[35] In a great number of documented cases, the report continues, local governments along the Spanish coasts have elaborated urban development plans not out of any real need created by population growth or tourism demand but to satisfy their own ambition and greed.

Corruption on the Costa del Sol and Jesús Gil as Cultural Icon

For Antonio Romero and Miguel Díaz in *Costa Nostra: Las mafias en la Costa del Sol*, urban corruption is (and has been) a core cultural value that pervades development projects along the Mediterranean coasts, but especially in southern Spain where they describe corruption as a "fantasma que recorre la Costa del Sol" (a ghost that courses through the Costa del Sol).[36] They call attention to a kind of vicious circle in which the urban habitat, geo-political location, and economic prioritization of tourism have fostered the conditions for criminality and corruption to thrive there more than anywhere else in Spain by driving further land speculation and what they call "criminalidad inmobiliaria" (speculation criminality) that thereby deepens and extends the roots of corruption.[37] The proximity of the Costa del Sol to Gibraltar, they note, attracts criminal elements and mafias whose need for secrecy is met by the 80,000 front businesses there (in contrast with only 30,000 residents), along with numerous law firms and financial agencies that specialize in the creation of offshore enterprises, actual front companies, and ghost businesses all designed to protect individuals from taxes as well as launder money. In cities and towns all along the Costa del Sol, the authors assert, the zoning of urban land is the source of most corruption and the origin of one of the largest corruption scandals in Spanish (or even European) history. The progressive erosion of regulations that safeguarded speculative practices, coupled with the promise of ever-increasing revenue derived from the tourism industry, has fostered fertile habitat where local political leaders collude with criminal mafias to launder millions of euros through unbridled land development practices. Not only do such practices undermine the urbanistic legality of construction projects but they also negatively impact the socioeconomic environment and degrade the quality of life of society more broadly.[38] Romero and Díaz note that officials in Málaga had projected an additional 600,000 properties being developed over the next decade, which would almost double the existing 800,000 homes. In the province of Málaga, they state, there is 60 percent more construction than in the Autonomous Community of Madrid, the western part of the Costa del Sol being the area most affected with 13,358 hectares of urbanized land. Marbella is the most saturated with about 62 percent of the first kilometer of coastline occupied with artificial use. Another manifestation of the uncontrolled speculation are golf courses and leisure ports, whose planificatión goes hand in hand with speculation interests and "megalómanos proyectos urbanos" (megalomaniacal urban projects). At the time of the writing of their book in 2009, the authors state that there were fifty new golf courses under construction along the Costa del Sol, all of which were conceived as tourist attractions.[39] The "dictadura del ladrillo" (tyranny of bricks) forged a perverse symbiosis, the authors declare, between constructors, politicians, and mafias in which real estate and speculation are responsible for at least 20 percent of dirty money circulating in Spain and the purchase of properties with undeclared money is an extensive and widely accepted practice.[40] Loosening regulations on speculation through such laws such as the Ley del Suelo in 1998 impelled uncontrolled growth that was driven by rampant corruption and undermined democratic processes. These factors congealed to impose a zeitgeist in the 1990s and 2000s throughout Spain, but especially along the coasts, that transformed the old Francoist dictum "España: una, grande, y libre" (Spain: one, great, and free) into "una, grande, y urbanizable" (one, great, and developable).[41]

If the Costa del Sol is, as Romero and Díaz assert, the money-laundering paradise of Europe and Marbella is its omnipresent epicenter, then one man reifies the cultural values that typified the boom years in Spain during the 1990s and 2000s: Jesús Gil. [42] In his book *Ghosts of Spain: Travels through Spain and its Silent Past*, Giles Tremlett juxtaposes the model of tourism in Benidorm with that of Marbella: the former a "massive eyesore" that appeals to working class Brits with fish'n'chips and stand-up comedians and the latter a "monument to corruption and uncontrolled greed" with designer boutiques and ostentatious wealth.[43] Jesús Gil, he states, is the man responsible for molding Marbella into what it is now. Tremlett describes him as a corrupt, medallion-wearing property developer, football club owner, and all-around thug who ran for mayor of Marbella because he was sick of paying bribes to city hall officials while still getting many of his properties blocked. Tremlett offers Gil's Marbella as an example of the perfection of a system of corruption but also asserts that it is a "temptation" to all Spanish town halls, especially along the coast where revenue from construction and tourism have bound the two in a symbiotic relationship.[44] Most land, he states, needs to be reclassified from rural to urban, and that power rests almost entirely with the town hall that depends on the taxes from new building and the revenue from licenses it sells, not to mention the boom to local business more tourism promises. Gil's populist rhetoric and charismatic personality, his flagrant disregard for the rule of law, and his unbridled desire for accumulation epitomize the neoliberal tenets of the Aznar years and the motto "España va bien."[45] Jesús Gil is the iconic cultural manifestation par excellence of the collapse between political power and economic interests, pervasive corruption, and uncontrolled land speculation that characterized the construction boom years. The fact that Gil orchestrated the initials of the Grupo Independiente Liberal (GIL) to coincide with his own surname attests to the political bossism rampant within the neoliberal practices in Spain, especially along the coasts. Jesús Gil may be understood in hindsight as both promoter and product of the systematization of corruption, an emblem of an era as well as an archetype that informs (and is even parodied) representations of corruption in cultural production including film, novel, and pop music (for example, "Marbella y la bestia" by the group Los Muertos de Cristo). The cornerstone of this chapter is the legacy of the infamous figure Jesús Gil y Gil (often referred to as Trump before Trump), a charismatic property tycoon, soccer mogul, and former mayor of Marbella where vast urban corruption scandals such as Caso Malaya, a prelude to the 2008 financial collapse, may hardly be considered anomalies but have flourished within the political and economic ecosystem of urban coastal tourism in Spain. Jesús Gil y Gil not only serves as an archetype for the systematized corruption that has plagued the coasts or as an emblem for unbridled land speculation driven by unquenchable greed, but he also epitomizes the new manifestation of "caciquismo" to which Naredo referred and he became a cultural icon that embodies the social values of excess and accumulation driving Spanish society in the 1990s and early 2000s.

In *Torrente 2: Misión en Marbella*, many references allude to Jesús Gil and parody his lifestyle as mayor as well.[46] First, both Gil and Torrente are sexist, fascist, racist, party-loving, Atletico de Madrid fans. The titular detective drives a sports car with the logo of the Atlético de Madrid football club that Jesús Gil oversaw as its president. The emblem of the Atlético de Madrid appears throughout the film and even plays a role in a major plot point when a lapel pin with the logo hides a computer chip that will launch missiles to destroy Marbella. Additionally, Torrente (Santiago Segura) resembles Jesús Gil physically, with his obese physical form as well as his open shirt, hairy chest, and the noticeable gold chain that he always wore. In one scene, Torrente is in a jacuzzi surrounded by half-naked women, evoking Gil's appearances on his late-night talk show *Las noches de tal y tal*, which he hosted surrounded by bikini-clad women in a jacuzzi. In another scene, when the dim-witted mayor of Marbella hears from his secretary that agents from Interpol are there to speak with him, he quickly starts shredding documents but is relieved ironically when they inform him that they are not there to talk about illegal rezoning but have uncovered a plot by an evil villain to destroy Marbella with missiles if Spanish authorities do not cede to his blackmail demand. That a villain threatens destruction through extortion may be viewed as highly ironic considering the pervasive corruption, embezzlements, extortions, bribery, and more that led to the dissolution of the city government in 2006. Throughout the film, many recognizable celebrities including movie stars, models, and other figures make cameo appearances. But at the end, after Torrente is reinstated in the Madrid police force as a traffic cop, actress Ariadna Gil tries unsuccessfully to convince him not to write her a ticket. That her surname evokes Jesús Gil and that she attempts to sidestep the law, even in the most trivial of circumstances, is a veiled reference to the atmosphere of illegality that pervaded Marbella during Gil's time as mayor and beyond. *Torrente 2* was the highest grossing of all the Torrente films (five in total) and is considered the eighth highest grossing Spanish film, having earned 22,142,173 euros with 5,321,969 spectators.[47]

That HBO produced and distributed worldwide a four-part documentary series about the life of Jesús Gil y Gil is a testament to Gil's iconic status not only in Spain but globally. Titled *El Pionero*, the documentary directed by Enric Bach explores the polemic and charismatic figure of Jesús Gil over four hour-long episodes comprised of original news footage from the 1990s, legal documents, clips from Gil's tv show *Las noches de tal y tal*, interviews, and panoramic aerial shots of Marbella's coastline.[48] Through juxtaposed images and quick edits, the documentary seeks to connect the past with the present to assert a cultural trajectory in which the current atmosphere of crisis may be perceived as a result of the excesses and corruption of the 1990s and early 2000s in the construction industry along the coast and in Marbella specifically. Yet, another message the documentary film communicates is that although Jesús Gil was removed as mayor of Marbella in 2002 (and barred from ever holding political office again) and died in 2004, his legacy extends a long shadow over contemporary Spain. Additionally, Gil represents a prototype or precursor of the kind of corrupt conservative politician that has emerged many times since in figures like Silvio Berlusconi or Donald Trump, who blur the line between politics and business, acquire wealth and political capital through real estate, and maintain power and control through a blend of media savvy, national populist rhetoric, and personal charisma. The documentary connects the past to the present to convey a sense of cultural, economic, and political trajectory through interviews with Gil's sons, activists, political opponents, journalists, former soccer players, Marbella residents, and others who knew Gil in the 1990s. Often in the documentary, clips of news footage or interviews from the past cut to an interview with the same person in the present in ways that offer a retrospective evaluation of the past. High-resolution aerial footage of today's overdeveloped Marbella coastline would often follow an interview or segment from the past and invite the viewer visually to draw conclusions about the lasting impact, influence, and imprint of Jesús Gil on the Costa del Sol and Spain, and to imagine alternative possible outcomes for development along the Spanish coastline.[49]

In Rafael Aníbal's *Aquellos maravillosos años: Escándalos de corrupción y despilfarro en España durante la última década,* the author similarly invites the reader to re-evaluate the impact of the previous decade on Spain's political and economic crisis.[50] Aníbal states that his purpose is not only to single out and draw attention to shameless politicians who have sacked the reserves of the State, pilfering millions for their personal wealth while cutting social services like education and public health. The author's intent is also to unsettle and incite the reader through dark humor, a "sonora y maliciosa carcajada" (resounding and malicious guffaw), by exposing an esperpentic landscape in Spanish politics where greed, lust, and vanity guide policymaking, not any interest in well-being, ethics, or the common good. [51] Each chapter reconstructs the biggest (and most surreal) corruption cases from specific regions of Spain, a "grotesco 'tour' por esa geografía de la corrupción" (grotesque tour of that geography of corruption), of the first decade of the twenty-first century.[52] A kind of forensic anthropology manual, then, this book seeks to dissect Spain's political class in a style inspired by the picaresque literature of the Spanish Golden Age from the seventeenth century, which approaches miserable characters through satire to depict a decaying society. The decay of the decrepit political landscape of Spain acquires a physical manifestation that I will discuss at the end of this chapter where the lavish mega-construction projects—airports, train stations, and especially hotels—were abandoned in the wake of the 2008 financial crisis and now sit in limbo, incomplete ruins that monumentalize the corruption and greed that guided real estate and development practices since the 1950s in Spain through a perversion of Enlightenment ideals of well-being or the common good.[53]

Aníbal himself writes the chapter about Marbella and the imprint left by Jesús Gil in his chapter, "Gil Babá y los 40 cabrones: un cuento de malayos, cupletistas y axiomas Marbella." The chapter on Gil and his impact in Marbella starts with a quote from the mayor of Marbella himself that states, "Me presento a la alcaldía de Marbella para vender más pisos" (I am presenting myself as candidate for Mayor of Marbella so I can sell more properties). Aníbal asserts that Marbella establishes the axiom of corruption in Spain and there is no other greater corruption scandal than the so-called Caso Malaya.[54] He asserts that nothing in Marbella is as it seems, but it is much worse; and one cannot understand the decadence of Marbella or the culture of corruption behind the "Caso Malaya" without analyzing one of the "figuras políticas más nocivas y perniciosas que jamás haya pisado la Administración pública de este país: Jesús Gil y Gil" (most harmful and pernicious figures to ever step foot in Public Administration in this country: Jesús Gil y Gil. Gil arrived at Marbella in the early 1990s with a checkered past as a businessman, having spent time in prison for his culpability in faulty building project that collapsed killing dozens of people in Segovia, and his boisterous outbursts as president of the Football Club, el Atlético de Madrid made him a nationally recognized media figure. After creating a political party that carried his own surname, GIL (Grupo Independiene Liberal), he presented himself as a candidate in the Marbella mayoral elections in 1991 which he won handily with an absolute majority. With a "carácter populista y conservador, histriónico y fanfarrón" (populist and conservative, theatrical and boastful character), Gil took advantage of the poor public management of previous administrations with a simple message that criticized the traditional political parties, the Partido Popular (PP) and the Partido Socialista Obrero Español (PSOE), complained of the inattention paid to localized crime and corruption, and bemoaned the overall bad state in which the city of Marbella found itself.[55] Aníbal states that Gil transformed Marbella into his own private playground where his aggressive tone, his defiant bravado, and his shamelessness erected him as one of the most charismatic and popular figures "de la fatídica y poco edificante década de los 90" (the fateful and uninspiring decade of the 1990s).[56] Aníbal asserts that Gil and his acolytes would be the first to establish a new business model that would later extend throughout the entire nation, especially along the coasts that combined land speculation and urban development with public administration driven by a deep personal interest for wealth and power. Under Gil, and after him, Marbella became the prime example and the model for institutionalized corruption and Jesús Gil the archetype, an "abominable prototipo" (abominable prototype) that we find over and over again throughout the Iberian peninsula.[57]

In the early 1990s, Marbella was a city plagued by unemployment and crime, immersed in economic crisis, and abandoned by the Junta de Andalucía. When Gil arrived, he implemented the so-called "Operación Limpieza" (Operation Clean Up) to "clean" Marbella of transients, miscreants and petty criminals, and the homeless. The objective, asserts Aníbal, was to transform Marbella into the perfect window dressing for tourism by offering clean streets, safe commercial districts, opulent hotels, and beautiful vistas. Much of Gil's populist appeal derived from his ability to address the immediate needs of citizens, such as public safety, as well as his flamboyant rhetoric that allied him with the "common citizen" against the interests of corporate elites and political enemies who could not understand the needs of the working class. Gil, moreover, was media savvy and understood the value of spectacle. He even had a late night television show titled *Las noches de tal y tal* that he hosted from a jacuzzi and used as a vehicle to attack anyone who dared criticize him.

A second component of Gil's populism was to endow citizens with a sense that if the city prospered then they did as well, and that they were a part of the success of Marbella, individually as well as collectively. Under Gil's mayorship,

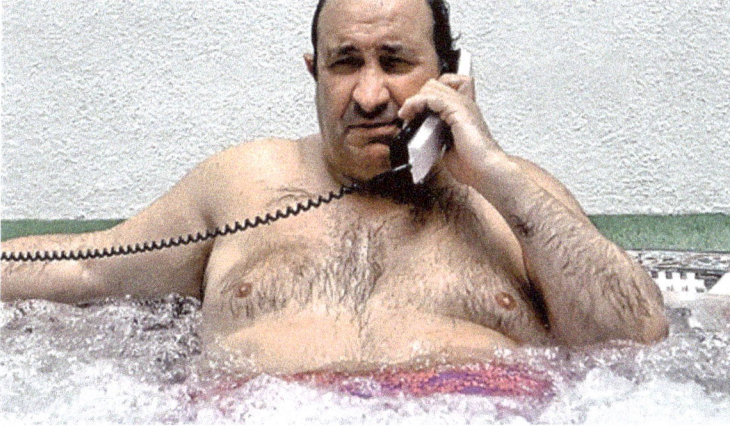

FIGURE 4.1. *Jesús Gil en una jacuzzi*, Deklan Enaut. Wikimedia Commons

Marbella sought to attract an elite clientele and became the tourist destination for the "jet set," appearing highlighted in glamour magazines, that filled the city's coffers with tourist capital and catalyzed unbridled construction and a thorough "cirugía estética" (plastic surgery) that changed every aspect of Marbella, physically and ideologically.[58] An iconic representation of this physical transformation of the city were the bridges constructed on the highways entering the city that were shaped in the form of the letters "Marbella," thus inscribing the space with a sort of national pride at the local level by branding the location and defining its purpose. In his biography *Salvaje: La imperiosa historia de Jesús Gil y Gil*, Iván Castelló writes that before Gil arrived at the Costa del Sol, Marbella was all but forgotten, a dim echo of a city that had once attracted movie stars like Audrey Hepburn, Kim Novak, Gina Lollobrigida, Brigitte Bardot, and Sean Connery (who ended up moving to the Costa del Sol) to the luxury hotel the Marbella Club.[59] He began a series of urban development projects in 1986 that changed the face of Marbella as well as its reputation. In the process, Gil acquired power both financially and politically to become mayor in 1991 with almost 70 percent of the vote. Gil, a self-made man, declared that as mayor his priority was expanding urban development and Castelló quotes him saying, "Me da igual que las zonas sean verdes, azules o amarillas" (I don't care if the areas are green, blue, or yellow).[60] Though Marbella presented an outward image that was clean and inviting to attract tourism, internally, asserts Aníbal, capital overtly dictated the direction of city managers who benefited from illegal gains obtained through urban development. Moreover, while petty crime all but disappeared, there was a level of lawlessness in which frequent disappearances, suicides, and vendettas would be reported. Aníbal states clearly, "El ladrillo se había convertido en la mina de oro de la ciudad y Jesús Gil en su particular Rey Midas" (Construction had become the gold mine for the city and particularly Jesús Gil was its King Midas).[61] Urban development agreements would mask a shadow contract with the construction companies, which allowed Gil and his followers to erect an elaborate network that brought a tsunami of revenue not for the city but for personal gain. Motivated by greed, Gil committed "verdaderas atrocidades urbanísticas" (true urban atrocities) constructing indiscriminately in protected green zones, flood plains, natural parks, and any open land that the city could declare developable to build.[62]

Although Gil won the 1999 municipal elections and his party expanded its presence in Andalucía (with representation in thirteen other towns as well as the mayorships in the Spanish territories of Ceuta and Melilla in North Africa), legal pressure from Andalusian authorities made him increasingly isolated. Some believed that the expansion of the GIL political party to the Spanish cities in Northern Africa was part of a larger scheme Jesús Gil concocted to transform Ceuta and Melilla into a kind of Mediterranean Hong Kong tourist paradise with hotels, casinos, and night clubs that would attract the many leisure cruises that traveled through the Strait of Gibraltar but also offer a "paraíso fiscal" similar to Marbella. Over the years, Gil had evaded many accusations including embezzlement, fraud, Social Security scams, and falsifying documents among others, but in 2000 Málaga district attorneys sentenced him to twenty-eight years of probation and six months in prison as the result of the "Caso Camisetas." Ironically, the "Caso Camisetas" bore no relation to urban development projects or shadow construction contracts, but instead accused Gil of not consulting with the city council before diverting 450 million pesetas from the Marbella government to the Atlético de Madrid Football Club in order to place the logo for the city on the team's uniforms. On April 5, 2002, Spain's Supreme Court upheld the sentence and Gil was forced to resign as mayor, leaving in his wake a legacy of moral and political corruption that infected government systems and set a model for collusion that spread along the coasts and throughout the country.

The "Caso Malaya" and the Legacy of Jesús Gil

The legacy of Jesús Gil is clearly manifested in the "Caso Malaya," to date the largest corruption scandal in Spanish history. In 2005, the Anti-Corruption

Prosecutors' office uncovered the money-laundering operation, "Ballena Blanca" (White Whale), that was the largest ever in Europe filtering almost 2.5 billion euros from countries like Russia and Tunisia through more than one thousand enterprises, all of which were connected to drug trafficking and organized crime, and funneled through the law offices of Fernando del Valle. In various wiretap recordings, prosecutors discovered several cases of urbanistic corruption in Marbella and along the Costa del Sol, which put into motion an investigation that would become the "Caso Malaya." What they discovered was a deep, complex, and widespread infrastructure of enterprises that siphoned funds derived from illegal activities, bribed judges and other public officials, obstructed justice, and embezzled public funds among other crimes. Juan Antonio Roca, Jesús Gil's right-hand man who served as his Director of Urban Development in Marbella from 1992 to 2003, oversaw the entire Malaya operation that was based in Marbella but stretched along the Costa del Sol as well as Madrid, Murcia, and other areas of Spain. The scandal implicated businessmen such as Rafael Gómez, builder and owner of the theme park Tívoli World in Torremolinos, and Fidel San Román, manager of Las Ventas bullfight stadium in Madrid, who were among the most recognizable names associated with the Caso Malaya. By 2012, the Caso Malaya led to 195 volumes of proceedings, almost 100 indictments, and thousands of hours of investigation and interrogation, and unveiled the largest corruption scheme and money-laundering operation in European history.

In the Fundación Alternativa's *Informe sobre la democracia en España 2007: La estrategia de la crispación*, directed by Joaquín Estefanía Moreira, the Caso Malaya (and Marbella in general) is highlighted as a magnificent example of the level of degradation that public institutions can reach when officials take advantage of the opportunities generated by the impunity that surrounds them.[63] The macro-police investigation known as Operación Malaya broke on March 29, 2006, with the arrest of more than twenty people including Marisol Yagüe, mayor of Marbella; two city councillors; Juan Antonio Roca, director of urbanism; Leopoldo Barrantes, council secretary; and fifteen other people, including lawyers and other responsible figures that participated in a network of crimes including misuse of public funds, bribery, influence trafficking, price-fixing, and money laundering. Roca began working under Jesús Gil in 1992 as the manager of urbanism overseeing the municipal project Planeamiento 2000. During those fifteen years, more than 900 urban development contracts were signed and more than 10,000 construction licenses were granted. The municipal government would sign construction contracts that established financial payments or in-kind payment (such as real estate) that were well below market value. While the agreements appeared legitimate, the unofficial contract set much higher amounts that were paid with dark money that was delivered in three installments: upon the signing of the agreement, after obtaining the license, and when the construction was finished. An army of lawyers and front men served to hide the illegal activities by creating a network of more than 120 organizations that laundered the money obtained illegally through investments in real estate properties. Prosecutors estimate that, during those fifteen years, Roca amassed a fortune that surpassed 2.4 billion euros.[64]

The report argues that the vast corruption network that Roca oversaw could not have been possible without the creation of a necessary organizational structure. Although his term as mayor of Marbella ended in 2002 and he died in 2004, Jesús Gil y Gil created the administrative organization within the local government of Marbella that not only allowed widespread corruption but promoted it by treating city hall as another of his many businesses whose purpose was to generate personal revenue. With the excuse of improving the efficiency of local government, the first thing GIL did was to create a parallel administrative structure within city hall. The purpose of this was to strip the government offices of any authority or oversight and to deactivate any mechanisms of control over the local government's actions on two fronts: judicial processes and public opinion. On the latter front, Jesús Gil and the GIL party-controlled Marbella media outlets and even created a series of municipal communication initiatives, such as *La Tribuna*, to control the narrative about the actions of the government. With regard to the former, GIL implemented a strategy that rewarded judges who favored the party and punished those who did not. From the beginning, the primary objective for Jesús Gil and the GIL party was complete control of urban development in Marbella in a "ritmo frenético" (frenetic rhythm) that signed hundreds of construction agreements and rezoned thousands of square kilometers of forest land for development.[65]

The authors of the report pose the question: How does one explain the prevalence and persistence of such a vast web of corruption and the continuation of the GIL party's control (and its expansion to other municipalities including Ceuta and Melilla) even after Gil's tenure as mayor? The report offers two explanations. First, it asserts that between 1991 and 2003 Jesús Gil's party received wide and continued support from the electorate in Marbella. Gil's populist and anti-party message along with general employment and wealth generated by the construction boom, as well as his focus on citizen's safety and the virtual inexistence of street crime, consolidated the backing

of the majority of voters.⁶⁶ A second condition that contributed to the persistence of this "red delictiva" (web of crime) is the excessively passive role
played by the the major political parties, the PSOE and the PP, as well as
certain State institutions.⁶⁷ Both major political parties approved without
question urban development plans that expanded the construction efforts
of Marbella in exchange for political pacts that sought support from the GIL
party on other initiatives. The report notes certain institutional effects that
weakened the role played by the Junta de Andalucía that was not able to ini-
tiate a process to impede the municipality's urban planning competitions
until 2005. Additionally, housing and tax authorities (Hacienda) suffered from
scarce resources that meant they did not have the personnel or the authority to investigate such types of complicated crimes. Lastly, the report points
to slow judicial processes that contributed to the "caos urbanístico actual"
(current urbanism chaos) and a pervasive "clima de impunidad entre los
responsables del ayuntamiento de Marbella" (climate of impunity among
the responsible parties in the Marbella local government).⁶⁸ Property regis-
trars, notaries, banks, and other bad actors exacerbated the atmosphere of
chaos and corruption through their real estate operations by continuing to
sell properties that lacked legal licenses and refusing to collaborate with the
Junta de Andalucía.

   Such an atmosphere of legal impunity and pervasive corruption, which
catalyzed the dialectic between tourism and construction, is not relegated to
just Andalucía and the Costa del Sol. While perhaps not reaching the scale
of the Caso Malaya, other similar scandals have emerged in the wake of the
2008 financial collapse that have revealed a rotten economic and political
system guided by a short-sighted ideology of greed and power. In 2009, the
Caso Gürtel in Valencia uncovered a vast network of construction companies, businessmen, and politicians that had been funneling capital gained
from speculation related to tourism during the real estate boom into funds
that financed electoral campaigns for the Partido Popular (PP) since the late
1990s. The Caso Gürtel intersects with another corruption scandal, the Caso
Bárcenas, in which Luis Bárcenas, treasurer for the Partido Popular chosen
personally by Prime Minister Mariano Rajoy, has amassed a fortune of 48.2
million euros that were hidden in a Swiss bank account. Ultimately, Bárcenas
was imprisoned along with dozens of others and Mariano Rajoy was forced
to resign because of his association with Bárcenas and the political embar-
rassment for his party. The so-called Bárcenas papers published in the news-
papers *El Mundo* and *El País* revealed that the PP had maintained shadow
accounts to hide slush money from illegal donations that was then used to

pay off PP leaders with undeclared money. In Murcia, the "Caso Camelot" uncovered bribes and embezzlement schemes in 2007, where politicians were reclassifying lands near the area of Manga del Mar Menor and elsewhere to accommodate Polaris World's plans to construct a series of golf resorts along the coast. Founded in 2001, Polaris World sought to capitalize on the construction boom of the late 1990s to import Miami's tourism model to Murcia by establishing a "golf trail" with courses designed by Jack Nicklaus. After the 2008 financial crisis and the Spanish real estate bubble, though Polaris World was able to refinance the company failed to avoid bankruptcy. More recently, the "Operación Testudo" uncovered a money-laundering network centered in Benidorm (with some connections to Marbella) in which the Russian mafia colluded with politicians from the Partido Popular, builders, and businessmen to invest in the tourist properties. The "Caso Gürtel," the "Caso Bárcenas," the "Caso Camelot," and "Operación Testudo" are only a few of many other corruption scandals that have emerged along the coasts in the years since the financial crisis. They underscore Amando de Miguel's declaration, "España no es que sea diferente; es que es inverosímil" that I cited in the epigraph.

Ghost Hotels as Monuments to Crisis and Corruption

Ironically, Rafael Chirbes's award-winning yet understudied novel *Crematorio* (made into an acclaimed TV series in 2011) may now be considered a prophetic anticipation of the in-credible and un-believable (inverósimil) corruption that emerged after 2008 like dead fish after an atomic blast in the ocean.[69] Like much of Chirbes's literary works, this novel asserts that corruption, both moral and political, has served as a foundational value upon which Spanish society has constructed its modern identity, physically and ideologically. Beneath the façade of a tourist paradise, a world of mafias, bribes, greed, corruption, and crime not only undergird Spain's modernization project but have steered it into the vortex of economic and political crises that have dominated Spanish society in the last two decades. Throughout his literary career, the late Valencian author Rafael Chirbes critiqued the hypocrisies of the Transición by focusing on the origins of social, economic, and political crises in the 1950s. Set in the fictional town of Misent, a small village that has transformed into a tourist destination along the Costa Blanca in Valencia, Chirbes's *Crematorio* follows the corrupt dealings of the inscrupulous Rubén Bertomeu, a construction magnate and real estate mogul in some ways reminiscient of Jesús Gil, whose tentacles reach into all social institutions (including the Russian mafia) and move politics, economy, and society from the shadows. The novel's structure moves back and forth in time and across various narrative voices to present a scathing panorama of contemporary Spanish society through the Bertomeu family memories propelled by the death of Rubén's brother, Matías Bertomeu, who had rejected greed and instead kept a modest plot of land on the family property where he cultivated crops.[70] Through these two brothers, Chirbes questions a Spain that is and one that could have been if those in power had not developed the coasts with such a fervor to urbanize every possible open space. Though fictional, the transformation of the Mediterranean town Misent (which appears in virtually all of his novels) mirrors the changes in similar towns all along the coast, and on the islands too, where land speculation urbanized the natural habitat into an artificial tourist paradise. In its conclusion, Chirbes's novel ponders what had been gained and what has been lost in the process of urbanizing the Mediterranean coasts of Spain, and it finds in construction the perfect metaphor for capitalism that erects "arquitecturas sin verdad."[71] Construction and destruction entwine in a dialectic relationship within the logic of late capitalism that has bound urbanization and tourism in an insatiable vicious circle, "Crecer supone destruir (. . .) crecer es no parar de crecer y construir es no parar de destruir. Se destruye algo para construir algo" (Growth implies destruction . . . growth is to never stop growing and constructing means to never stop destroying. You destroy something to build something).[72]

Today, so-called ghost hotels and construction projects abandoned in the wake of the 2008 economic crisis stand ironically as monuments to their own destruction. Their hollowness reifies the ideological emptiness of urban coastal tourism, and they stand today, I argue, as monuments of the crisis that announce the endgame of Spain's modernization project that began in the late 1950s. Some consider the hotels constructed in the 1960s like the Don Pepe (and other hotels from that era) as sites that evoke the vibrant and dynamic early years of costal tourism in Spain. The physical constructions as well as postcards and other types of ephemera (including films themselves) may be seen now as relics of the past where material culture offers a kind of depository for a collective nostalgia to reside. The locations, objects, and images that evoke the Golden Age of Spanish tourism and that typified the ludic hedonism and the culture of leisure tied to costal tourism now ironically offer a kind of "lieux de mémoire," both figuratively and literally. Alberto

García-Moreno, Carlos Rosa-Jiménez, and María José Márquez-Ballesteros read the city of Torremolinos across different modes of cultural production from cinema to literature to art and architecture as an archive that preserves and projects a heritage identity through its banality. The buildings and their architectural design as well as urban spaces intimately tied with coastal tourism offer, the authors propose, monuments to a past that today is barely recognizable. Bars and pubs, restaurants, discotheques, and especially hotels, the authors suggest, offer a cartography of past cultural values that are made tangible in the physical presence of the objects themselves.

Moreover, they argue, these remnants of "pop" culture and their association with the perceived banality of leisure subvert the elitist hierarchies typically associated with the concept of heritage and cultural patrimony. Tourism and the mass movement of peoples around the globe in the interest of leisure, they continue, has impacted social organization and hierarchies, has led to cultural hybridization, has provoked profound and lasting alterations to local lifestyles, has generated material and immaterial goods, and has defined modern life in the second half of the twentieth century to today. Moreover, tourism supposes a characterization of modernity that is capable of producing "una historia, un folklore, una arquitectura, unos paisajes, unos eventos y unas costumbres, en una conjunción que diseña una cultura propia y alternativa" (a history, a folklore, an architecture, landscapes, events and customs, all in conjunction that design its own alternative culture).[73] While the system of Parador hotels described in relation to the conclusion of *El turismo es un gran invento* seek to recover and monumentalize a narrative of the rural past in Spain, hotels like the Pez Espada, the Hotel Cervantes, and the Don Pepe along with urbanized areas like the Nogalera in Torremolinos reify the values of Spain's transition away from its agrarian identity toward modernity and an incipient consumer capitalism. The hotels in Torremolinos like the ones mentioned here and many others (even those that no longer exist) stand as monuments that evoke a bygone era whose dynamic vitality, exultation of pleasure, and even its banality offer an escape from the perpetual atmosphere of crisis in contemporary Spain and engage Svetlana Boym's notion of modern nostalgia. In *The Future of Nostalgia*, Boym understands nostalgia as a dislocation from time more than space and views it as the characteristic condition of the modern age in which the steady march of progress denies human beings the mythic return home they yearn for on an individual and collective level. What Gaviria called the "materialization of welfare" when he referred to the architecture, buildings, and physical spaces associated with coastal tourism in Spain during the 1960s and 1970s now manifest the bygone ideals and vitality of that era that offer an escape from the pervasive atmosphere of crisis in the present. As monuments of banality, the hotels intimately connected with the Golden Age of Spanish tourism engage the viewer's gaze and invoke Boym's notion of modern nostalgia that she says "is a mourning for the impossibility of mythical return, for the loss of an enchanted world with clear borders and values; it could be a secular expression of a spiritual longing, a nostalgia for an absolute, a home that is both physical and spiritual, the edenic unity of time and space before entry into history."[74] Ironically, then, industrialization and modernization have accentuated the persistence of nostalgia with the concept of progress dependent on a notion of "unrepeatable and irreversible" time.[75] The accelerated pace of the modern world intensified the collective and individual yearnings for "the slower rhythms of the past, for continuity, social cohesion and tradition."[76]

If we understand the hotels built along the Spanish coasts during the 1960s and 1970s as cultural heritage whose physical space and visual design serve as monuments that evoke the viewer's nostalgic gaze and entice an escape from the crises, pressures, and pace of the modern world, then we confront a series of paradoxes. On one hand, the hotels were designed as destinations for Northern European tourists to escape from the mundane routines and everyday stresses of their industrialized, modern life through the consumerist mentality and ludic hedonism of the Spanish coasts. That these hotels now offer a nostalgic escape from the persistent atmosphere of crisis in contemporary Spain attests to the alluring ideological force of their physical built spaces. Additionally, these hotels stand as monuments to the modernization projects in Spain in which unregulated urbanization not only redefined the coasts as sites of consumption but also served as a model for urban renewal that extended throughout Spain from the 1960s to now. The intimate connection between urban renewal, tourism, and economic revitalization has been constant for over fifty years with the hotel as the iconic destination for visitors. Yet, in the economic crisis after the 2008 global financial crash, the dimensions of the hotel's iconic status have shifted and the hotel's monumental impact serves as a visual metaphor for the endgame of Spain's modernization project. If we understand the hotel to be the "destino" (both destination and destiny) of Spain's modernization project during the last sixty years, it may also be emblematic of the endgame of this modernization project and its broken dreams in the aftermath of the current economic crisis.

Take as evidence the Hotel Cruiser Tres Carabelas Gran Lujo that was approved for construction in 2006 on a large plot of land in Torremolinos.

The antiquated Hotel Meliá was demolished and an entire neighborhood razed to allow the construction of a hotel that was hoped to mark a watershed moment for tourism on the Costa del Sol. At a cost of 120 million euros, the edifice was planned as three interconnecting buildings, two thirteen-story flanks with a fifteen-story futuristic circular construction at its center. Truly a *Torremolinos Gran Hotel,* it was to have 439 rooms with boutique stores and other high-end commercial shopping along with a spa and even a heliport. However, Arcosur, the firm overseeing the construction, ran into financial problems in 2007 soon after construction began, when the Junta de Andalucía suspended their license after discovering their plans did not conform with the Plan General de Ordenación Urbana. While that issue was ultimately resolved, the financial crisis of 2008 created a series of obstacles, the municipal permits expired, and today the property sits half constructed, in decay, vandalized, and doomed never to be completed.[77] The empty shell of the abandoned hotel project stands as a monument to the failed promises of Spain's modernization project begun in the 1960s. That the structure now serves as shelter for the homeless and the indigent, overrun with rats and populated with pools of stagnant water, exposes the fragility of Spain's economic miracle and the precarity of Spanish citizens and their economic and physical well-being. Far from creating the 4-star environment advocated by the PNIT, the presence of the incomplete Hotel Cruiser Tres Carabelas actually threatens the safety of the neighborhood and paradoxically undermines a vital component of the urbanization projects of coastal tourism: to attract capital by engaging the tourist's gaze and appealing to escape modern life and indulge their desire for leisure, luxury, and pleasure.

In their 2018 book *Playa Burbuja: Un viaje al reino de los señores de ladrillo*, investigative journalists Ana Tudela and Antonio Delgado undertake a 15,000 kilometer journey by motorcycle along the Mediterranean coasts to trace the "cicatrices que dejó en el levante el fin de la burbuja inmobiliaria, un catálogo de hormigón y ladrillo" (scars left on the levant by the real estate bubble, a catalog of concrete and brick).[78] For Tudela and Delgado, the distance they travel is as much a journey through time as it is through space in which they capture the most iconic stories about the consequences and effects of the urbanistic policies that not only allowed but actively fomented unregulated speculation of land along the Mediterranean coasts in Spain. Marbella, they assert, is ground zero for where the tourist boom began but also where the urbanistic model accompanied it and radiated outward along the coasts over decades and, especially in the 1990s under the politics of Jesús Gil, infused urban development with collusion and corruption. Similar to the Hotel Cruiser

FIGURE 4.2. Hotel Algarrobico, Playa Carboneras, Almería, Andalucía, Spain. Greenpeace

Tres Carabelas Gran Lujo many other unfinished construction and urbanization projects, often described as "hoteles fantasma" (ghost hotels), stand as
unofficial monuments to the economic crisis in Spain and the consequence
of a real-estate bubble founded on illegal practices, unrestrained greed, rampant corruption, and unregulated speculation. What Tudela and Delgado call
"aberraciones arquitectónicas" (architectural aberrations) stretch along the
coast from Marbella to Barcelona as urbanistic disasters that offer evidence of
the endgame of Spain's modernization project begun along the coasts in the
1960s.[79] Among these urbanistic abominations the Hotel Algarrobico stands
out. The Algarrobico, located in Carboneras along the coast in Almería, was
not only constructed in clear violation of the "ley de costas" (law of the coasts)
that banned construction within one hundred meters of the shoreline but it
also situated the future hotel within the confines of the Parque Natural del
Cabo de Gata-Níjar. Construction of the hotel halted in 2006 amidst legal
and financial battles and still stands despite ecological protests by Greenpeace (most notably one incident in 2014 when Greenpeace activists painted
the façade of the hotel with enormous letters that read "Hotel Ilegal" (Illegal
Hotel)) and promises by the municipal government and the Junta de Andalucía to raze the structure.[80] In "Algarrobico, símbolo de la destrucción de la
costa," Greenpeace declares that in more than 8000 kilometers of Spanish

coastline there are numerous examples of ecological destruction, but the illegal hotel on the Algarrobico beach is one of the biggest urbanistic scandals at the coasts.[81] The construction of the hotel, Greenpeace points out, was allowed to proceed by the local government in the town of Carboneras as well as the regional Junta de Andalucía. With 21 floors, 411 rooms, and only 14 meters from the sea, its location in a natural park has blighted one of the few remaining unurbanized natural areas along the Mediterranean coast in Spain. Although there are currently twenty legal judgements against the illegal construction, the hotel's future remains in limbo; there are no funds nor legal permissions to finish the project and tearing it down is too costly. So, it stands as a monument to the greed and excess that drove the construction boom of the 1990s and 2000s.

In other areas along the coast, the drive to develop protected land has not only led to the construction of illegal hotels but also entire "urbanizaciones" (neighborhoods) of golf courses, restaurants, night clubs, chalets, and more that were conceived to entice tourists with the promise of a four-star resort experience but which now lie in ruins. Casares Costa (referred to as the "chernóbil of Málaga" by Idealista News), the Playa de Macenas in Almería, the so-called "macrourbanizaciones" of Marbella, and more lay as wastelands in the aftermath of the financial crisis yet offer visual testimonies to the myopic mentality of modernization that began a half-century ago in Spain with the idea to build the coasts without conscience laid out in the 1963 law "Centros Zonas de Interés Nacional" that I described in the introduction.[82] These more contemporary "ruins" serve as curious bookends to the skeletal remains of once thriving hotels from the early years of Spanish tourism. From the Hotel Ten-Bel along the Costa del Silencio in the Canary Islands to the Hotel de los Arenales in Alicante, many of the hotels that first drew tourists from Northern Europe with the promise of paradise now stand as abandoned ruins covered in graffiti and strewn with trash. Similarly the unfinished projects of Antonio Bonet's failed dream to create a luxury destination like the Costa del Sol's Puerto Banús in Murcia's Manga del Mar Menor exemplify the fervor to attract capital by constructing sites of leisure and consumption but also demonstrate the lasting negative ecological impact of unconstrained growth along the fragile coastlines of Spain. All of these sites, whether recent or not, act as places of public memory where their materiality is both a consequence of the past but also a symbolic reminder of trauma and loss. In *Places of Public Memory: The Rhetoric of Museums and Memorials* Dickinson, Blair, and Ott understand monuments as "mediated representations" that anchor an individual and collective consciousness in a partial, if not partisan, representations of the past whose stories are animated by affect and anxiety.[83] The intended design of the sites mentioned earlier was not to articulate a place of public memory but actually quite the opposite: to construct a ludic non-place that would attract tourists seeking an escape from everyday life. Now, the shells of these urban projects that stretch from the 1960s to today inadvertently offer physical spaces that reify yet also symbolize the economic and ecological trauma of Spain's modernization project. The abandoned hotels, empty urban spaces, and decayed buildings along the coast serve as physical reminders of the "desastre financiero" (financial disaster) predicted by Carlos Moraleda, owner of the three-star Hotel Estrella del Pacífico, in Ángel Palomino's 1971 novel *Torremolinos Gran Hotel*.

Conclusion

If Spain's story of economic transformation in the 1960s is indeed miraculous, then the various forms of cultural production, especially those visual media that engage the tourist's gaze, construct and fortify the ideological foundations upon which the built landscape of the Mediterranean coasts is erected. The images that populate brochures, tourism guidebooks, postcards, and even popular film frame the viewer's understanding of urban coastal spaces and projects the hedonistic ambience and the modern amenities the tourist may anticipate upon their arrival. Scenes of sun-soaked tourists lounging under palm trees along the sandy beaches or around crystal blue pools convey an atmosphere of leisure and seek to entice the tourist gaze with the promise of physical restoration and, subsequently, emotional salvation from the stresses of modern life. Photographs of interior spaces like restaurants, bars, lobbies, and other amenities as well as the modern architecture of the exterior mark the luxurious environs of hotels that offer modern conveniences and, at the same time, frame the tourist experience as a commercial transaction. Flamenco dancers dressed in the traditional "vestido de gitana" and men donning a cordobés hat who pose with Andalusian horses present a sense of authenticity that packages an exotic otherness to entice tourists by marketing difference and the promise of purity. Parallel and complementary to the urbanization of the coasts and the construction of necessary infrastructure to support it with roads and sanitation services, communication networks, air travel, and housing is the construction of the narrative that bolsters the urban development projects and bolsters the ideology of consumption that drives it.

Thus, by building on the foundations laid in both tourism and urban studies, this book has forged new ground that examines the ways in which cultural production offers an alibi of sorts for the paradox of destroying the natural beauty of the coasts in order to fabricate paradise. The visual media I discussed suppress any social conflict and erase authenticity to add another layer of paradox to the creation of paradise. The creative destruction behind the development of paradise along the coasts is likewise reflected in the visual culture associated with coastal tourism in which authenticity is staged and Spain's tourism narrative is solidified. By combining the fields of tourism and urban studies, then, we are not only better able to discern the subtle ideological practices that coincide with and support the political and economic policies that push urban development along the coasts, but we can lay bare the unseen power dynamics that simultaneously dismantle difference and repackage it as a commodity for consumption. Lefebvre's observation that "consumption of space" creates a "space of consumption" along Spain's Mediterranean coasts is not only visible in the material construction along the shoreline but in the cultural production that accompanies it as well. The discourse latent in cultural production whether material, visual, plastic, or textual offers us an entry point from which to contemplate the possibility to resist the values of consumption propagated by the narrative of development that has been and continues to be tied to tourism in Spain.

Looking backward, we can see the trajectory of urban development along the Spanish coasts from the early 1960s to today in the physical growth of buildings and cement that have corrupted, literally and figuratively, the Mediterranean coastline. By studying the cultural production associated with coastal tourism, we can perceive a similar trajectory but—even more poignant—we can point to concerns posed that sought to pierce the illusion of transparency and questions raised that attempted to point out the paradoxes inherent within the dominant narrative of development. While Palomino's *Torremolinos Gran Hotel* expresses a prescient concern for overdevelopment guided by the blind greed of land speculation and back-room deals, Manegat's *Spanish Show* anticipates and laments, from a conservative point of view, the loss of authenticity as culture is progressively commodified with the expansion of tourism and the growth of urban spaces along the coast. Photographers like Martin Parr and Carlos Pérez Siquier upend and invert the visual grammar of postcards and tourism propaganda to expose the dislocation of space and place, and through social media platforms like Instagram current photographers including María Moldes and Roberto Alcaraz continue to explore the ironies of tourism iconography that frames a concept of "place" at the same time that global communication networks erase the boundaries of space. Lastly, cultural icons such as Jesús Gil emblematize the corruption, collusion, and greed that Palomino anticipated as the logical outcome of rampant land speculation and the guiding principle to "forrarse" (make a killing). The ghost hotels that populate the Spanish landscape along the coasts (and in the interior of the peninsula as well) may be understood culturally as monuments that commemorate the pervading atmosphere of crisis since the financial meltdown of 2008 but also harken back to Carlos Moraleda's prophetic depiction of catastrophe at the end of Palomino's novel.

That tourism and urban development have been intimately intertwined to construct, literally and figuratively, the dominant narrative for modernization in Spain for over the last half-century is not really at question. What is, has been, and continues to be the question at the heart of the story told about Spain's development revolves around agency and authorship, who is included and who is excluded from the story and why. A close examination of the various types of cultural production, some of which reflect that narrative and others that resist it, allows us not only to see more clearly the paradox of paradise but also to explore the possibility for telling a different story, forging an alternative narrative, and taking back, as David Harvey urges, the right to the city.

NOTES

INTRODUCTION

1. Dean MacCannell, *The Tourist: A New Theory of the Leisure Class*, 9th ed. (New York: Schocken Books, 1976).
2. MacCannell, *The Tourist*, 2.
3. MacCannell, *The Tourist*, 2.
4. MacCannell, *The Tourist*, 13.
5. Sasha D. Pack, *Tourism and Dictatorship: Europe's Peaceful Invasion of Franco's Spain* (New York: Palgrave Macmillan, 2006).
6. Pack, *Tourism and Dictatorship: Europe's Peaceful Invasion of Franco's Spain (New York: Palgrave Macmillan, 2006)*, 1.
7. Pack, *Tourism and Dictatorship*, 108.
8. Pack, *Tourism and Dictatorship*, 10–15.
9. Eugenia Afinoguénova and Jaume Martí-Olivella, eds., *Spain Is (Still) Different: Tourism and Discourse in Spanish Identity* (Lanham, MD: Lexington Books, 2008).
10. Afinoguénova and Martí-Olivella, *Spain Is (Still) Different, xiv*.
11. Justin Crumbaugh, *Destination Dictatorship: The Spectacle of Spain's Tourist Boom and the Reinvention of Difference* (Albany: State University of New York Press, 2009).
12. Crumbaugh, *Destination Dictatorship*, 10.
13. Alicia Fuentes Vega, *Bienvenido, Mr. Turismo: Cultura visual del boom en España* (Madrid: Ediciones Cátedra, 2017).
14. Jordi Puig Castellano, *1960s–1970s Costa Brava: Postals, postales, cartes postales, postcards* (Girona, Spain: Úrsula Llibres, 2017).
15. Francisco Franco, *Ley 197/1963 Centros y zonas de interés turístico nacional*, BOE-A-1963-22673 (Madrid, Spain: Boletín Oficial del Estado, 1963).
16. Javier Sola Teyssiere, *Ordenación territorial y urbanística de las zonas turísticas*, 2nd ed. (Seville, Spain: Instituto Andaluz de Administración Pública, 2007).
17. Teyssiere, *Ordenación territorial y urbanística*, 45.

18. Teyssiere, *Ordenación territorial y urbanística*, 45.

19. Teyssiere, *Ordenación territorial y urbanística*, 46.

20. Teyssiere, *Ordenación territorial y urbanística*, 47.

21. Pack, *Tourism and Dictatorship*, 120.

22. Pack, *Tourism and Dictatorship*, 121.

23. Ángel Palomino, *El milagro turístico* (Barcelona, Spain: Plaza and Janes, Editores, 1972).

24. Palomino, *El milagro turístico*, 220.

25. Palomino, *El milagro turístico*, 222. For more on the urban development on the coasts and the impact on local culture, ecology, and economy, see M. Barke, J. Towner, and M. T. Newton, eds., *Tourism in Spain: Critical Issues* (Wallingford, UK: CAB International, 1996). See also John Pollard and Rafael Domínguez Rodríguez, "Unconstrained Growth: The Development of a Spanish Resort," *Geography* 80, no. 1 (January 1995): 33–44, and Mar Loren, *Costa-grafías: El litoral turístico como sistema de diferencias* (Seville: Universidad de Sevilla, 2014).

26. Palomino, *El milagro turístico*, 210–13. This reference to the creation of an "earthly paradise" is just one of many cultural connections between modern tourism and the medieval pilgrimage. In both instances, large masses of people are motivated to find salvation from a broken world through travel and the search for a utopic space. As Peter Osborne notes in *Traveling Light: Photography, Travel, and Visual Culture*, both the modern tourist and the medieval pilgrim extol a faith in the "potency of visual images and the ritual aims of traveling" and thus their desire to recover a perceived lost wholeness often manifests in a penchant for sacred objects. Souvenirs for the modern tourist, Osborne states, are like relics to pilgrims that reify the salvation experience and offer means to relive that sense of transcendence repeatedly through nostalgia after the journey is complete. The distinction Osborne makes, however, is that while the tourist and the pilgrim may be seeking a sense of connectedness in a fragmented world, most tourists understand that they move through a fiction where images and objects are "symbolic devices which invent their own world." Peter D. Osborne, *Travelling Light: Photography, Travel, and Visual Culture* (New York: Manchester University Press, 2000), 87–89.

27. Rafael Esteve Secall, *Ocio, turismo, y hoteles en la Costa del Sol* (Málaga, Spain: University of Málaga, 1982), 19–20.

28. Esteve Secall, *Ocio, turismo*, 25.

29. Manuel Planelles, "La urbanización de la primera línea de costa crece un 33% en 24 años," *El País*, August 22, 2016.

30. Tomás Mazón, "Benidorm: Un destino turístico de altura," *Gran Tour: Revista de Investigación Turísticas* 2 (2010): 9.

31. Manuel Vázquez Montalbán, *La literatura en la construcción de la ciudad democrática* (Barcelona: Crítica [Grijalbo Mondadori], 1998), 94.
32. Sharon Zukin, *Point of Purchase: How Shopping Changed American Culture* (New York: Routledge, 2004).
33. Zukin, *Point of Purchase*, 33.
34. Zukin, *Point of Purchase*, 34.
35. See also "The Politics of 1992" by Helen Graham and Antonio Sánchez in *Spanish Cultural Studies: An Introduction,* ed. Helen Graham and Jo Labanyi (New York: Oxford University Press, 1995), and Emilio Lamo de Espinosa's "La normalización de España: España, Europa y la modernidad," *Claves de Razón Práctica*, no. 111 (April 2001).
36. Vázquez Montalbán, *La literatura*, 94.
37. Ramón Fernández Durán, *El tsunami urbanizador español y mundial* (Barcelona: Virus Editorial, 2006).
38. Fernández Durán, *El tsunami*, 30–32. In 2001, José Luis Guerín, a Spanish documentary filmmaker, released his now iconic film *En construcción* that followed the experiences of several inhabitants of Barcelona's working-class neighborhood known as the Raval as the area in the heart of the city gentrified and transformed into a bright, shiny modern urban space that marketed itself to upper middle-class professionals. The 2018 documentary from Laura Álvarez titled *City for Sale* may be thought of as a kind of sequel to Guerín's classic film about the invisible hands that reconstruct the built environment. Álvarez's film offers a chronicle of the harmful effects of what she calls the tourism real estate complex (paraphrasing Eisenhower's notion of the military-industrial complex) that has transformed Barcelona's historic city center, Ciutat Vella, into a site of consumption and has outnumbered the neighborhood's lifelong residents with a crush of tourists. Laura Álvarez, dir., *City for Sale* (Spain: Bausan Films 2018).
39. Fernández Durán, *El tsunami*, 32–34.
40. In "Turismo y libertad," Vázquez Montalbán states that the turn to tourism "presagiaba la llegada de la libertad" which was also accelerated by the ministerial changes in 1962. By calling it a "neolibertad" (neoliberty), he draws the connection between the political freedom associated with democracy and the economic policies of neoliberalism that emerge in Spain after the dictatorship. Tourism in the 1960s, Vázquez Montalbán asserts, offered a prelude to this connection in which Spaniards measured freedom through leisure and consumption. Yet, he concludes that this is an "equivalencia falsa" (false equivalent) fabricated through the desire to appeal to the gaze of the European tourist who is only interested in "esta España turística, con paella

y cordero a la chilindrón con sol y paisaje destrozado por los rascacielos de verano" (this touristic Spain, with paella and lamb with tomatoes and peppers, with sun and a landscape destroyed by the skyscrapers of summer). Manuel Vázquez Montalbán, *Crónica sentimental de España* (Barcelona: Grijalbo Mondadori, 1998), 193.

41. Ana Penyas, *Todo bajo el sol* (Barcelona: Penguin Random House Grupo Editorial, 2021).

42. Henri Lefebvre, *The Production of Space*, trans. Donald Nicholson-Smith (Malden, MA: Blackwell, 1991), 353.

43. Lefebvre, *The Production of Space*, 354. In "Cultural Geography, Consumption, and the City," Mark Jayne interrogates how "cities shape consumption and consumption shapes cities" to understand urban spaces not as mere backdrops to human relations but to reconceptualize them as factors that actively influence political and economic formations, human social relations, and even individual and collective identities. The decline of manufacturing industries and the upsurge of service industries in conjunction with social and demographic forces have led to increased competition between cities to attract businesses, speculators, and consumers by fabricating a brand image and a "place myth" that promotes the city as culturally rich and diverse. The urban space itself becomes a spectacle designed for and developed around the consumption practices of the new middle classes. Mark Jayne, "Cultural Geography, Consumption and the City," *Geography* 91, no. 1 (2006): 36–39. See also Mark Jayne's *Cities and Consumption* (London: Routledge, 2005).

44. Mario Gaviria et al., *España a go-gó: Turismo charter y neocolonialismo del espacio* (Madrid: Ediciones Turner, 1974), 277.

45. Gaviria et al., *España a go-gó*, 279.

46. See Gaviria's book *Benidorm*, in which he asserts the city as a model for other tourist cities, defends it against criticism, and contradicts prejudices of those who malign the city as vulgar and banal. This book is interesting because it is presented as a kind of coffee table book, large and hard-covered, with big, glossy photos by Bianca Berlín that engage the viewer's gaze as if to market the city. Gaviria was one of the key protagonists in the unlikely and unsuccessful application to declare Benidorm a UNESCO World Heritage Site for its value as a urbanist, social, and tourist model for development. Mario Gaviria, *Benidorm* (Benidorm, Spain: Benidorm City Council and Lunwerg Editores, 1990).

47. Henri Lefebvre, *Toward an Architecture of Enjoyment*, trans. Robert Bononno (Minneapolis: University of Minnesota Press, 2014), 99.

48. Lefebvre, *Toward an Architecture of Enjoyment*, 99.

49. Dean MacCannell, *Empty Meeting Grounds: The Tourist Papers* (London: Routledge, 1992).

50. MacCannell, *Empty Meeting Grounds*, 230–40.

51. Manuel Delgado, *La ciudad mentirosa: Fraude y miseria del "modelo Barcelona*, 3rd ed. (Madrid: Los Libros de la Catarta, 2017), 165.

52. Delgado, *La ciudad mentirosa*, 274.

53. Lefebvre, *The Production of Space*, 28.

54. Edward Relph, *Place and Placelessness* (London: Pion Limited, 1976), 93.

55. Relph, *Place and Placelessness*, 93.

56. David Harvey, *The Urban Experience* (Baltimore, MD: Johns Hopkins University Press, 1989), 249.

57. Harvey, *The Urban Experience*, 249–50.

58. Harvey, *The Urban Experience*, 250.

59. China C. Cabrerizo, *La ciudad negocio: Turismo y movilización social en pugna* (Madrid: Cisma Editorial, 2016), 22.

60. Despite massive investments since the 1960s, Andalucía continues to be one of the poorest provinces in the European Union.

61. Cabrerizo, *La ciudad negocio*, 61–62.

62. Iván Murray Mas, *Capitalismo y turismo en España: Del "milagro económico" a la "gran crisis"* (Barcelona: Alba Sud Editorial, 2015), 18–19.

63. Murray Mas, *Capitalismo y turismo*, 19.

64. The term was coined by Manuel Delgado in a column in *El País*. Manuel Delgado, "Turistofobia," *El País*, July 11, 2008 2008, https://elpais.com/diario/2008/07/12/catalunya/1215824840_850215.html. See the UNWTO's report: United Nations World Tourism Organization, *'Overtourism'?: Understanding and Managing Urban Tourism Growth beyond Perceptions* (Madrid, Spain: UNWTO, 2018). In *Ciudad de vacaciones: Conflictos urbanos en espacios turísticos*, Claudio Milano and José Mansilla designate 2014 as year 0 when "turismofobia" first emerged. Their book offers a transatlantic analysis of the manifestation of "turismofobia" in cities in the Iberian Peninsula as well as Latin America where many cities, not necessarily on the coast, have integrated tourism as an essential paradigm of their urban development strategies and policies. The city as a marketplace, the authors assert, epitomizes the neoliberal character of late capitalism yet by juxtaposing case studies of urban social activism from cities in Spain, Portugal, and Latin America the authors hope to find some strategies for resistance. Claudio Milano and José A. Mansilla, eds., *Ciudad de vacaciones: Conflictos urbanos en espacios turísticos* (Barcelona: Pol*len edicions, 2018).

65. See Ian Brossat, *Airbnb: La ciudad uberizada*, trans. Sagrario Ruiz Elizalde (Pamplona, Spain: Katakrak Liburuak, 2018).

66. Francisco Carballo-Cruz, "Causes and Consequences of the Spanish Economic Crisis: Why the Recovery Is Taken [*sic*] So Long?," *Panoeconomicus* 3 (2011): 310–12.

67. Carballo-Cruz, "Causes and Consequences," 313.

68. Puneet Dhaliwal, "Public Squares and Resistance: The Politics of Space in the Indignados Novement," *Interface: A Journal for and about Social Movements* 4, no. 1 (May 2012): 256–59.

69. *Manifiesto de la Assemblea del Raval* (Barcelona: Assemblea del Raval, 2014), https://asamblearaval.files.wordpress.com/2014/08/viscalabarceloneta_ manifiesto-comunicado.pdf. Also known as the "Barrio Chino" (Red Light District), the Raval neighborhood figures prominently in the writings of Manuel Vázquez Montalbán, especially in the Pepe Carvalho detective series. The physical transformations of this area of Barcelona as well as other areas epitomize the promises and failures of modernity in Spain and are intimately tied with memory as the city changes and places of the past disappear. In the prologue to the English translation of *Barcelonas*, Váquez Montalbán acknowledges the effects of the urban reconstruction projects in preparation for the 1992 Olympics on the solidarity of residents in Barcelona and questions the narrative of modernization that is so intimately tied to urban development: "Has it not turned what might have been a model of democratic urban expansion into a speculative frenzy, determined by the 'city as market' model which posits urban development as a process tailor-made to benefit the wealthiest social classes?" Manuel Vázquez Montalbán, *Barcelonas*, trans. Andy Robinson (London: Verso, 1992), 7.

70. MacCannell, *Empty Meeting Grounds*, 5.

71. MacCannell, *Empty Meeting Grounds*, 9.

CHAPTER 1

1. Secretaría General de Turismo, *Turismo 2020: Plan del turismo español horizonte 2020* (Madrid: Ministerio de Industria, Turismo, y Comercio, 2007), 10, https:// www.tourspain.es/es-es/Conozcanos/Documents/HistoricoPoliticaTuristica/ Horizonte%202020%20-%20Plan%20Turismo%20Espa%C3%B1ol%200812. pdf.

2. Secretaría General de Turismo, *Turismo 2020*, 7.

3. Secretaría General de Turismo, *Turismo 2020*, 22–27.

4. Secretaría de Estado de Turismo, *Plan nacional e integral de turismo (PNIT): 2012–2015*, (Madrid: Ministerio de Industria, Energía y Turismo, 2012), 69,

https://turismo.gob.es/es-es/servicios/Documents/Plan-Nacional-Integral-Turismo-2012-2015.pdf. In *España a go-gó*, Mario Gaviria lays out the blueprint for a resort hotel from the cost of the land to the services offered to the proximity to restaurants, train stations, airports, and shopping districts.

5. Ignacio Lillo, "El alcalde respalda el hotel del puerto y lo ve como un nuevo icono para la ciudad," *Diario Sur* (Málaga, Spain), May 30, 2015, https://www.diariosur.es/malaga-capital/201505/30/alcalde-respalda-hotel-puerto-20150530153744.html.

6. Nowhere is the iconic importance of the hotel more noticeable than in Benidorm where the tallest hotel in Europe is located. The Gran Hotel Bali is a four-star hotel that opened in 2002 and is 610 feet tall (690 ft. with the hotel spire). It was the tallest building in Spain until the Torre Espacio opened in 2006, but it continues to be the tallest building on the Mediterranean Sea. It is now the second tallest building in Benidorm after the residential Intempo building, which opened in 2014. The Gran Hotel Bali also plays an important role in the Bigas Luna film *Huevos de oro* (1993). At the time of filming it was under construction, but in the film the hotel represents the dream of the protagonist Benito González (Javier Bardem) to create the tallest building in Benidorm.

7. Marc Augé, *Non-places: An Introduction to Supermodernity*, trans. John Howe, 4th ed. (New York: Verso, 1995).

8. Augé, *Non-places*, 63.

9. Augé, *Non-places*, 70.

10. *Costa Ibérica: Hacia la ciudad del ocio*, a book developed by students and professors at the Escuela Superior de Arquitectura (ESARQ) in Barcelona and based on studies performed during a three-week workshop in 1998, combines cartography, urban planning, population analysis and graphic design to analyze the effects of the "sueño californiano" (California dream). Urban development has sought and continues to seek, the authors argue, to combine gastronomy, leisure, nature and construction, while disregarding their ecological impact, to increase population density while maximizing area in order to skyrocket land value and attract capital, making the Iberian coast the "equivalente europeo de California" (the European equivalent of California). *Equipo de Arquitectos MVRDV, Costa Ibérica: Hacia la Ciudad del Ocio* (Barcelona: Actar, 2001), 172–73.

11. "Estilo del relax" is a term coined by Juan Antonio Ramírez and Diego Santos in 1987 to describe the architectural style that proliferated along the N-340 national highway that stretches over one thousand kilometers from Cádiz along the coast to Barcelona. Characterized by chic, undulating shapes and

unsymmetrical forms that fuse a kind of art deco style with other modern-
ist aesthetics, the so-called "estilo del relax" privileges form over function,
design over planning in ways that mirror and also promote the ideology of
leisure and pleasure along the coasts. For a more detailed understanding of
the "estilo del relax" and the ideological implications of its aesthetic, see Tecla Lumbreras, *El estilo del relax: N-340. Málaga, b. 1953–1965* (Málaga, Spain:
Colegio Oficial de Arquitectos en Málga, Ayuntamiento de Málaga, Observatorio de Medio Ambiente Urbano, 2009), and Tecla Lumbreras, *El relax expandido: La economía turística en Málaga y la Costa del Sol* (Málaga, Spain: Colegio Oficial de Arquitectos en Málga, Ayuntamiento de Málaga, Observatorio
de Medio Ambiente Urbano, 2009). See also Jordi Granell I March et al., *La
arquitectura del sol / Sunland Architecture* (Valencia: Col·legi d'Arquitectes de
Catalunya, 2002), and Maite Méndez Baiges, ed., *Arquitectura, ciudad y territorio en Málaga (1900–2011)* (Málaga, Spain: Geometría Asociación Cultural,
2012), in particular her chapter "La arquitectura del sol: El Movimiento Mod-
erno durante los años cincuenta y sesenta" (187–224).

12. Wolfgang Iser was a German literary critic famous for his contributions to
Reader Response Theory in texts like *The Implied Reader* (1972) and *The Act of
Reading* (1976). He outlined reading as a dynamic process in which the reader
plays an active role in creating meaning by filling in the text's unwritten gaps.

13. The term *ludic* used here and throughout this book refers to the atmosphere
of play, pleasure, and leisure associated with the hotel's physical space where
everyday stresses, political or social conflicts, and mundane concerns disappear often through acts of conspicuous consumption.

14. Hal Foster, *Recodings: Art, Spectacle, Cultural Politics* (Seattle: Bay Press, 1985),
83.

15. Julio Manegat, *Spanish Show* (Barcelona: Editorial Planeta SA, 1965), 21–23.

16. While the narrator does not indicate that don Feliciano García is corrupt in
any way, Rafael Chirbes scrutinizes the generation after the Spanish Civil War
that exploited Spain's impoverished conditions for their own individual enrichment and empowerment. The theme of a generation that betrayed the
painful memories and experiences of the Spanish Civil War for their own
individual social mobility appears in virtually every novel he has written. In
an interview with Chirbes, he commented, "Para subir al escalón de arriba
tienes que aplastar a él del escalón de abajo y empujar a él que ocupa el escalón de arriba. Digamos, hay una violencia latente en esta sociedad apacible
que asume la violencia y el ascenso el subir al escalón de arriba" (To move
up a step you need to crush the one who is below you and push out the one
who is above you. Let's just say, there is a latent violence in this supposedly

peaceful society that internalizes the violence and the ascent to the next social class). William Nichols, "Sifting through the Ashes: An Interview with
Rafael Chirbes," *Arizona Journal of Hispanic Cultural Studies* 12 (2008): 231.

17. Manegat, *Spanish Show*, 22.

18. Coincidentally, the narrator in Manegat's novel details the history of the land
along the coast that was being developed. The property was divided between
two brothers, Quimet and Pedro, in the Blanch family who had lived in the
area for generations. Quimet, who owned the property perceived to be more
valuable near the beach, had disappeared years earlier. Pedro, a simple farmer
used his inherited land for his own subsistence but because it was not near
the shoreline it was not perceived as valuable by others in the tourism industry. The narrator notes the invasion of outsiders drawn to the land speculation
of the coasts, "Pero otros muchos cobraron carta de ciudadanía: construc-
tores, hoteleros, dirigentes de empresas inmobiliarias, agentes de compra y
venta de fincas. Muchos de ellos buscaron el camino de la casa de los Blanch
y hablaron con el dueño. No, aquellos terrenos baldíos de la playa no le pert-
enecían a él, sino a su hermano; y de éste nada se sabía. Años atrás recibieron
una carta desde Gerona en la que ni siquiera indicaba sus señas." (But many
others gained their citizenship: constructors, hoteliers, real estate agents,
mortgage brokers. Many of them sought the road to the Blanch household
and spoke with the owner. No, those empty lands on the beach don't belong
to him, rather his brother; and nobody knew anything about him. Years earlier they received a letter from Gerona in which he didn't even indicate his
address.) Manegat, *Spanish Show*, 259. The tension between brothers over
rights to the land being developed is echoed in Rafael Chirbes's novel *Crematorio* (Barcelona: Anagrama, 2007).

19. Manegat, *Spanish Show*, 258.

20. Manegat, *Spanish Show*, 23.

21. Manegat, *Spanish Show*, 25. Don Feliciano may be viewed from a certain perspective as a precursor to someone like Jesús Gil, the corrupt real estate mogul from Marbella who rose to fame in the 1990s and early 2000s. Although
Manegat's novel never portrays don Feliciano as politically corrupt, he is criticized for his boundless greed and the narrator remarks on his economic and
political influence in the region.

22. In a Bakhtinian way, Manegat includes the voices of workers in *Spanish Show*
with conversations where characters who were farmers and miner discuss
their reasons for migrating to the coast to work in construction or as waiters.
They articulate their reasons for moving but also express a sense of loss that
connects the economic and urban transformations of Spain in the 1960s with

a tremendous shift in the demands for labor. In one scene, the narrator describes two construction workers who comment that "gracias a las construcciones de aquí hemos podido levantar cabeza" (thanks to the constructions around here we have been able to get ahead). As they lay bricks, the wall they build is infused with their memories of misery but also, the narrator asserts, embodies the hopes they, and thousands of others all along the coast, have invested in tourism. Manegat, *Spanish Show*, 49.

23. Manegat, *Spanish Show*, 264.
24. Manegat, *Spanish Show*, 265.
25. Manegat, *Spanish Show*, 265.
26. Manegat, *Spanish Show*, 267.
27. Manegat, *Spanish Show*, 131.
28. Manegat, *Spanish Show*, 257.
29. John L. Comaroff and Jean Comaroff, *Ethnicity, Inc.* (Chicago: University of Chicago Press, 2009), 19–20.
30. In Berlanga's 1953 classic satirical film *Bienvenido Mr. Marshall*, the residents of a rural northern Spanish town attempt to entice the gaze, and economic investment, of Americans in the post-war Marshall Plan by erecting the whitewashed façade of an Andalusian village and donning the polka dot flamenco dresses and the traditional wide-brimmed Cordobés hats associated with Andalusian popular culture and folkloric practices.
31. Manegat, *Spanish Show*, 258. In her introduction to *Constructing Identity in Contemporary Spain*, Jo Labanyi notes the paradox of the development of a "national culture" as a concept during the Romantic period that is also accompanied by the mythification of folk culture that are resemanticized as an expression of the national "soul." Jo Labanyi, ed., *Constructing Identity in Contemporary Spain: Theoretical Debates and Cultural Practice* (New York: Oxford University Press, 2002), 5. In *The Sublime South: Andalusia, Orientalism, and the Making of Modern Spain*, José Luis Venegas studies the shift in the rhetoric of the Franco regime's attitude toward Andalusia from the autarkic period in the 1940s to the technocratic development policies of the 1950s and 1960s. Through orientalist representations of Andalusia, Venegas asserts, the Franco state maintained its policy of evasion in the 1940s by projecting Spain as impervious to modernization and change through folkloric images in blockbuster films that reinforced the country's rural identity. As Spain established military and economic agreements with the United States, opened to foreign investments, and promoted tourism, the country's difference, Venegas asserts, became a marketable commodity, and Andalusia was

"gradually transformed from an archaic land populated by dancing gypsies to an appealing destination for sun-starved northern Europeans." José Luis Venegas, *The Sublime South: Andalusia, Orientalism, and the Making of Modern Spain* (Evanston, IL: Northwestern University Press, 2018), 98.

32. Manegat, *Spanish Show*, 90.
33. If the decoration of the bars and hotels evoke stereotypes of Andalusia through their mise en scène, the flamenco dancers Gavilán and Paloma emphasize the performative aspect of the Andalusian stereotypes they project in their show, literally a spectacle. Gavilán admits his identity and their flamenco show is a lie that only serves to "hipnotizar" a los turistas" (hypnotize tourists) Manegat, *Spanish Show*, 74.
34. In Manegat's novel, Miguel Olives is able to pay off his loans in just a year not because the bar has proven itself a lucrative success but because it has become a site for the sale and consumption of illicit drugs, namely marijuana and heroin. Manegat highlights that even from the early days of Spain's tourism industry, the ludic atmosphere of sand and sun fomented the expansion of an underground network of illicit drug trade and trafficking.
35. Jean Baudrillard, *Simulacra and Simulation*, trans. Sheila Faria Glaser (Ann Arbor: University of Michigan Press, 1994), 77.
36. Manegat, *Spanish Show*, 40.
37. Manegat, *Spanish Show*, 43.
38. Manegat, *Spanish Show*, 145.
39. Comaroff, *Ethnicity, Inc.*, 20.
40. Before dedicating himself full-time to writing, Palomino worked as an entrepreneur in the tourism industry overseeing direction of different hotel chains, in particular the Meliá. Ángel Palomino, *Torremolinos Gran Hotel* (Barcelona: Editorial Planeta, 1971), 16.
41. Palomino, *Torremolinos Gran Hotel*, 122.
42. Lefebvre, *The Production of Space*, 28.
43. Palomino, *El milagro turístico*, 210.
44. Palomino, *Torremolinos Gran Hotel*, 40.
45. Palomino, *Torremolinos Gran Hotel*, 12–16.
46. Palomino, *Torremolinos Gran Hotel*, 13.
47. Palomino, *Torremolinos Gran Hotel*, 87–88.
48. Palomino, *Torremolinos Gran Hotel*, 88.
49. Palomino, *Torremolinos Gran Hotel*, 154.
50. Palomino, *Torremolinos Gran Hotel*, 68.
51. Palomino, *Torremolinos Gran Hotel*, 148.

52. Palomino, *Torremolinos Gran Hotel*, 153; Fredric Jameson, *Postmodernism, or, The Cultural Logic of Late Capitalism* (Durham, NC: Duke University Press, 1992), 27.

53. Palomino, *Torremolinos Gran Hotel*, 163.

54. Palomino's conservative politics emerge more clearly with a notably moralistic tone when he describes the perceived loss of solemnity associated with a traditional Catholic mass as it is celebrated along the Costa del Sol. Rather than sport coats and ties, he implies would be appropriate, the significance of the church seems lost on attendees who wear mini-skirts, short pants, and short sleeves.

55. Palomino, *Torremolinos Gran Hotel*, 180.

56. Lefebvre, *The Production of Space*, 353.

57. For an analysis of the impact of the audiovisual industry in Spain to promote tourism in Spain through the representation of tourist spaces, see Jorge Nieto Ferrando, Antonia del Rey Reguillo, and Eugenia Afinoguenova, "Narration and Placement of Tourist Spaces in Spanish Fiction Cinema (1951–1977)," *Revista Latina de Comunicación Social* 70 (2015): 584–610.

58. Palomino delves deeper into the myth of the "sueca" in his book *Carta abierta a una sueca*. Ángel Palomino, *Carta abierta a una sueca* (Madrid: Ediciones 99, 1974).

59. Palomino, *Torremolinos Gran Hotel*, 88.

60. Claudio Minca and Tim Oakes, eds., *Travels in Paradox: Remapping Tourism* (Lanham, MD: Rowman and Littlefield, 2006), 10.

61. Despite this distinction, there is a connection between Foucault's reading of the panopticon and the surveillance within the hotel in which both serve as "political technology" that "define power relations in terms of the everyday life of men." Michel Foucault, *Discipline and Punish: The Birth of the Prison*, trans. Alan Sheridan (New York: Vintage, 1977), 205. As I outline, the construction of spectacle, its consumption, and its surveillance ultimately serve the capitalist desires of the Board of Directors and the economic system itself.

62. Palomino, *Torremolinos Gran Hotel*, 132.

63. Palomino, *Torremolinos Gran Hotel*, 132.

64. Palomino, *Torremolinos Gran Hotel*, 212–13.

65. David Harvey, "The Right to the City," *New Left Review* 53 (2008): 38.

66. In "The Art of Rent" Harvey specifically mentions the hotel industry as an example of the mechanisms of monopoly rent in which commercial capitalists purchase land, but revenue is generated through the resources offered on that land and the selling of shares for stakes in the company that oversees the services produced by the hotel. He writes, "The locational version would

be centrality (for the commercial capitalist) relative to, say, the transport and communications network or proximity (for the hotel chain) to some highly concentrated activity (such as a financial centre). The commercial capitalist and the hotelier are willing to pay a premium for the land because of accessibility. These are the indirect cases of monopoly rent. It is not the land, resource or location of unique qualities which is traded but the commodity or service produced through their use. In the second case, the land or resource is directly traded upon (as when vineyards or prime real estate sites are sold to multinational capitalists and financiers for speculative purposes)" David Harvey, "The Art of Rent: Globalization, Monopoly and the Commodification of Culture," *Social Register* 38 (2002): 94.

67. Hernando de Soto, *The Mystery of Capital: Why Capitalism Triumphs in the West and Fails Everywhere Else* (New York: Basic Books, 2000).
68. Palomino, *Torremolinos Gran Hotel*, 13.
69. Alfred Chandler, *The Visible Hand: The Managerial Revolution in American Business* (Boston, MA: Harvard University Press, 1977).
70. In Alfredo Taján's novel *Pez Espada* (2010), the hotel serves as an emblem for the social, political and economic transformations of Spain, far removed from the "juerga interminable" of the Costa del Sol during the early years of the tourist boom. In the novel, Gustavo Marín, a retired economist returns to the hotel after fifty years and ruminates about the "transitions" and transformations of the locale, the region, and the country. Marín narrates in first person and directs his comments to an implied "ustedes" to suggest a shared memory and nostalgia for a Proustian lost past in which the "especulación inmobliaria" has transformed the Costa del Sol into the "Costa del Cemento." He describes the Hotel Pez Espada in the present as a "catacumba" and decides to narrate its past "cuando la Costa del Sol estaba libre de los vuelos chárter que hoy vomitan millones y millones de turistas, que no de viajeros, turistas productivos, víctimas de la masificación, símbolos vivientes del gran instinto capitalista que expande el ocio para hacer negocio." Alfredo Taján, *Pez Espada* (La Coruña, Spain: Ediciones del Viento, 2010), 38.
71. Palomino, *Torremolinos Gran Hotel*, 214.
72. Palomino, *Torremolinos Gran Hotel*, 280.
73. Sally Faulkner, *A Cinema of Contradiction: Spanish Film in the 1960s* (Edinburgh, Scotland: Edinburgh University Press, 2006).
74. Crumbaugh, *Destination Dictatorship*, 20.
75. Rafael Gómez Alonso, "El turismo no es un gran invento: Aperturismo y recepción del ocio y consumo a través del cine español de los 60," *Área Abierta* 15 (Noviembre 2006): 9. See also Nieto Ferrando, del Rey Reguill,

and Afinoguenova, "Narration and Placement of Tourist Spaces," and Gorka Zamarreño Aramendia, Elena Ruiz Romero de la Cruz, and Elena de los Reyes Cruz Ruiz, "Málaga y la marca territorio en el cine del turismo del Franquismo," *International Journal of Scientific Management and Tourism* 3, no. 3 (2017).

76. In "La construcción de la imagen de la arquitectura del relax," Maite Méndez Baiges and Inmaculada Hurtado Suárez suggest that the "lenguaje de la arquitectura turística" (language of the tourist architecture) along the Costa del Sol, emerged as a hybridization of high and low styles whose visually provocative, chic international sensibility sought to appeal to the consumerist inclinations of foreign tourists. The architecture itself, the authors assert became the "escenificación de la modernidad y la normalidad" (staging of modernity and normality) of Francoist Spain in the 1960s whose symbolic and ideological charge made them prime protagonists for the promotion of tourism both economically and culturally through diverse visual media outlets including the NO-DO newsreels, film, television, print publications, and even postcards. Maite Méndez Baiges and Inmaculada Hurtado Suárez, "La construcción de la imagen de la arquitectura del relax" (paper presented at the Territorios del turismo: El imaginario turístico y la construcción del paisaje conemporáneo, Universidad de Girona, Girona, Spain, 2014), 254.

77. See Alberto García Moreno, *Cine, ciudad y patrimonio en Torremolinos (1959–1979)* (Málaga, Spain: UMA Editorial, 2017); Alberto E. García-Moreno, Carlos Rosa-Jiménez, and María José Márquez-Ballesteros, "Lo banal como patrimonio de la Costa del Sol: Torremolinos 1959–1979," *Pasos: Revista de turismo y patrimonio cultural* 14, no. 1 (2016); and Lourdes Royo Naranjo "Paisaje, patrimonio y arquitectura en los destinos turísticos litorales: Notas sobre la Costa del Sol," *Anales de Historia del Arte* 24 (December 2014).

78. Pedro Lazaga, dir., *El turismo es un gran invento* (Madrid: Pedro Masó Producciones Cinematográficas, 1968); Pedro Lazaga, dir., *El abominable hombre de la Costa del Sol* (Madrid: Pedro Masó Producciones Cinematográficas, 1969).

79. Edward W. Soja, *Thirdspace: Journeys to Los Angeles and Other Real-and-Imagined Places* (Oxford, UK: Blackwell Publishers, 1996).

80. Soja, *Thirdspace*, 243–55. Soja also refers to the exopolis as a "scamscape" where space is not only falsified but fraudulent, masking the corruption of savage capitalism that flows under the luminous "radiant surface" of the exopolis (279). In the case of the Spanish Coasts, one only need think of the infamous corrupt former mayor of Marbella, Jesús Gil, and the widespread presence of global mafias all along the Mediterranean Sea in Spain to see them as "scamscapes."

81. Soja, *Thirdspace*, 81.
82. Soja, *Thirdspace*, 68.
83. Soja, *Thirdspace*, 249–78.
84. Soja, *Thirdspace*, 249.
85. Tatjana Pavlovic, *The Mobile Nation: España cambia de piel (1954–1964)* (Chicago: Intellect, 2011). An especially poignant example of Spain's desire for mobility and modernity may be found in Juan Antonio Bardem's film *El Puente*, when Juan travels across half the country to reach Torremolinos. In one scene, he encounters two American women who leave him behind when his sputtering motorcycle is unable to keep up with their fast convertible, offering an unmistakable visual metaphor for Spain's journey on the road to modernity. Juan Antonio Bardem, dir., *El puente* (Spain: Euromedia Visión, 1976).
86. This abrupt juxtaposition of place, the vibrant modern Costa del Sol and the slow-paced rural Aragón, exemplifies the "sociospatial tensions" Nathan Richardson points to that underlie many of the Spanish comedies from the 1960s, what he calls "paleto cinema," and expose deeper concerns about modernization in Spain, the progressive urbanization of Spanish society, and the assimilation of consumerist values. Nathan E. Richardson, *Postmodern Paletos: Immigration, Democracy, and Globalization in Spanish Narrative and Film, 1950–2000* (Lewisburg, PA: Bucknell University Press, 2002), 71.
87. Harvey, *The Urban Experience*, 256.
88. Guy Debord, *The Society of the Spectacle*, trans. Donald Nicholson-Smith, 8th ed. (New York: Zone Books, 1994), 33.
89. Jean Baudrillard, "The Ecstasy of Communication," in *The Anti-Aesthetic: Essays on Postmodern Culture*, ed. Hal Foster (New York: The New Press, 1983), 131.
90. Baudrillard, "The Ecstasy of Communication," 131.
91. In *Destination Dictatorship*, Justin Crumbaugh explains the origins of the Parador Nacional hotels throughout Spain to commodify Spain's patrimonial heritage and to render it a mediated spectacle through cultural tourism Crumbaugh, *Destination Dictatorship*, 54.
92. Méndez Baiges and Hurtado Suárez, "La construcción de la imagen de la arquitectura del relax," 259.
93. David Harvey, *The Condition of Postmodernity* (Boston, MA: Blackwell, 1990), 284–85.
94. Harvey, *The Condition of Postmodernity*, 286.

CHAPTER 2

1. Osborne, *Travelling Light*, 107. For Osborne the destination as an Edenic utopian ideal links tourism and its imagery to medieval religious pilgrimages

that also emphasized the power of visual images and valued the ritual purpose of travel. In both modern tourism and religious pilgrimages, individuals exhibit a desire to restore wholeness and view themselves as fragments
in a broken world. Osborne asserts that visual iconography frames the experience for both tourist and medieval pilgrim. He states that souvenirs for the
modern tourist are sacred objects akin to the relics sought by the pilgrim.
Travelling Light, 87–88.

2. Osborne, *Travelling Light*, 79.

3. In the case of Spain, the NO-DO (Noticiero Documental) newsreels also served
as a propaganda vehicle to establish a commonly held narrative that promoted the coasts as a paradisiacal space that attracted international tourism and as a result brought "salvation" to Spanish society through the re-
sultant economic boom. See, for example, Rafael R. Tranche and Vicente
Sánchez-Biosca's *NO-DO: El tiempo y la memoria*, 7th ed. (Madrid: Cátedra
and Filmoteca Española, 2005). See also Durante Asensio and Aliaga Cárceles's article "La creación del mito de La Manga del Mar Menor a través de la
promoción turística de NO-DO," *Cuadernos de turismo* 44 (2019). Also, Eric
Storm's "A More Spanish Spain: The Influence of Tourism on the National
Image," in *Metaphors of Spain: Representations of Spanish National Identity in
the Twentieth Century*, ed. Javier Moreno-Luzón and Xosé M. Núñez Seixas
(New York: Berghahn Books, Inc, 2017). In "Fotografía para la promoción
turística: El archive fotográfico de Turespaña," Lucia Domingo Barral and
Asunción Muñoz Montalvo study the evolution of images from the Archivo
Fotográfico de Turespaña that have been used for tourism promotion both
internally and internationally in brochures, posters, guidebooks, and magazines. With the establishment of the Patronato Nacional de Turismo in 1928,
the authors note that photographic images played a vital role in tourism ad-
ministratively and were the primary means to communicate an understanding of Spanish cultural identity internally as well as to promote and attract
tourism internationally. Lucia Domingo Barral and Muñoz Montalvo, "Fotografía para la promoción turística: El archivo fotográfico de Turespaña,"
Estudios Turísticos, no. 213-214 (2017).

4. Osborne, *Travelling Light*, 81–82.

5. Osborne, *Travelling Light*, 84.

6. Norman Stevens attributes the lack of serious scholarly attention on postcards
to their status as "ephemeral items intended to be used and discarded" and
the perception that they were "trivial and insignificant." "Introduction: Welcome to the World of Postcards," in *Postcards in the Library: Invaluable Visual
Resources*, ed. Norman D. Stevens (New York: Haworth Press), 2. Similarly,

Mark Simpson asserts that scholarly attention to postcards has been inconsistent at best, recognizing a paradox that revolves around postcards: "The very materiality of the form (purely a thing) seems, for many, to confirm its immateriality (merely a thing)." Mark Simpson, "Postcard Culture in America: The Traffic in Traffic," in *The Oxford Collection on Visual Culture: Volume Six: U.S. Popular Print Culture 1860–1920*, ed. Christine Bold (New York: Oxford University Press, 2012), 170.

7. Steven Dotterer and Galen Cranz, "The Picture Postcard: Its Development and Role in American Urbanization," *Journal of American Culture* 5, no. 1 (1982): 49.

8. MacCannell, *The Tourist*, 148.

9. Roland Barthes, *Camera Lucida: Reflections on Photography* (New York: Hill and Wang, 1980), 6, 84.

10. Travel and the symbolic power of the trinkets, souvenirs, and postcards acquired by the tourist embodies Bourdieu's notion of "habitus" and the strategies and practices that individuals employ to make sense of their place in the world and to distinguish themselves from other social classes precisely through their consumption of such objects. In essence, said objects acquire an evidentiary value that demonstrates the accumulation of cultural capital through travel that attest to the "taste and distinction of their owner." The experience of travel and tourism, then, conveys a symbolic power akin to literacy and education that offer a legitimating discourse that attests to an individual's accumulation of cultural capital. Pierre Bourdieu, *Outline of a Theory of Practice* (Cambridge: Cambridge University Press, 1977), 197.

11. Barthes, *Camera Lucida*, 88–89.

12. Lefebvre, *The Production of Space*, 353. Winiwarter states that postcard images stand on the verge between dream and reality. See Verena Winiwarter, "Buying a Dream Come True," *Rethinking History* 5, no. 3 (2001), and Verena Winiwarter, "Nationalized Nature on Picture Postcards: Subtexts of Tourism from an Environmental Perspective," *Global Environments* 1, no. 1 (2008): 194.

13. Jonas Larsen, "Geographies of Tourist Photography," in *Geographies of Communication: The Spatial Turn in Media Studies* (Gothenburg: Nordicom, 2006), 241.

14. Larsen, "Geographies of Tourist Photography," 242.

15. See Derrida's epistolary satire *The Post Card* (Chicago: University of Chicago Press, 1980).

16. Naomi Schor, "'Cartes Postales': Representing Paris 1900," *Critical Inquiry* 18, no. 2 (Winter 1992): 237.

17. John Urry, *The Tourist Gaze,* 2nd ed. (London: Sage Publications, 1990).

18. Dean MacCannell, *The Ethics of Sight-Seeing* (Berkeley: University of California Press, 2011), 22.

19. Puig Castellano, *1960s–1970s Costa Brava;* Fuentes Vega, *Bienvenido, Mr. Turismo*. The focus on picture postcards from Spain is starting to draw more attention. See a recent article by Mercè Picornell titled "The back side of the postcard: Subversion of the island tourist gaze in the contemporary Mallorcan imaginary," *Island Studies Journal* 15, no. 2 (2020).
20. Stevens, "Introduction: Welcome to the World of Postcards."
21. Stevens, "Introduction: Welcome to the World of Postcards," 3.
22. Especially the Hotel Tahiti reminds us of the French painter Paul Gauguin who moved away from what he perceived to be the artificial and conventional trappings of modern life in Copenhagen in 1891 to pursue the romantic image of Tahiti in French Polynesia as an untouched paradise where he hoped to rediscover the spirituality and poetic purity of his painting by immersing himself in the perceived authenticity of the island's native cultures. Manuel Vázquez Montalbán's 1979 novel *Los Mares del Sur (The Southern Seas)* rewrites Gauguin's search for cultural authenticity within the class struggles of post-Franco Spain, where unbridled urban speculation threatens traditionally proletariat neighborhoods with capitalist renewal projects and gentrification.
23. The reincarnation of the Don Juan stereotype in Spanish film, especially those from the 1960s and 1970s starring actors like Alfredo Landa or Manolo Escobar, became known as Don Juan Turístico in which the predatory "macho ibérico" (Iberian male) pursues foreign female tourists in the permissive sexual culture (permissive for Spanish men and foreign women not Spanish women) along the coasts.
24. See Jane C. Desmond's *Staging Tourism: Bodies on Display from Waikiki to Sea World* (Chicago: University of Chicago Press, 1999). Desmond examines the development of tourism in Waikiki and the "staging" of Hawaiian culture, specifically through the iconic image of the "hula girl" and in-person live hula performances on the island.
25. In "The Mediterranean Pool: Cultivating Hospitality in the Coastal Hotel," Pau Obrador Pons confirms the prominent position of the coastal hotel, both physically and symbolically, yet also recognizes that the significance of the coastal hotel in the tourist experience has been consistently overlooked. While many in the social sciences have studied the spaces of the hotel, such as the lobby, by emphasizing their anonymous nature and inhabitability, drained of meaning and sociability, Obrador Pons looks at the pool as a site of communality and meaningful hospitality within the commodified spaces of the hotel. Pau Obrador Pons, "The Mediterranean Pool: Cultivating Hospitality in the Coastal Hotel," in *Cultures of Mass Tourism: Doing the Mediterranean*

in the Age of Banal Mobilities, ed. Pau Obrador Pons, Mike Crang, and Penny Travlou (Surrey, England: Ashgate, 2009), 91.

26. In her introduction to *Constructing Identity in Contemporary Spain*, Jo Labanyi examines the appropriation and resemanticization of popular and mass culture during the Franco regime (and its re-appropriation by directors like Pedro Almodóvar after Franco) as a means to create a national narrative through folklore, cinema, and sports. Flamenco, specifically, became a means to forge a Nationalist ideology under Franco in order to attract tourism through the fetishization of the "gypsy" figure and its transformation into a symbol of Spanish national identity. See Storm, "A More Spanish Spain"; William Washabaugh, *Flamenco Music and National Identity in Spain Flamenco Music and National Identity in Spain* (Farnham, UK: Ashgate, 2012); Luis Fernández Cifuentes, "Southern Exposure: Early Tourism and Spanish National Identity," *Journal of Iberian and Latin American Studies* 13, no. 2 (2007).; Lou Charnon-Deutsch's *The Spanish Gypsy: The History of a European Obsession* (University Park, PA: Pennsylvania State University Press, 2004).; and José Colmeiro, "Exorcising Exoticism: "Carmen" and the Construction of Oriental Spain," *Comparative Literature* 54, no. 2 (2002).

27. In this way, the photos of this type of "mosaic" postcard resemble certain aspects of comics or graphic novels in which panels offer discrete pieces of information that, when taken together, communicate motion through time and space to create meaning through a story. Moreover, as Scott McLoud notes in his classic book the creation of meaning and story happens in the blank spaces between the panels where the reader fills in information about time, place, and action to create story. Scott McLoud, *Understanding Comics: The Invisible Art* (New York: Harper Perennial, 1993).

28. The crest is actually a simulacrum. It may evoke a sense of history inherited from a medieval past, but in reality it was created in 1954 by Pedro Zaragoza as part of the marketing strategy to sell tourism in Benidorm.

29. Mythic figures of flamenco would perform in Torremolinos at hotels like the iconic Hotel Miami or the Pez Espada and in *tablaos* (bars that specialized in flamenco performances,like the Bodega Andaluza, El Piyayo, and Las Cuevas de la Alhambra—actually built into a cave to simulate the spaces associated with the "gypsies" of Sacromonte near Granada). The most famous tablao flamenco in Torremolinos was El Jaleo (today the Taberna Flamenca Pepe López) that opened in 1965 and was directed by the famous flamenco dancer Mariquilla (stage name for María Guardia Gómez) and her husband Luis Javier Garrido. Many flamenco superstars performed at El Jaleo such as Camarón de la Isla, guitarrist Paco de Lucía, Habichuela, Manuela Carrasco

among many others. Little has been written about the interconnections between flamenco performances and the surge in coastal tourism in the 1960s.

30. Luis Clemente, *Kitsch y flamenco* (Seville, Spain: Casa de la Provincia, Diputación de Sevilla, 2009), 12.

31. The same coastline appears on a different yet equally fabricated and falsified postcard in which a smiling, bikini-clad woman clings to a pole and seems to wave to the viewer welcomingly. She is situated on the right side of the post-card while the left lower quadrant shows prickly pear cacti, not uncommon in southern Spain, which seem to be encroaching on the beach scene that extends into the distance with the Playamar towers in the background. The image is visible on the Torremolinos Chic website, at http://www.torremolinoschic. com/wp-content/uploads/playa-del-bajondillo.jpg. There is information about the web site at http://www.torremolinoschic.com/presentacion.

32. Constructed by architect Antonio Lamela Martínez, the Playamar complex comprises twenty-one buildings (each one fifteen stories) that sit on fifty-four thousand square meters of land; it includes apartments, commercial zones, and sports areas. Winner of the 1969 Gold Plate for Tourist Merit, the project design reflects the notion that every apartment offers an "optimum view of the sea, ample ventilation, and direct sunlight." Granell I March et al., *La Arquitectura del Sol*, 268. A wide boulevard that runs perpendicular to the sea connects the various apartment blocks to each other, to communal areas, and to the sea, while another avenue circles the perimeter of the apart-ment blocks, allowing access to parking. Each building complex is comple-mented by pool and tennis court facilities, a night club, restaurant, and a small shopping center.

33. Despite the fact that the vast majority of postcard images offer a heteronor-mative view of sexuality along the coasts in Spain, the sexual permissiveness in tourist sites like Torremolinos allowed for the development of so-called "gay tourism" during the 1960s. It is no coincidence that the first openly gay bar in Spain, Tony's, opened in Torremolinos in 1962. A clandestine gay tourist industry emerged in Torremolinos despite the strict morality of the Franco regime, until a police raid in the neighborhood known as the Pasaje Begoña in 1971 led to the closure of many gay establishments to appease the conser-vative elements in the regional government. Not only were the raids a blow to sexual freedom, but they brought a deep and lasting economic impact to Torremolionos. In the wake of the raids, gay tourism declined in Torremoli-nos because tourists in the LGBTQ+ community sought more liberal locales such as Ibiza. In 2018 the Andalusian government unanimously approved

the recognition of the Pasaje Begoña as a Place of Historical Memory and established the Pasaje Begoña Association (https://pasajebegona.com/). For more history on LGTBI+ tourism in Spain, especially in Torremolinos and the Costa del Sol, see José María Valcuende del Río y Rafael Cáceres, "Memória LGTBI+ y Contextos Turísticos: El caso de Torremolinos en la Costa del Sol (España)," in *Quando a história acelera: Resistência, movimentos sociais e o lugar do futuro*, ed. João Carlos Louçã and Paula Godinho (Lisbon, Portugal: Instituto de História Contemporânea, 2021).

34. When Alfredo discovers a postcard titled "Torremolinos 73" in Pablo Berger's *Torremolinos 73*, he not only finds the inspiration for a feature-length film set in the city, but he acknowledges the market appeal Carmen demands outside of Spain and affirms the coast's status as a ludic non-place defined by heterosexual desire. By affixing her face to the body of the woman on the postcard, Alfredo unwittingly recognizes Carmen as a constructed, mediated non-place, similar to Torremolinos, to be consumed by the male gaze. Incidentally, I discovered a postcard from Roses, Spain, along the Costa Brava that included a silhouette of a naked woman on the beach posing with her hand on her head and the sea behind her. Alongside the anonymous woman, the sender inscribed the name of his wife, Cynthia.

35. See Karl Spracklen's book *Whiteness and Leisure* in which the author explores whiteness as a particular hegemonic but invisible power relation that privileges yet normalizes the culture and position of white people. He explores many aspects of leisure from spots to tourism where "white cultural norms" become "universal norms" that obscure the historical inequalities of power. Karl Spracklen, *Whiteness and Leisure* (New York: Palgrave MacMillan, 2013). See also Daniel Burdsey's book *Race, Place, and the Seaside: Postcards from the Edge*, the first academic monograph to focus exclusively on issues of race, ethnicity, whiteness, and multiculture at the English seaside. Burdsey introduces the notion of "coastal liquidity" to detail shifting ethno-racial demographics, the politics of migration, and the spatial dynamics along the seaside. Daniel Burdsey, *Race, Place, and the Seaside: Postcards from the Edge* (London: Palgrave MacMillan, 2016).

36. Augé, *Non-places*, 27.

CHAPTER 3

1. Osborne, *Travelling Light, 79*.
2. Daniel Michael Levin, *Modernity and the Hegemony of Vision* (Berkely: University of California Press, 1993), 2.
3. Levin, *Modernity and the Hegemony of Vision*, 6.

4. Paul Rodaway, *Sensuous Geographies: Body, Sense, and Place* (London and New York: Routledge, 1994).

5. Rodaway, *Sensuous Geographies*, 159.

6. Rodaway, *Sensuous Geographies*, 160.

7. Rodaway, *Sensuous Geographies*, 161.

8. In *The Tourist Gaze,* John Urry states that the photographic tourist gaze produces an aesthetics that "excludes as much as it includes" in which postcards never exhibit landscapes of "waste, disease, dead animals, poverty, sewage, and despoilation" (129).

9. Rodaway refers to shopping malls, leisure or theme parks, and heritage areas as "themescapes" that are manipulated in ways similar to film and photographic images. The leisure areas along the Spanish coasts adhere to Rodaway's understanding of themescapes in that they exemplify the kind of artificial, textured environment that is constructed as a simulation based on a theme and disconnected from reality. Rodaway, *Sensuous Geographies,* 164.

10. Jonas Larsen, "(Dis)connecting Tourism and Photography: Corporeal Travel and Imaginative Travel," *Journeys* 5, no. 2 (2004): 27.

11. Larsen, "(Dis)connecting Tourism and Photography," 27.

12. Larsen, "(Dis)connecting Tourism and Photography," 29.

13. Larsen, "(Dis)connecting Tourism and Photography," 29. In her classic study *On Photography*, Susan Sontag states that industrial societies have turned their citizens into "image-junkies," the "most irresistible form of mental pollution." Susan Sontag, *On Photography* (New York: Farrar, Straus, and Ciroux), 24.

14. In "Geographies of Tourist Photography," Larsen refers to photography, especially tourism advertising, as a "technology of world making" in which the viewer is not a passive recipient but enacts "imaginative geographies" through the cognitive exercise of interpreting, evaluating, comparing, and drawing connections between signs and referents. Gazing, he asserts, is not merely seeing but is a practice (242–48).

15. Urry, *The Tourist Gaze*, 132.

16. Urry, *The Tourist Gaze*, 137.

17. Urry, *The Tourist Gaze*, 137. In this way one could view contemporary tourist public spaces as a kind of logical extension of the urban renewal projects in nineteenth-century Paris directed by Georges-Eugène Haussmann. By destroying decrepit overcrowded medieval neighborhoods overrun with crime and disease, Haussmann oversaw the construction of fountains, aqueducts, parks, squares, and wide boulevards where the Parisian bourgeoisie, most notably Baudelaire's flaneur, could stroll public spaces both to see and be seen, consuming urban environments from the comfort of anonymity. The

reconstruction of Paris and the displacement of the working class led to residential segregation, what we would call gentrification today, in which high rents of luxury apartments were out of reach for long-time residents. For a more detailed analysis of the impact of urban renewal projects in Paris, see David Harvey, *Paris: Capital of Modernity* (New York: Routledge, 2003).

18. John Urry, *The Tourist Gaze 3.0*, 3rd ed. (Los Angeles: Sage, 2011), 135.

19. Urry, *The Tourist Gaze 3.0*, 136.

20. Urry, *The Tourist Gaze 3.0*, 141.

21. Tom Selwyn, ed., *The Tourist Image: Myth and Myth Making in Tourism* (Chichester: John Wiley & Sons, 1996).

22. David Crouch and Nina Lübbren, eds., *Visual Culture and Tourism* (Oxford: Berg, 2003), 5.

23. Crouch and Lübbren, *Visual Culture and Tourism*, 10.

24. Crouch and Lübbren, *Visual Culture and Tourism*, 11.

25. Michel de Certeau, *The Practice of Everyday Life*, trans. Steve Rendall (Berkeley: University of California Press, 1984), 117.

26. de Certeau, *The Practice of Everyday Life*, 117.

27. de Certeau, *The Practice of Everyday Life*, 117.

28. de Certeau, *The Practice of Everyday Life*, 117.

29. de Certeau, *The Practice of Everyday Life*, 118.

30. John Taylor, *A Dream of England: Landscape, Photography and the Tourist's Imagination* (Manchester: Manchester University Press, 1994), 240.

31. Taylor, *A Dream of England*, 241.

32. Martin Parr, *Small World: A Global Photographic Project* (Stockport, England: Dewi Lewis Publishing, 1995); Martin Parr, *Common Sense* (Stockport, England: Dewi Lewis Publishing, 1999); Martin Parr, *Benidorm: Über die Welt / Benidorm: About the World*," ed. Sprengel Museum Hannover (Hannover, Germany: Sprengel Museum Hannover, 1999).

33. Carlos Pérez Siquier, *La Playa: 1972–1996* (Almería, Spain: Fundación de Arte Ibáñez-Cosentino, 2019).

34. Carlos Pérez Siquier, Carlos Gollonet, and Carlos Martín, *Pérez Siquier* (Madrid: Fundación MAPFRE Área de Cultura, 2020), 74.

35. Osborne, *Travelling Light*, 71.

36. Crouch and Lübbren, *Visual Culture and Tourism*, 8.

37. Crouch and Lübbren, *Visual Culture and Tourism*, 5–11.

38. Martin Parr, *The Last Resort: Photographs of New Brighton* (Wallasey, UK: Promenade Press, 1986).

39. See Douglas R. Nickel's book *Francis Frith in Egypt and Palestine: A Victorian Photographer Abroad* (Princeton, NJ: Princeton University Press, 2004). Nickel

offers an interdisciplinary approach to the impact of Frith's entrepreneurial integration of photography and travel. Interestingly, Frith started one of the first postcard companies to market tourism through publicly disseminated images that individuals could send each other. Curiously, Martin Parr published a book titled *Boring Postcards USA* (New York: Phaidon Press, 2004). Parr's ironic approach upends the notion and purpose of the postcard to entice the tourist's gaze with the mystery and beauty of exotic, distant lands. Rather, the images in Parr's collection are actual postcards of highways, airports, commercial districts, and other forgotten, and forgettable, non-places that have now become invisible pieces of everyday modern life.

40. Paul Fussel marks the start of jet travel as 1957 when "safe and efficient uniform international jet service began in earnest" and marked the beginning of a new era of "human passivity." Paul Fussel, *Abroad: British Literary Traveling between the Wars* (New York: Oxford University Press, 1980), 45. For Daniel Boorstin in *The Image, or, What Happened to the American Dream*, the advent of jet travel transforms the "traveler" into "tourist" through "magical modern machinery" that clears the world of its commonplaceness and making the exotic part of the everyday. For Boorstin, the traveler is one who goes to faraway places to see strange sights because their imagination impels them. In the jet age, he argues, this experience has been "diluted, contrived, and prefabricated" through the "multiplication, improvement, and cheapening of travel." As a result, Boorstin asserts, the modern tourist fills their experience with pseudo-events where the exotic and the familiar can be made to order and they approach travel through a consumerist mindset expecting to have all their demands met because they have paid for it. Daniel Boorstin, *The Image, or, What Happened to the American Dream* (New York: Atheneum, 1962), 77–79.

41. Geoff Dyer, introduction to *Small World* (Stockport, England: Dewi Lewis Publishing, 2007), 5.

42. Dyer, introduction, 7.

43. In their article "Martin Parr: A Traveller-Critic and a Professional Post-Tourist in a Small World," Theopisti Stylianou-Lambert and Elena Stylianou describe Parr as an "oppositional photographer" who remains outside the group of tourists in a privileged position of observer in order to problematize the tourist gaze and the tourist stage. In this way he acts as a traveller-critic "who adopts the rhetoric of globalization in order to critique contemporary consumption and reveal the discrepancies between promotional material and reality." Theopisti Stylianou-Lambert and Elena Stylianou, "Martin Parr: A Traveller-Critic and a Professional Post-Tourist in a Small World," *Travel, Tourism and Art* (2016): 167.

44. "Martin Parr, 'Common Sense' 1995–9," Tate, February 2004, https://www.tate. org.uk/art/artworks/parr-common-sense-p78371.
45. Parr, *Benidorm: Über die Welt.*
46. Daisy Woodward, "Martin Parr's Benidorm," Magnum Photos, May 21, 2021, https://www.magnumphotos.com/arts-culture/society-arts-culture/martin-parr-benidorm.
47. The photos from the shoot can be found online: "Vogue España: I Love Benidorm by Martin Parr," Models, June 2019, https://models.com/work/vogue-espana-i-love-benidorm-by-martin-parr/1130002.
48. In the program for the exhibition of work produced by AFAL at the Museo Nacional Centro de Arte Reina Sofía from May 30 to November 7, 2016, Laura Terré described AFAL as "uno de los colectivos fotográficos más importantes del siglo xx en España" (one of the most important photographic collectives from Spain in the twentieth-century) Laura Terré, *Historia del grupo fotográfico AFAL: 1956/1963*, ed. Museo Nacional Centro de Arte Reina Sofía (Madrid: Ministerio de Arte, Cultura, y Deporte, 2016), 3. From 1956 to1963, their independent thinking and fresh tone attracted photographers from all over the country, she states, who were unfulfilled with the state of photography and visual art at the time in Spain and through the AFAL journal became the catalyst to revolutionize Spanish photography after the Spanish Civil War. Terré states that AFAL offered an artistic, cultural, and physical space for an eclectic blend of documentary and subjective photographers to collaborate through their shared interest in the social function of photography and its implication in the reality of their era.
49. In 1985, Maxine Feifer coined the term "post-tourism" in her book *Tourism in History: From Imperial Rome to the Present* (New York: Stein and Day Publishers, 1986). She highlighted a new and symbolically playful mode of travelling, one in which the traveler (typically a middle-class Western consumer) was reflexively aware of the staged nature of mass tourism and deliberately performed tourism according to media imageries. She characterizes the post-tourist as a traveler whose experiences are mediated through televised images (or now massified images on the Internet) and though travel propaganda (magazines, pamphlets, brochures, postcards, and other forms of mass publication), consuming sites through their gaze without any physical mobility. The post-tourist perceives the genre codes latent in global tourism and understands what it means to play the role of a tourist within the realm of staged authenticity as described by MacCannell. Moreover, the post-tourist is acutely aware of the gaze, their own and that of others, that frames tourist experiences. In his article, "The 'Other' Postmodern Tourism: Culture, Travel, and the New

Middle Classes," Ian Munt builds on Feifer's notion of the post-tourist to interrogate wider practices within what he calls "postmodern tourism" and the
role of the new middle class as both "producers and consumers of new forms
of travel, particularly to Third World destinations" to establish and maintain
social differentiation. Ian Munt, "The 'Other' Postmodern Tourism: Culture,
Travel, and the New Middle Classes," *Theory, Culture, & Society* 11, no. 3 (1994):
101–2. Citing Bourdieu, Munt argues that tourism has emerged as a key commodity or "cultural good where it is primarily experiences and symbols that
are consumed" (109). To confer the coveted "distinction" and "taste" that
Bourdieu associates with the symbolic capital of class differentiation, Munt
describes how tour operators market and cater to the interests of a new kind
of traveller who seeks "tourist-free" experiences that is "real and true" (116).

50. During the Spanish Civil War, this area of Almería was heavily bombed by
German squadrons, and in the postwar period languished in oblivion during
the so-called "Años de Hambre" (Years of Hunger). Ironically, Franco's Fa-
lange party traveled to the area of La Chanca in the 1940s to photograph the
caves in the Cerro del Hambre (Hill of Hunger), document the impoverished
conditions, and justify a hygienic cleansing of the area as part of a proposed
urban renewal project that never materialized.

51. In their article "Fotografía para la promoción turística: El archivo fotográfico
de Turespaña," Lucía Domingo Barral and Asunción Muñoz Montalvo examine the role of photographic images in the administration and development
of tourism in Spain from the 1960s to the present. The article mentions that
Pérez Siquier served as a prominent photographer within the tourism industry in Spain along with many other renowned photographers like Juan Manuel Castuera, Francisco Ontañón, and Francesc Catalá-Roca. Domingo Barral
and Muñoz Montalvo, "Fotografía para la promoción turística."

52. Europa Press Andalucía, "'La playa', de Carlos Pérez Siquier, recoge una colección inédita de imágenes de la costa almeriense," *Europa Press*, April 3,
2019 2019, https://www.europapress.es/andalucia/diputacion-almeria-01014/
noticia-playa-carlos-perez-siquier-recoge-coleccion-inedita-imagenes-costa-
almeria-20190403160744.html. Referred to as the "Hollywood of Spain," Almería opened the airport in 1968 to facilitate travel for the film industry that
had first discovered the arid landscapes of southern Spain for the settings of
the so-called "Spaghetti Westerns." Iconic Westerns like *A Fistful of Dollars*
(1964), *For a Few Dollars More* (1965), *The Good, the Bad, and the Ugly* (1966), and
Once Upon a Time in the West (1968) found ideal filming locations in the dusty
deserts of Almería that mirrored those of the Southwest in the United States.
Earlier films like *Cleopatra* (1963) and *Lawrence of Arabia* (1962) also filmed

scenes in Almería. Subsequently, Almería has served as a filming location for many other films, including *Conan the Barbarian* (1982) and *Indiana Jones and the Last Crusade* (1989). More recently, television shows like *Black Mirror* and *Game of Thrones* have filmed scenes in Almería. Because of the film industry's interest, Almería has developed a component of the tourism industry that is focused on "film tourism," in which visitors may travel to the desert landscapes or see the beaches and coves from scenes of their favorite movies.

53. Rafael Doctor Roncero, "La playa," in *La playa: 1972–1996*, ed. Carlos Pérez Siquier (Almería, Spain: Fundación de Arte Ibáñez-Cosentino, 2019), 13.

54. Parr states that when he asked Pérez Siquier if his shift from black and white to color photography occurred because he had seen or studied the work of other colorists, the answer was an "emphatic no." Martin Parr, "Pérez Siquier," *Impresiones* 1 (2013): 4. Parr himself admits that he would love to claim that he himself was influenced by the work of Pérez Siquier but says he never saw the images when he started shooting at beaches in color with a ring flash and macro lens. The clear overlap in the visual language of Parr's and Pérez Siquier's photos led the former to believe erroneously that two photographers were contemporaries yet he states, "I was amazed when I saw they were taken in the early 1970s." Parr, "Pérez Siquier," 8.

55. Valle-Inclán's 1924 play *Luces de bohemia* establishes the *esperpento* genre as one inspired by the techniques and composition of silent films. Most notably, the deformed cityscapes of expressionist German films like *The Cabinet of Dr. Caligari* informed a dystopic view of modern society that was reflected also in the corporal deformation of various characters. The grotesque obesity of the bureaucrat in Valle-Inclán's play, for example, conveys the dehumanization and inner immorality of social institutions like government that mold society and its citizens.

56. Carlos Gollonet, "Pérez Siquier, pionero del color," in *Pérez Siquier* (Madrid: Fundación MAPFRE, 2020), 50.

57. Patrizia Toscano, "Instagram-City: New Media and the Social Perception of Public Spaces," *Visual Anthropology* 30, no. 3 (2017): 276.

58. Toscano, "Instagram-City," 277.

59. Toscano, "Instagram-City," 280.

60. Joan Fontcuberta, "Por un manifiesto posfotográfico," *La vanguardia*, May 11, 2011 2011, http://www.lavanguardia.com/cultura/20110511/54152218372/por-un-manifiesto-posfotografico.html.

61. Henry Jenkins, *Convergence Culture: Where Old and New Media Collide* (New York: New York University Press, 2008), 2. In the introduction to *Convergence Culture*, Henry Jenkins argues against the idea that convergence be

understood as solely a technological process that only focuses on media functions on digital devices. Rather, he conceptualizes convergence within the flow of content that instigated deep cultural shifts and has provoked social changes. Before the dot.com bubble, Jenkins asserts, the now antiquated paradigm of the 1990s erroneously believed that new media would displace old media, but the emerging convergence paradigm believes that old and new media will interact in increasingly complex ways where an old concept will not disappear but will take on new meanings (6). He also makes a distinction between the delivery systems that are simply technologies and the media itself which represents a cultural system. A medium's content may shift, its audience may change, and its status may rise or fall, but Jenkins states that once a medium establishes itself as satisfying a core human need, it continues to function within the larger system of communication options and is forced to coexist with the emerging media (14). Media convergence from Jenkins's perspective is less a technological shift and more a transformation of the relationship between existing technologies, industries, markets, genres, and audiences. Understood as a process not an endpoint, convergence impacts both how media is produced and how it is consumed (16).

62. As an example of how official tourism accounts on Instagram manipulate hashtags to brand their destination and call tourists to action by framing their emotional connection to the locale, see the article "#ILoveLondon: An exploration of the declaration of love towards a destination on Instagram." Raffaele Filieri, Dorothy A. Yen, and Qionglei Yu, "#ILoveLondon: An exploration of the declaration of love towards a destination on Instagram," *Tourism Management* 85 (2021).

63. Rubén Esquitino, "La belleza radiactiva de Benidorm triunfa en Instagram," *El País*, December 5, 2014 2014, https://elpais.com/elpais/2014/12/05/album/1417784722_556720.html#foto_gal_5. Subsequent photo exhibits like "Gamma City" (2015), "Bloop" (2018), and "Ultimátum a la Tierra" (2019) by María Moldes similarly invite the viewer into a seemingly alternate reality that offers an ironic, even esperpentic, view of contemporary consumerist society and especially the ecological impact of our modern lifestyle.

64. Founded on October 6, 2010, Instagram currently counts over 1 billion users with over 500 million posting daily Instagram stories. More than 50 billion photos have been uploaded since the inception of Instagram with an estimated 1074 photos uploaded to Instagram every second. "Instagram by the Numbers: Stats, Demographics & Fun Facts," accessed October 26, 2021, https://www.omnicoreagency.com/instagram-statistics. These statistics endow Susan Sontag's musings in *On Photography* with a prescient poignancy

"By furnishing this already crowded world with a duplicate one of images, photography makes us feel that the world is more available than it really is. . . . Industrial societies turn their citizens into image-junkies; it is the most irresistible form of mental pollution" (24).

65. Sontag, *On Photography*, 14.

66. Elena Velasco, "Benidorm Dreamin: el paraíso kitsch de Roberto Alcaraz," *Kluid Magazine*, 2020, https://kluidmagazine.com/benidorm-dreamin-el-paraiso-kitsch-de-roberto-alcaraz. The New Topographic Movement in photography emerged in 1975 with the landmark exhibition titled *New Topographics: Photographs of a Man-Altered Landscape* at the International Museum of Photography, George Eastman House. Photographers such as Lewis Baltz, Robert Adams, Nicholas Nixon, and Frank Gohlke broke with the images of romanticized American landscapes most typically associated with Ansel Adams. Instead, the "new topographics" focused on ugly, ordinary elements of everyday environments to offer ironic critiques of suburban sprawl and concerns about the ways in which humans have transformed the landscape within the framework of consumer capitalism. For more information on New Topographic photography, see Greg Foster-Rice and John Rohrback, *Reframing the New Topographics* (Chicago, IL: Center for American Places at Columbia College Chicago and University of Chicago Press, 2013). See also Britt Salvesen, *New Topographics* (Göttingen, Germany: Steidl and Partners, 2010).

67. Joaquín Rodríguez et al., eds., *Ensayo y error Benidorm* (Seville, Spain: Editorial Barrett, 2019).

68. Rodríguez et al., *Ensayo y error Benidorm*, 128–29.

69. Rodríguez et al., *Ensayo y error Benidorm*, 132–35.

CHAPTER 4

1. "Marbella, segundo acto," *El País,* June 28, 2006, http://elpais.com/diario/2006/06/28/opinion/1151445601_850215.html.

2. Palomino, *Torremolinos Gran Hotel*, 40.

3. Víctor Santos, *Intachable: 30 años de corrupción* (Girona, Spain: Panini España, 2020).

4. Mario Gaviria, *La séptima potencia: España en el mundo* (Barcelona, Spain: Ediciones B, 1996).

5. In normative economics, *welfare* and *well-being* are usually taken to be synonyms. These terms do not refer to the so-called welfare state and the social services attached to it. Rather, these concepts represent a mental state, a condition of happiness or good feeling. This is a very important link between the two concepts and justifies their interchangeable use. The well-being concept

seeks to acknowledge how long-term goals, like the desire to establish a family, influence individual and collective economic stability. Behind this general outlook on happiness is a desire-satisfaction measure where the "good life" results from the satisfaction of as many as possible of these desires. If welfare is to buy many objects of consumption (cars, houses, clothes, etc.), well-being is to have as many life-driven factors (family, job, friendships, etc.) as possible. See Amartya Sen's chapter titled "Capability and Well-Being," in *The Philosophy of Economics: An Anthology*, ed. Daniel M. Hausman (Cambridge: Cambridge University Press, 2008).

6. Gaviria, *La séptima potencia*, 189.
7. Gaviria, *La séptima potencia*, 335.
8. Gaviria, *La séptima potencia*, 335.
9. Íñigo Domínguez Gabiña, *Mediterráneo descapotable: Viaje ridículo por aquel país tan feliz* (Madrid: Libros del K.O., 2015).
10. María Angulo Egea, "El cielo enladrillado. Paisajes y figuras de la crisis española (2008–2015). Discursos y narrativas de no ficción actuales," in *Crisis, comunicación y crítica política*, ed. Carlos Del Valle Rojas and Víctor Silva Echeto (Quito, Ecuador: Ediciones Ceispal, 2017), 106.
11. Javier López Menacho, *Yo, precario* (Barcelona: Los libros del lince, 2013).
12. Domínguez Gabiña, *Mediterráneo descapotable*, 191.
13. Domínguez Gabiña, *Mediterráneo descapotable*, 7.
14. Domínguez Gabiña, *Mediterráneo descapotable*, 25.
15. Domínguez Gabiña, *Mediterráneo descapotable*, 15.
16. Domínguez Gabiña, *Mediterráneo descapotable*, 67.
17. The chapter on Marina D'Or is particularly scathing. Domínguez Gabiña invokes Tolkien renaming it Mord'Or whose falsified landscape he imagines was designed by Javier Mariscal (the mastermind behind Cobi, the mascot of the 1992 Barcelona Olympics) and where he fantasizes that mad scientists work in underground laboratories to obtain the DNA of tourists to clone them for winter travel and thus boost attendance for promotional videos. Domínguez Gabiña asserts, golf is a "fiebre and delirio" (fever and delirium) in Andalucía. *Mediterráneo descapotable*, 107. According to statista.com, in 2020 there were 446 golf courses throughout Spain, and 106 are located in Andalucía alone. Castilla y León has the second most golf courses with 45. "Número de campos de golf en España en 2020, por comunidad autónoma," Statista Research Department, 2021, https://es.statista.com/estadisticas/670013/numero-de-campos-de-golf-por-region-espana.
18. Domínguez Gabiña, *Mediterráneo descapotable*, 122.

19. Fernando Roch, "La ciudad inmobiliaria y el precio de la vivienda," *Papeles de la FIM*, no. 20 (January 2004).
20. Domínguez Gabiña, *Mediterráneo descapotable*, 284.
21. Domínguez Gabiña, *Mediterráneo descapotable*, 276.
22. José Manuel Naredo and Antonio Montiel Márquez, *El modelo inmobliiario español y su culminación en el caso valenciano* (Barcelona: Icaria Editorial, 2011). The book is divided in two parts. The first, written by José Manuel Naredo, is titled "El modelo inmobliario español y sus consecuencias." The second, written by Antono Montiel Márquez is titled "El modelo inmobiliario valenciano: Marco institucional, actores, resultados y perspectivas."
23. Naredo and Montiel Márquez, *El modelo inmobliiario español*, 7–9, 13.
24. Naredo and Montiel Márquez, *El modelo inmobliiario español*, 13–15.
25. Naredo and Montiel Márquez, *El modelo inmobliiario español*, 19.
26. Naredo and Montiel Márquez, *El modelo inmobliiario español*, 29–30.
27. Naredo and Montiel Márquez, *El modelo inmobliiario español*, 35–36.
28. After the 15-M protests in 2011 against austerity measures during the Spanish financial crisis, many of the so-called Indignados coined the term "El Régimen del 78" (Regime of 1978) to refer to the political class responsible for forging Spain's constitution after the death of Franco. The term refers to a dominant class that controlled not only the social, political, and economic institutions during the incipient democracy, but also directed the discourse about the transition from dictatorship to democracy. Often projected as a rupture, the notion of the "Régimen del 78" is that a strong desire among the elites to maintain the status quo infused the policies of the era with a sense of "continuismo" (continuism) that ignored critical voices, marginalized the working class, and quelled any possibility for reparations from the Spanish Civil War and political persecution during the Franco dictatorship.
29. Naredo and Montiel Márquez, *El modelo inmobliiario español*, 40. "Caciquismo" refers to a political system where power rests in the hands of a local boss, or chieftan, who maintains control through domination, influence, corruption, and voter suppression, but also, oftentimes, with charisma and populism. Often, these local bosses occupied rural areas and ascended to power through their ownership of wide swaths of land. The cacique figure has been seen throughout Spanish history and has cultural importance in Latin America as well. Within the context of coastal urban development, local figures like Jesús Gil comply with the idea of a cacique because they wield tremendous political power through corruption, fraud, and intimidation as well as populist rhetoric and a charismatic personality. In the case of the

coasts, while not rural areas, the power these figures acquire is related to land ownership, specifically their control over real estate, speculation, and urbanization processes.

30. Fernando Jiménez Sánchez, "Boom urbanístico y corrupción política en España," *Mediterráneo Económico* 14 (2008): 266.

31. Jiménez Sánchez, "Boom urbanístico," 266.

32. Centro de Inteligencia contra el Crimen Organizado (CICO) was only founded in 2006, suggesting that until the eruption of scandals in Marbella and the Costa del Sol between 2005 and 2007, not much attention was given to the issue of organized crime in Spain from a judicial, investigatory, or prosecutorial point of view. The CICO was reorganized in 2014 to include terrorism and changed its name to the Centro de Inteligencia contra el Terrorismo y el Crimen Organizado (CITCO).

33. Jiménez Sánchez, "Boom urbanístico," 273.

34. Jiménez Sánchez, "Boom urbanístico," 277.

35. Jiménez Sánchez, "Boom urbanístico," 279.

36. Antonio Romero and Miguel Díaz, *Costa Nostra: Las mafias en la Costa del Sol* (Seville: Atrapasueños Editorial, 2009).

37. Romero and Díaz, *Costa Nostra*, 31.

38. Romero and Díaz, *Costa Nostra*, 31.

39. Romero and Díaz, *Costa Nostra*, 32–33.

40. Romero and Díaz, *Costa Nostra*, 37.

41. Romero and Díaz, *Costa Nostra*, 36.

42. The authors cite a report from the Ministry of the Interior that eight in ten money laundering operations in Europe related to Spain have some aspect rooted in Marbella.

43. Giles Tremlett, *Ghosts of Spain: Travels Through Spain and Its Silent Past* (New York: Walker & Company, 2006).

44. Tremlett, *Ghosts of Spain: Travels Through Spain and Its Silent Past*, 113.

45. José María Aznar served as Prime Minister of Spain from 1996 to 2004 during which time he promoted policies that loosened state regulation of the construction industry and fomented the construction boom at the same time it weakened social benefits like public health, education, and retirement pensions. In 1997, Aznar famously declared "España va bien" (Spain is doing great!) and predicted that the country had entered an unstoppable trajectory of economic growth. At the time, Spain's GDP, employment, and the IBEX (the Spanish stock market) were all increasing and the country, he asserted, was entering the era of a new economic miracle. Aznar oversaw the strategic privatization of numerous public companies including Tabacalera, Endesa,

and Repsol as well as labor reforms that sought to introduce "una mayor competencia en la mejora del bienestar social, la reducción de las hipotecas, la bajada de las tarifas aéreas, la liberalización de las telecomunicaciones, la reducción de la inflación que mejora las rentas familiares y finalmente la disminución de las tarifas eléctricas" (greater ability to improve social welfare, the reduction of mortgage rates, the lowering of airline tariffs, the liberalization of telecommunications, the reduction of inflation to improve family income, and finally the decrease of tariffs related to electricity." Josep Maria Cortes, "Aznar anuncia en Barcelona una reforma laboral en 1997 para establecer un contrato flexible," *El País*, November 22, 1996, https://elpais.com/diario/1996/11/23/espana/848703616_850215.html. Mariano Rajoy, from the rightwing Partido Popular, as is Aznar, served as prime minister of Spain from 2011 until his resignation in 2018 after a vote of no confidence in the wake of the Gürtel corruption scandal. During the first half of his administration, Rajoy oversaw major restructuring efforts in the banking and labor systems during the peak years of Spain's financial crisis. He adopted Aznar's "España va bien" and adapted it to "España va mejor" (Spain is doing better).

46. Santiago Segura, *Torrente 2: Misión en Marbella* (Madrid, Spain: Amiguetes Entertainment, 2001).

47. "Torrente (saga)," Taquilla España, May 27, 2020, https://www.taquillaespana.es/sagas/torrente-saga.

48. Enric Bach, *El pionero* (Spain: HBO España, 2019).

49. There is also a documentary about Pedro Zaragoza, the mayor of Benidorm from 1951 to 1967 who famously rode his Vespa to lobby Franco in the 1950s to lift the ban on the bikini. The documentary titled *El hombre que embotelló el sol* (2016; The man who bottled the sun) is a sixty-four-minute film directed by Óscar Bernàcer and produced by Nakamura Films and Televisión Española. It explores one of the foundational myths of Benidorm, the famous Vespa ride to Madrid, and delves into Zaragoza's vision and resolve to open the city to tourism against the political pressures, ideological opposition, and administrative constraints of the Franco regime and the Catholic Church. The film examines the origins of the mythic tourism destination and portrays Zaragoza as an expert promoter who invented Benidorm's brand through music festivals, popular films, charter tours, and even by designing the city's coat of arms that marketed the city as a spectacle in and of itself. The documentary was nominated for ten Goya awards in 2017.

50. Rafael Aníbal, ed., *Aquellos maravillosos años: Escándalos de corrupción y despilfarro en España durante la última década* (Madrid: Editorial Continta Me Tienes, 2012).

51. Aníbal, *Aquellos maravillosos años*, 9. The notion of "esperpento" appropriately captures the absurdity and the horror of Spain's coastal transformations, where the grotesquely deformed bodies in the photographs of Carlos Pérez Siquier and María Moldes mirror the grotesque changes to the
physical landscape. In this chapter, the grotesque elements extend to deep
political (and moral) corruption that both derives from and drives the construction projects that destroy the natural beauty of the coasts weaking ecological disaster.

52. Aníbal, *Aquellos maravillosos años*, 9. The author recognizes that had they detailed every corruption case in Spain from this era, it would have required
volumes and volumes.

53. Widespread corruption has forged a new vocabulary that has been introduced
into Spanish vernacular. Bernardo Vergara's *Corrupcionario: Diccionario en
viñetas de la corrupción española* (Barcelona: Random Comics, 2018). satiri-
cally collects and explains terminology related to corruption through comics. Drawings complement textual definitions with dark humor to expose
the absurd, esperpentic nature of Spanish politics through grotesque exag-
gerations whose deformed appearance communicates a society perverted
by corruption. Phrases include *tráfico de influencias* (influence trafficking),
paraíso fiscal (fiscal paradise or tax haven), or *blanqueo de dinero* (money
laundering) among many others.

54. For a complete retelling of the origins and outcomes of the investigation, see
Miguel Ángel Ordóñez's book *El Caso Malaya: Los elefantes asolaron Marbella*
(Granada, Spain: Ultramarina, 2010).

55. Aníbal, *Aquellos maravillosos años*, 30.

56. Aníbal, *Aquellos maravillosos años*, 30.

57. Aníbal, *Aquellos maravillosos años*, 31. Unlike the ironic title of Pedro Lazaga's 1969 film, Jesús Gil may be considered the true "abominable hombre
de la Costa del Sol."

58. Aníbal, *Aquellos maravillosos años*, 32.

59. *Salvaje: La imperiosa historia de Jesús Gil y Gil* (Barcelona: Contraediciones,
S.L., 2017).

60. Castelló, *Salvaje*, 225.

61. Aníbal, *Aquellos maravillosos años*, 33.

62. Aníbal, *Aquellos maravillosos años*, 33.

63. Joaquín Estefanía Moreira, dir., *Informe sobre la democracia en España 2007:
La estrategia de la crispación*, Fundación Alternativas (Madrid, 2007), 233.

64. Estefanía Moreira, *Informe sobre la democracia*, 233–36.

65. Estefanía Moreira, *Informe sobre la democracia*, 239.

66. Estefanía Moreira, *Informe sobre la democracia*, 240.

67. Estefanía Moreira, *Informe sobre la democracia*, 241.

68. Estefanía Moreira, *Informe sobre la democracia*, 241.

69. Chirbes, *Crematorio*.

70. The relationship to the land and the diverging notions about the meaning of the land itself are tropes that have appeared in Spanish film, tv, and literature, often with regard to the urbanization of the coasts. For example, in the Mariano Ozores film *En un lugar de la Manga* (1970) an important real estate developer company proposes to expand along the coastline. However, Juan (Manolo Escobar) refuses to sell his property because the land holds sentimental value for him due to its association with childhood memories. Similarly, in the television series *Verano Azul* set in Nerja, the fisherman Chanquete (Antonio Ferrandis) similarly refuses to sell his land because of its connection to family and memory.

71. Chirbes, *Crematorio*, 401.

72. Chirbes, *Crematorio*, 409.

73. García Moreno, Rosa-Jiménez, and Márquez-Ballesteros, "Lo banal como patrimonio," 256.

74. Svetlana Boym, *The Future of Nostalgia* (New York: Basic Books, 2001), 8.

75. Boym, *The Future of Nostalgia*, 13.

76. Boym, *The Future of Nostalgia*, 16.

77. Carmen Romera, "Cruiser: de gran lujo a refugio de indigentes," *La Opinión de Málaga* (Málaga, Spain), November 11, 2012, https://www.laopiniondemalaga.es/costa-sol-occidental/2012/11/11/cruiser-gran-lujo-refugio-indigentes/547506.html.

78. Ana Tudela and Antono Delgado, *Playa Burbuja: Un viaje al reino de los señores del ladrillo* (Madrid, Spain: Datista, 2018), 17.

79. Ana and Delgado Tudela, Antono, "Las mayores aberraciones arquitectónicas de la costa española," *El país* (Madrid), August 8, 2019, ICON Design, https://elpais.com/elpais/2019/08/06/icon_design/1565078918_545121.html.

80. The *New York Times* featured a story recently about the Hotel Algarrobico: Raphael Minder, "Haunting the Coast of Spain: The Ghost Hotel of Algarrobico," *New York Times*, Dec. 29. 2021, https://www.nytimes.com/2021/12/29/travel/spain-abandoned-hotel.html.

81. "Algarrobico, símbolo de la destrucción de la costa," Greenpeace, accessed January 16, 2022, https://es.greenpeace.org/es/trabajamos-en/oceanos/costas/algarrobico-simbolo-de-la-destruccion-de-la-costa.

82. See Redacción, "Errores/horrores urbanos: Casares costa o el llamado 'Chernóbil de Málaga,'" Idealista, May 23, 2012, https://www.idealista.com/news/inmobiliario/vivienda/2012/05/23/455083-errores-horrores-urbanos-casares-costa-o-el-llamado-chernobil-de-malaga.

83. Gregg Dickinson, Carole Blair, and Brian L. Ott, eds., *Places of Public Memory: The Rhetoric of Museums and Memorials* (Tuscaloosa: University of Alabama Press, 2010), 12.

BIBLIOGRAPHY

Afinoguénova, Eugenia, and Jaume Martí-Olivella, eds. *Spain Is (Still) Different: Tourism and Discourse in Spanish Identity*. Lanham, MD: Lexington Books, 2008.

"Algarrobico, símbolo de la destrucción de la costa." Greenpeace, accessed January 16, 2022, https://es.greenpeace.org/es/trabajamos-en/oceanos/costas/algarrobico-simbolo-de-la-destruccion-de-la-costa.

Álvarez, Laura, dir. *City for Sale*. Spain: Bausan Films, 2018.

Aníbal, Rafael, ed. *Aquellos maravillosos años: Escándalos de corrupción y despilfarro en España durante la última década*. Madrid: Editorial Continta Me Tienes, 2012.

Augé, Marc. *Non-Places: An Introduction to Supermodernity*, 4th ed. Translated by John Howe. London: Verso, 1995.

Bach, Enric. *El Pionero*. Spain: HBO España, 2019.

Bardem, Juan Antonio, dir. *El Puente*. Spain: Euromedia Visión, 1976.

Barke, M., J. Towner, and M. T. Newton, eds. *Tourism in Spain: Critical Issues*. Wallingford, UK: CAB International, 1996.

Barthes, Roland. *Camera Lucida: Reflections on Photography*. New York: Hill and Wang, 1980.

Baudrillard, Jean. "The Ecstasy of Communication." In *The Anti-Aesthetic: Essays on Postmodern Culture*, edited by Hal Foster, 126–34. New York: The New Press, 1983.

———. *Simulacra and Simulation*. Translated by Sheila Faria Glaser. Ann Arbor: University of Michigan Press, 1994.

Berger, Pablo. *Torremolinos 73*. Madrid, Spain: Estudios Picasso, 2003.

Bermúdez, Silvia, and Geist, Anthony L., eds. *Cartographies of Madrid: Contesting Urban Spaces at the Crossroads of the Global South and Global North*. Nashville, TN: Vanderbilt University Press, 2019.

Boorstin, Daniel. *The Image, or, What Happened to the American Dream.* New York: Atheneum, 1962.

Bourdieu, Pierre. *Outline of a Theory of Practice.* Cambridge: Cambridge University Press, 1977.

Boym, Svetlana. *The Future of Nostalgia.* New York: Basic Books, 2001.

Brossat, Ian. *Airbnb: La ciudad uberizada.* Translated by Sagrario Ruiz Elizalde. Pamplona, Spain: Katakrak Liburuak, 2018.

Burdsey, Daniel. *Race, Place, and the Seaside: Postcards from the Edge.* London: Palgrave MacMillan, 2016.

Cabrerizo, China C. *La ciudad negocio: Turismo y movilización social en Pugna.* Madrid: Cisma Editorial, 2016.

Carballo-Cruz, Francisco. "Causes and Consequences of the Spanish Economic Crisis: Why the Recovery Is Taken [*sic*] So Long?" *Panoeconomicus* 3 (2011): 309–28.

Castelló, Iván. *Salvaje: La imperiosa historia de Jesús Gil Y Gil.* Barcelona: Contraediciones, 2017.

Chandler, Alfred. *The Visible Hand: The Managerial Revolution in American Business.* Boston, MA: Harvard University Press, 1977.

Charnon-Deutsch, Lou. *The Spanish Gypsy: The History of a European Obsession.* University Park: Pennsylvania State University Press, 2004.

Chirbes, Rafael. *Crematorio.* Barcelona: Anagrama, 2007.

Clemente, Luis. *Kitsch y flamenco.* Seville, Spain: Casa de la Provincia, Diputación de Sevilla, 2009.

Colmeiro, José. "Exorcising Exoticism: "Carmen" and the Construction of Oriental Spain." *Comparative Literature* 54, no. 2 (2002): 127–44.

Comaroff, John L., and Jean Comaroff. *Ethnicity, Inc.* Chicago: University of Chicago Press, 2009.

Cortes, Josep Maria. "Aznar anuncia en Barcelona una reforma laboral en 1997 para establecer un contrato flexible." *El País*, November 22, 1996. https://elpais.com/diario/1996/11/23/espana/848703616_850215.html.

Crouch, David, and Nina Lübbren, eds. *Visual Culture and Tourism.* New York: Berg, 2003.

Crumbaugh, Justin. *Destination Dictatorship: The Spectacle of Spain's Tourist Boom and the Reinvention of Difference.* Albany: State University of New York Press, 2009.

de Certeau, Michel. *The Practice of Everyday Life.* Translated by Steve Rendall. Berkeley: University of California Press, 1984.

de Soto, Hernando. *The Mystery of Capital: Why Capitalism Triumphs in the West and Fails Everywhere Else.* New York: Basic Books, 2000.

Debord, Guy. *The Society of the Spectacle*, 8th ed. Translated by Donald Nicholson-Smith. New York: Zone Books, 1994.

Delgado, Manuel. *La ciudad mentirosa: Fraude y miseria del "modelo Barcelona,"* 3rd ed. Madrid: Los Libros de la Catarta, 2017.

———. "Turistofobia." *El País*, July 11, 2008. https://elpais.com/diario/2008/07/12/catalunya/1215824840_850215.html.

del Valle-Inclán, Ramón. *Luces de Bohemia.* Madrid: Colección Austral, Espasa Calpe, 1999.

Derrida, Jacques. *The Post Card.* Chicago: University of Chicago Prss, 1980.

Desmond, Jane. *Staging Tourism: Bodies on Display from Waikiki to Sea World.* Chicago: University of Chicago Press, 1999.

Dhaliwal, Puneet. "Public Squares and Resistance: The Politics of Space in the Indignados Movement." *Interface: A Journal for and about Social Movements* 4, no. 1 (May 2012): 251–73.

Dickinson, Gregg, Carole Blair, and Brian L. Ott, eds. *Places of Public Memory: The Rhetoric of Museums and Memorials.* Tuscaloosa: University of Alabama Press, 2010.

Doctor Roncero, Rafael. "La Playa." In *La Playa: 1972–1996*, edited by Carlos Pérez Siquier, 11–15. Almería, Spain: Fundación de Arte Ibáñez-Cosentino, 2019.

Domingo Barral, Lucia, and Asunción Muñoz Montalvo. "Fotografía para la promoción turística: El archivo fotográfico de Turespaña." *Estudios Turísticos* 213–214, no. 3-4 (2017): 137–54.

Domínguez Gabiña, Íñigo. *Mediterráneo descapotable: Viaje ridículo por aquel país tan feliz.* Madrid: Libros del K.O., 2015.

Dotterrer, Steven, and Galen Cranz. "The Picture Postcard: Its Development and Role in American Urbanization." *Journal of American Culture* 5, no. 1 (1982): 44–52.

Durante Asensio, Isabel, and José Javier Aliaga Cárceles. "La creación del mito de La Manga del Mar Menor a través de la promoción turística de NO-DO." *Cuadernos de turismo* 44 (2019): 111–28.

Dyer, Geoff. Introduction to *Small World*. Stockport, England: Dewi Lewis Publishing, 2007.

Egea, María Angulo. "El cielo enladrillado: Paisajes y figuras de la crisis española (2008–2015). Discursos y narrativas de no ficción actuales." In *Crisis, comunicación y crítica política*, edited by Carlos Del Valle Rojas and Víctor Silva Echeto, 62–109. Quito, Ecuador: Ediciones Ceispal, 2017.

Esquitino, Rubén. "La belleza radiactiva de Benidorm triunfa en Instagram." *El País*, December 5, 2014. https://elpais.com/elpais/2014/12/05/album/1417784722_556720.html#foto_gal_5.

Estefanía Moreira, Joaquín, dir. *Informe sobre la democracia en España 2007: La estrategia de la crispación*. 2007. Madrid: Fundación Alternativas.

Esteve Secall, Rafael. *Ocio, turismo, y hoteles en la Costa del Sol*. Málaga, Spain: University of Málaga, 1982.

Europa Press Andalucía, "'La Playa', de Carlos Pérez Siquier, recoge una colección inédita de imágenes de la Costa Almeriense." *Europa Press*, April 3, 2019. https://www.europapress.es/andalucia/diputacion-almeria-01014/noticia-playa-carlos-perez-siquier-recoge-coleccion-inedita-imagenes-costa-almeria-20190403160744.html.

Faulkner, Sally. *A Cinema of Contradiction: Spanish Film in the 1960s*. Edinburgh: Edinburgh University Press, 2006.

Feifer, Maxine. *Tourism in History: From Imperial Rome to the Present*. New York: Stein and Day Publishers, 1986.

Fernández Cifuentes, Luis. "Southern Exposure: Early Tourism and Spanish National Identity." *Journal of Iberian and Latin American Studies* 13, no. 2 (2007): 133–48.

Fernández Durán, Ramón. *El tsunami urbanizador español y mundial*. Barcelona: Virus Editorial, 2006.

Filieri, Raffaele, Dorothy A. Yen, and Qionglei Yu. "#Ilovelondon: An Exploration of the Declaration of Love towards a Destination on Instagram." *Tourism Management* 85 (2021): 1–21.

Fontcuberta, Joan. "Por un manifiesto posfotográfico." *La vanguardia*, May 11, 2011. http://www.lavanguardia.com/cultura/20110511/54152218372/por-un-manifiesto-posfotografico.html.

Foster, Hal. *Recodings: Art, Spectacle, Cultural Politics*. Seattle, WA: Bay Press, 1985.

Foster-Rice, Greg, and John Rohrbach, eds. *Reframing the New Topographics*. Chicago: Center for American Places at Columbia College Chicago and University of Chicago Press, 2013.

Foucault, Michel. *Discipline and Punish: The Birth of the Prison*. Translated by Alan Sheridan. New York: Vintage, 1977.

Franco, Francisco. *Ley 197/1963 centros y zonas de interés turístico nacional*. Madrid, Spain: Boletín Oficial del Estado, 1963.

Fuentes Vega, Alicia. *Bienvenido, Mr. Turismo: Cultura visual del boom en España*. Madrid: Ediciones Cátedra, 2017.

Fussel, Paul. *Abroad: British Literary Traveling between the Wars*. New York: Oxford University Press, 1980.

García Moreno, Alberto E. *Cine, ciudad y patrimonio en Torremolinos (1959–1979)*. Málaga, Spain: UMA Editorial, 2017.

García Moreno, Alberto E., Carlos Rosa-Jiménez, and María José Márquez-Ballesteros. "Lo banal como patrimonio de la Costa del Sol: Torremolinos

1959–1979." *Pasos: Revista de turismo y patrimonio cultural* 14, no. 1 (2016): 253–73.

Gaviria, Mario. *Benidorm*. Beniorm, Spain: Benidorm City Council and Lunwerg Editores, 1990.

———. *La séptima potencia: España en el mundo*. Barcelona, Spain: Ediciones B, 1996.

Gaviria, Mario, José Miguel Iribas, Manuel Monterde, Françoise Sabbah, Juan Ramón Sanz, and Ernesto Udina. *España a go-gó: Turismo charter y neocolonialismo del espacio*. Madrid: Ediciones Turner, 1974.

Gollonet, Carlos. "Pérez Siquier, pionero del color." In Pérez Siquier, Gollonet, and Martín, *Pérez Siquier*, 38–55.

Gómez Alonso, Rafael. "El turismo no es un gran invento: Aperturismo y recepción del ocio y consumo a través del cine español de los 60." *Área Abierta* 15 (November 2006): 1–10.

Graham, Helen, and Antonio Sánchez. "The Politics of 1992." In *Spanish Cultural Studies: An Introduction*, edited by Helen Graham and Jo Labanyi, 406–18. Oxford: Oxford University Press, 1995.

Granell I March, Jordi, Andrés Martínez Medina, Antonio Luis, Juan Corral, José María López Martínez, Eusebio Villanueva Pleguezuelo, and Arsenio Pérez Amaral. *La arquitectura del sol / Sunland Architecture*. Valencia: Col·legi d'Arquitectes de Catalunya, Colegio Oficial de Arquitectos de la Comunidad Valenciana, Col·legi Oficial d'Arquitectes de les Illes Balears, Colegio Oficial de Arquitectos de Murcia, Colegio Oficial de Arquitectos de Almería, Colegio Oficial de Arquitectos de Granada, Colegio Oficial de Arquitectos de Málaga, Colegio de Arquitectos de Canarias, 2002.

Guerín, José Luis. *En construcción*. Spain: Oviedo TV, 2001.

Harvey, David. "The Art of Rent: Globalization, Monopoly and the Commodification of Culture." *Social Register* 38 (2002): 18.

———. *The Condition of Postmodernity*. Boston, MA: Blackwell, 1990.

———. *Paris: Capital of Modernity*. New York: Routledge, 2003.

———. "The Right to the City." *New Left Review* 53 (2008): 23–41.

———. *The Urban Experience*. Baltimore, MD: Johns Hopkins University Press, 1989.

"Instagram by the Numbers: Stats, Demographics & Fun Facts." Omnicore, last updated February 14, 2023, accessed October 26, 2021. https://www.omnicoreagency.com/instagram-statistics.

Jameson, Fredric. *Postmodernism, or, The Cultural Logic of Late Capitalism*. Durham, NC: Duke University Press, 1992.

Jayne, Mark. *Cities and Consumption*. London: Routledge, 2005.

————. "Cultural Geography, Consumption and the City." *Geography* 91, no. 1 (2006): 10.

Jenkins, Henry. *Convergence Culture: Where Old and New Media Collide.* New York: New York University Press, 2008.

Jiménez Sánchez, Fernando. "Boom urbanístico y corrupción política en España." *Mediterráneo Económico* 14 (2008): 263–85.

Labanyi, Jo, ed. *Constructing Identity in Contemporary Spain: Theoretical Debates and Cultural Practice.* Oxford: Oxford University Press, 2002.

Lamo de Espinosa, Emilio. "La normalización de España: España, Europa y la modernidad." *Claves de razón práctica* 111 (Abril 2001): 4–17.

Larsen, Jonas. "(Dis)connecting Tourism and Photography: Corporeal Travel and Imaginative Travel." *Journeys* 5, no. 2 (2004): 19–34.

————. "Geographies of Tourist Photography." In *Geographies of Communication: The Spatial Turn in Media Studies*, 241–57. Gothenburg: Nordicom, 2006.

Lazaga, Pedro. *El abominable hombre de la Costa Del Sol.* Madrid: Pedro Masó Producciones Cinematográficas, 1969.

————. *El turismo es un gran invento.* Madrid: Pedro Masó Producciones Cinematográficas, 1968.

Lefebvre, Henri. *The Production of Space.* Translated by Donald Nicholson-Smith. Malden, MA: Blackwell, 1991.

————. *Toward an Architecture of Enjoyment.* Translated by Robert Bononno. Minneapolis: University of Minnesota Press, 2014.

Levin, Daniel Michael. *Modernity and the Hegemony of Vision.* Berkely: University of California Press, 1993.

Lillo, Ignacio. "El alcalde respalda el Hotel del Puerto y lo ve como un nuevo icono para la ciudad." *Diario Sur* (Málaga, Spain), May 30, 2015. https://www.diariosur.es/malaga-capital/201505/30/alcalde-respalda-hotel-puerto-20150530153744.html.

López Menacho, Javier. *Yo, precario.* Barcelona: Los libros del lince, 2013.

Loren, Mar, ed. *Costa-Grafías.* Seville, Spain: Secretariado de Publicaciones de la Universidad de Sevilla, 2014.

Lumbreras, Tecla, ed. *El estilo del relax: N-340. Málaga, H. 1953–1965.* Málaga, Spain: Colegio Oficial de Arquitectos en Málaga, Ayuntamiento de Málaga, Observatorio del Medio Ambiente Urbano, 2009.

————, ed. *El relax expandido: La economía turística en Málaga y la Costa del Sol.* Málaga, Spain: Colegio Oficial de Arquitectos en Málaga, Ayuntamiento de Málaga, Observatorio del Medio Ambiente Urbano, 2009.

MacCannell, Dean. *Empty Meeting Grounds: The Tourist Papers.* London: Routledge, 1992.

————. *The Ethics of Sight-Seeing.* Berkeley: University of California Press, 2011.

————. *The Tourist: A New Theory of the Leisure Class.* 9th ed. New York: Schocken Books, 1976.

Manegat, Julio. *Spanish Show.* Barcelona: Editorial Planeta, 1965.

Manifiesto de la Assemblea del Raval. Barcelona: Assemblea del Raval, 2014.

"Marbella, segundo acto." *El País*, June 28, 2006. http://elpais.com/diario/2006/06/28/opinion/1151445601_850215.html.

"Martin Parr, 'Common Sense' 1995-9." Tate, February 2004, https://www.tate.org.uk/art/artworks/parr-common-sense-p78371.

Martinez, Ignacio, and Jorge L. Soria. "Gil sugiere en Estepona que convertirá en paraísos fiscales a Ceuta y Melilla." *El País*, April 17, 1999. https://elpais.com/diario/1999/04/18/andalucia/924387746_850215.html.

Mazón, Tomás. "Benidorm: Un destino turístico de altura." *Gran tour: Revista de investigación turísticas* 2 (2010): 8–22.

McLoud, Scott. *Understanding Comics: The Invisible Art.* New York: Harper Perennial, 1993.

Méndez Baiges, Maite, ed. *Arquitectura, ciudad y territorio en Málaga (1900–2011).* Málaga, Spain: Geometría Asociación Cultural, 2012.

Méndez Baiges, Maite, and Inmaculada Hurtado Suárez. "La construcción de la imagen de la arquitectura del relax." Paper presented at the Territorios del turismo: El imaginario turístico y la construcción del paisaje conemporáneo, Universidad de Girona, Girona, Spain, 2014.

Milano, Claudio, and José A. Mansilla, eds. *Ciudad de vacaciones: Conflictos urbanos en espacios turísticos.* Barcelona: Pol*len edicions, sccl, 2018.

Minca, Claudio, and Tim Oakes, eds. *Travels in Paradox: Remapping Tourism.* Lanham, MD: Rowman and Littlefield, 2006.

Munt, Ian. "The 'Other' Postmodern Tourism: Culture, Travel, and the New Middle Classes." *Theory, Culture, and Society* 11, no. 3 (1994): 101–23.

Murray Mas, Iván. *Capitalismo y turismo en España: Del "milagro económico" a la "gran crisis."* Barcelona: Alba Sud Editorial, 2015.

MVRDV, Equipo de Arquitectos. *Costa ibérica: Hacia la ciudad del ocio.* Barcelona: Actar, 2001.

Naredo, José Manuel, and Antonio Montiel Márquez. *El modelo inmobliiario español y su culminación en el caso valenciano.* Barcelona: Icaria Editorial, 2011.

Nichols, William. "Sifting through the Ashes: An Interview with Rafael Chirbes." *Arizona Journal of Hispanic Cultural Studies* 12 (2008): 219–33.

Nickel, Douglas R. *Francis Frith in Egypt and Palestine: A Victorian Photographer Abroad.* Princeton, NJ: Princeton University Press, 2004.

Nieto Ferrando, Jorge, Antonia del Rey Reguillo, and Eugenia Afinoguenova. "Narration and Placement of Tourist Spaces in Spanish Fiction Cinema (1951–1977)." *Revista Latina de Comunicación Social* 70 (2015): 585–610.

"Número de campos de golf en España en 2020, por comunidad autónoma." Statista Research Department, 2021, https://es.statista.com/estadisticas/670013/numero-de-campos-de-golf-por-region-espana.

Obrador Pons, Pau. "The Mediterranean Pool: Cultivating Hospitality in the Coastal Hotel." In *Cultures of Mass Tourism: Doing the Mediterranean in the Age of Banal Mobilities*, edited by Pau Obrador Pons, Mike Crang, and Penny Travlou, 91–109. Surrey, England: Ashgate, 2009.

Ordóñez, Miguel Ángel. *El caso Malaya: Los elefantes asolaron Marbella.* Granada, Spain: Ultramarina, 2010.

Osborne, Peter D. *Travelling Light: Photography, Travel, and Visual Culture.* Manchester: Manchester University Press, 2000.

Pack, Sasha D. *Tourism and Dictatorship: Europe's Peaceful Invasion of Franco's Spain.* New York: Palgrave Macmillan, 2006.

Palomino, Ángel. *Carta abierta a una sueca.* Madrid: Ediciones 99, 1974.

———. *El milagro turístico.* Barcelona, Spain: Plaza and Janes, 1972.

———. *Torremolinos Gran Hotel.* Barcelona: Editorial Planeta, 1971.

Parr, Martin. *Benidorm: Über Die Welt / Benidorm: About the World*, edited by Sprengel Museum Hannover. Hannover, Germany: Sprengel Museum Hannover, 1999. Exhibition catalog.

———. *Boring Postcards USA.* New York: Phaidon Press, 2004.

———. *Common Sense.* Stockport, England: Dewi Lewis Publishing, 1999.

———. *The Last Resort: Photographs of New Brighton.* Wallasey, UK: Promenade Press, 1986.

———. "Pérez Siquier." *Impresiones* 1 (2013): 1–81.

———. *Small World: A Global Photographic Project.* Stockport, England: Dewi Lewis Publishing, 1995.

Pavlovic, Tatjana. *The Mobile Nation: España Cambia de Piel (1954–1964).* Bristol, UK: Intellect, 2011.

Penyas, Ana. *Todo bajo el sol.* Barcelona: Penguin Random House, 2021.

Pérez Siquier, Carlos. *La Playa 1972–1996.* Almería, Spain: Fundación de Arte Ibáñez-Cosentino, 2019.

Pérez Siquier, Carlos, Carlos Gollonet, and Carlos Martín. *Pérez Siquier.* Madrid: Fundación MAPFRE Área de Cultura, 2020. Exhibition catalog.

Picornell, Mercè. "The Back Side of the Postcard: Subversion of the Island Tourist Gaze in the Contemporary Mallorcan Imaginary." *Island Studies Journal* 15, no. 2 (2020): 291–314.

Planelles, Manuel. "La urbanización de la primera línea de costa crece un 33% en 24 años." *El País*, August 22, 2016, 1–4.

Pollard, John, and Rafael Domínguez Rodríguez. "Unconstrained Growth: The Development of a Spanish Resort." *Geography* 80, no. 1 (January 1995): 33–44.

Puig Castellano, Jordi. *1960s–1970s Costa Brava: Postals, postales, cartes postales, postcards*. Girona, Spain: Úrsula Llibres, 2017.

Relph, Edward. *Place and Placelessness*. London: Pion Limited, 1976.

Richardson, Nathan E. *Postmodern Paletos: Immigration, Democracy, and Globalization in Spanish Narrative and Film, 1950–2000*. Lewisburg, PA: Bucknell University Press, 2002.

Río, José María Valcuende del, and Rafael Cáceres. "Memória LGTBI+ y contextos turísticos: El caso de Torremolinos en la Costa del Sol (España)." In *Quando a história acelera: Resist Resistência ncia, movimentos sociais e o lugar do futuro*, edited by João Carlos Louçã and Paula Godinho, 173–89. Lisbon, Portugal: Instituto de História Contemporânea, 2021.

Roch, Fernando. "La ciudad inmobiliaria y el precio de la vivienda." *Papeles de la FIM*, no. 20 (January 2004): 115–29.

Rodaway, Paul. *Sensuous Geographies: Body, Sense, and Place*. London: Routledge, 1994.

Rodríguez, Joaquín, et al. *Ensayo y error* Benidorm. Seville, Spain: Editorial Barrett, 2019.

Romera, Carmen. "Cruiser: De Gran Lujo a refugio de indigentes." *La Opinión de Málaga* (Málaga, Spain), November 11, 2012. https://www.laopiniondemalaga. es/costa-sol-occidental/2012/11/11/cruiser-gran-lujo-refugio-indigentes/547506. html.

Romero, Antonio, and Miguel Díaz. *Costa Nostra: Las mafias en la Costa del Sol*. Seville: Atrapasueños Editorial, 2009.

Royo Naranjo, Lourdes. "Paisaje, patrimonio y arquitectura en los destinos turísticos litorales: Notas sobre la Costa del Sol." *Anales de Historia del Arte* 24 (Diciembre 2014): 253–63.

Salvesen, Britt. *New Topographics*. Göttingen, Germany: Steidl and Partners, 2010.

Santos, Víctor. *Intachable: 30 años de corrupción*. Girona, Spain: Panini España, 2020.

Schor, Naomi. "'Cartes Postales': Representing Paris 1900." *Critical Inquiry* 18, no. 2 (Winter 1992): 188–244.

Secretaría de Estado de Turismo. *Plan nacional e integral de turismo (PNIT): 2012–2015*. Madrid: Ministerio de Industria, Energía y Turismo, 2012. https://turismo.gob.es/es-es/servicios/Documents/Plan-Nacional-Integral-Turismo-2012–2015.pdf.

Secretaría General de Turismo. *Turismo 2020: Plan del turismo español horizonte 2020*. Madrid: Ministerio de Industria, Turismo, y Comercio, 2007. https://www.tourspain.es/es-es/Conozcanos/Documents/HistoricoPoliticaTuristica/Horizonte%202020%20-%20Plan%20Turismo%20Espa%C3%B1ol%200812.pdf.

Segura, Santiago. *Torrente 2: Misión en Marbella*. Madrid, Spain: Amiguetes Entertainment, 2001.

Selwyn, Tom, ed. *The Tourist Image: Myth and Myth Making in Tourism*. Chichester, UK: John Wiley and Sons, 1996.

Sen, Amartya. "Capability and Well-Being." In *The Philosophy of Economics: An Anthology*, edited by Daniel M. Hausman, 270–94. Cambridge: Cambridge University Press, 2008.

Simpson, Mark. "Postcard Culture in America:The Traffic in Traffic." In *The Oxford Collection on Visual Culture: Volume Six: U.S. Popular Print Culture 1860–1920*, edited by Christine Bold, 169–90. New York: Oxford University Press, 2012.

Soja, Edward W. *Thirdspace: Journeys to Los Angeles and Other Real-and-Imagined Places*. Oxford, UK: Blackwell Publishers, 1996.

Sontag, Susan. *On Photography*. New York: Farrar, Straus, and Ciroux, 1973.

Spracklen, Karl. *Whiteness and Leisure*. London: Palgrave MacMillan, 2013.

Stevens, Norman D. "Introduction: Welcome to the World of Postcards." In *Postcards in the Library: Invaluable Visual Resources*, edited by Norman D. Stevens, 1–4. New York: Haworth Press, 1995.

Storm, Eric. "A More Spanish Spain: The Influence of Tourism on the National Image." In *Metaphors of Spain: Representations of Spanish National Identity in the Twentieth Century*, edited by Javier Moreno-Luzón and Xosé M. Núñez Seixas, 239–59. New York: Berghahn Books, Inc, 2017.

Stylianou-Lambert, Theopisti, and Elena Stylianou. "Martin Parr: A Traveller-Critic and a Professional Post-Tourist in a Small World." *Travel, Tourism and Art* (2016): 161–73.

Taján, Alfredo. *Pez Espada*. La Coruña, Spain: Ediciones del Viento, 2010.

Taylor, John. *A Dream of England: Landscape, Photography and the Tourist's Imagination*. Manchester: Manchester University Press, 1994.

Terré, Laura. *Historia del grupo fotográfico AFAL: 1956/1963*, edited by Museo Nacional Centro de Arte Reina Sofía. Madrid: Ministerio de Arte, Cultura, y Deporte, 2016.

Teyssiere, Javier Sola. *Ordenación territorial y urbanística de las zonas turísticas*. 2nd ed. Seville, Spain: Instituto Andaluz de Administración Pública, 2007.

"Torrente (saga)," Taquilla España, May 27, 2020, https://www.taquillaespana.es/sagas/torrente-saga.

Toscano, Patrizia. "Instagram-City: New Media, and the Social Perception of Public Spaces." *Visual Anthropology* 30, no. 3 (2017): 275–86.

Tranche, Rafael R. and Sánchez-Biosca, Vicente. *NO-DO: El tiempo y la memoria.* 7th ed. Madrid: Cátedra and Filmoteca Española, 2005.

Tremlett, Giles. *Ghosts of Spain: Travels through Spain and Its Silent Past.* New York: Walker and Company, 2006.

Tudela, Ana, and Delgado, Antono. "Las mayores aberraciones arquitectónicas de la costa española." *El país* (Madrid), August 8, 2019, ICON Design, 1–12. https://elpais.com/elpais/2019/08/06/icon_design/1565078918_545121.html.

———. *Playa burbuja: Un viaje al reino de los señores del ladrillo.* Madrid, Spain: Datista, 2018.

United Nations World Tourism Organization. *'Overtourism'?: Understanding and Managing Urban Tourism Growth beyond Perceptions.* Madrid, Spain: UNWTO, 2018.

Urry, John. *The Tourist Gaze.* 2nd ed. London: Sage Publications, 1990.

———. *The Tourist Gaze 3.0.* 3rd ed. Los Angeles: Sage Publications, 2011.

Vázquez Montalbán, Manuel. *Barcelonas.* Translated by Andy Robinson. London: Verso, 1992.

———. *Crónica sentimental de España.* Barcelona: Grijalbo Mondadori, 1998.

———. *La literatura en la construcción de la ciudad democrática.* Barcelona: Crítica (Grijalbo Mondadori), 1998.

Velasco, Elena. "Benidorm dreamin: El paraíso kitsch de Roberto Alcaraz." *Kluid Magazine.* (2020). https://kluidmagazine.com/benidorm-dreamin-el-paraiso-kitsch-de-roberto-alcaraz.

Venegas, José Luis. *The Sublime South: Andalusia, Orientalism, and the Making of Modern Spain.* Evanston, IL: Northwestern University Press, 2018.

Vergara, Bernardo. *Corrupcionario: Diccionario en viñetas de la corrupción española.* Barcelona: Random Comics, 2018.

Washabaugh, William. *Flamenco Music and National Identity in Spain.* Farnham, UK: Ashgate, 2012.

Winiwarter, Verena. "Buying a Dream Come True." *Rethinking History* 5, no. 3 (2001): 3.

———. "Nationalized Nature on Picture Postcards: Subtexts of Tourism from an Environmental Perspective." *Global Environments* 1 (2008): 192–215.

Woodward, Daisy. "Martin Parr's Benidorm." Magnum Photos, May 21, 2021. https://www.magnumphotos.com/arts-culture/society-arts-culture/martin-parr-benidorm.

Zamarreño Aramendia, Gorka, Elena Ruiz Romero de la Cruz, and Elena de los Reyes Cruz Ruiz. "Málaga y la marca territorio en el cine del turismo del

Franquismo." *International Journal of Scientific Management and Tourism* 3, no. 3 (2017): 541–4.

Zukin, Sharon. *Point of Purchase: How Shopping Changed American Culture.* New York: Routledge, 2004.

INDEX

panopticon, 48, 58, 64, 178n61
Parador hotels, 56, 61, 156, 181n91
paradox, 1, 2, 4, 52, 73, 102, 107,
115, 121, 128, 164, 165, 176n31,
183n6
paraíso fiscal, 29, 130, 131, 150, 200n53.
See also money laundering
Parr, Martin, 28, 95, 100–112, 189n39,
190n43, 193n54
pathos, 102
Penyas, Ana, 17, 170n41
Pérez Siquier, Carlos, 28, 100–103, 112–
20, 121–24, 164, 192n51, 192n52,
193n54, 200n51. *See also* La
Chanca, Almería
performance, 37, 82, 99, 102, 103, 118,
124, 125
periphery, 3, 6, 99, 113, 118
pilgrimage, 168n26, 182n1
pisos turísticos, 24, 37
Plan de Estabilización, 12
postmodernism, 37, 54, 75, 84, 116, 122,
126, 191n49
post-tourism, 191n49

Rajoy, Mariano, 31, 153, 199n45
Ramírez, Juan Antonio, 52, 173n11. *See
also* estilo del relax; Santos, Diego
Régimen del 78, 197n28

Santos, Diego, 34, 52, 173n11. *See also*
estilo del relax
satire, 28, 40, 96, 100, 101, 116, 120, 137,
147. *See also* humor; irony; self-
awareness
self-awareness, 28, 59, 63–69, 87, 96,
100, 103–5, 111, 116, 120–26. *See
also* humor; irony; satire
selfie, 111, 112, 121. *See also* anti-selfie
sightseeing, 3. *See also* MacCannell,
Dean
simulacra, 15–16, 49, 52, 53, 66, 86–87,
98–99, 105–6, 116, 126, 136. *See also*
hyperreal; spectacle
social media, 34, 75, 111, 112, 121, 123,
124, 164. *See also* Instagram

Soja, Edward, 53, 54, 59, 180n80. *See
also* Thirdspace
souvenirs, 8, 26, 27, 39, 41
space
consumption of, 17, 110–11, 164,
169n38
of consumption, 13, 17, 26, 33, 46, 48,
50, 63, 72, 164
fetishization of, 4, 15, 20, 54, 69, 91
and place, 17, 20, 52, 70, 97–100, 105,
109, 113, 170n43, 172n69
public, 16, 19–20, 25, 34, 98, 102–3,
112, 121, 124–25
speculation of, 16, 24, 38–39, 54, 131,
141–45, 148, 155, 175n18
"Spain is different," 6, 7, 130
Spanish Economic Miracle, 3, 8, 12, 18,
140
Spanish Show, 27, 35–38, 43, 44, 164,
175n18, 175nn21–22. *See also*
Manegat, José
spectacle
Debord, Guy, 59
and female body, 61, 91, 118
performance, 82–85, 148, 177n33
and representation, 37, 40–41, 45–50,
68, 91, 94–97, 102–3, 125
sites of, 16, 20, 34–37, 92, 170n43,
178n6, 181n91, 199n49
See also hyperreal; simulacra
staged authenticity, 70, 82, 84, 88,
97, 98, 105, 191n49. *See also*
authenticity; MacCannell, Dean
surveillance, 16, 48, 58, 112, 178n61

television, 97, 115, 132, 148, 180n76,
193n52, 201n70
theme park, 17, 19, 25, 34, 54, 61, 98,
102, 136, 151, 188n9
Thirdspace, 51, 53, 54, 61, 62, 65, 66,
180n80. *See also* Soja, Edward
torremolinoschic.com, 34, 75, 186n31
Torremolinos Gran Hotel, 27, 35, 36,
37, 43, 44, 45, 47, 49, 50, 51, 58,
64, 131, 158, 161, 164. *See also*
Palomino, Ángel

www.ingramcontent.com/pod-product-compliance
Lightning Source LLC
Chambersburg PA
CBHW050808270326

41926CB00026B/4638